A Chain of Events:

The Government Cover-up of the Black Hawk Incident and

The Friendly Fire Death of Lt. Laura Piper

Joan L. Piper

BRASSEY'S
Washington, D.C.

Library of Congress Cataloging-in-Publication Data

Piper, Joan L.
  A chain of events : the government cover-up of the Black Hawk incident and the friendly fire death of Lt. Laura Piper / Joan L. Piper.
    p. cm.
  Includes bibliographical references and index.
  ISBN 1-57488-231-7 (alk. paper)
  1. Black Hawk Friendly Fire Incident, Iraq, 1994. 2. Friendly fire (Military science)—Iraq. 3. Aerial reconnaissance, American—Iraq. 4. Black Hawk (Military transport helicopter)—Accidents—Investigation—United States. I. Title.

DS79.755.P56 2000
956.7044'4—dc21

                                                                                    99-086467

Printed in Canada on acid-free paper that meets the American National Standards Institute Z39-48 Standard.

Brassey's
22883 Quicksilver Drive
Dulles, Virginia 20166

First Edition

10 9 8 7 6 5 4 3 2 1

DEDICATION

This book is dedicated to my Laura. During her short life, she had become my role model and my inspiration. It is her tenacious spirit that has guided me through this enormous task of documenting the truth and telling this story.

This book is also dedicated to my family—my husband, Danny, and two sons, Dan and Sean—and to all the families who lost a loved one on the Black Hawks. As we all leaned on one another after the shoot down and the chain of events that followed, we became a part of the larger Black Hawk family.

IN MEMORY

Air Force Lieutenant Laura A. Piper
Army Staff Sergeant Paul N. Barclay
Army Specialist Cornelius A. Bass
Army Specialist Jeffrey C. Colbert
Army Private First Class Mark A. Ellner
Army Warrant Officer John W. Garrett Jr.
Army Chief Warrant Officer Michael A. Hall
Army Sergeant First Class Benjamin T. Hodge
Army Captain Patrick M. McKenna
Army Warrant Officer Erik S. Mounsey
Army Colonel Richard A. Mulhern
Army Specialist Michael S. Robinson
Army Staff Sergeant Ricky L. Robinson
Army Colonel Jerald L. Thompson
Barbara Schell, U.S. State Department
British Major Harry C. Shapland
British Lieutenant Colonel Jonathan C. Swann
French Lieutenant Colonel Guy Demetz
Turkish Colonel Hikmet Alp
Turkish Lieutenant Ceyhun Civas
Turkish Lieutenant Barlas Gultepe
Abdulsatur Arab, Kurdish Guard
Ghandi Hussein, Kurdish Guard
Bader Mikho, Kurdish Guard
Ahmad Mohammad, Kurdish Guard
Salid Said, Kurdish Interpreter

There is a special need in the military to make the killing of another as a result of simple negligence a criminal act. This is because of the extensive use, handling, and operation in the course of official duties of such dangerous instruments as weapons, explosives, aircraft, vehicles and the like. The dangers to others from such acts is so great that society demands protection.

—Rules for Courts-Martial, 303 Inquiry,
Uniform Code of Military Justice

Contents

Preface   vii
Acknowledgments   ix
1 • **San Antonio, Texas**   April 10, 1994   1
2 • **Incirlik Air Force Base, Turkey**   April 13, 1994   5
3 • **Incirlik Air Force Base, Turkey**   April 14, 1994   10
4 • **Incirlik Air Force Base, Turkey**   April 14, 1994   15
5 • **MCC Forward, Zakhu, Iraq**   April 14, 1994   20
6 • **No Fly Zone, Northern Iraq**   April 14, 1994   25
7 • **No Fly Zone, Northern Iraq**   April 14, 1994   35
8 • **Incirlik Air Force Base, Turkey**   April 14, 1994   40
9 • **Washington, D.C.**   April 14, 1994   54
10 • **San Antonio, Texas**   April 14, 1994   58
11 • **Incirlik Air Force Base, Turkey**   April 14, 1994   67
12 • **Black Hawk Crash Site, Iraq**   April 15, 1994   74
13 • **San Antonio, Texas**   April 15, 1994   80
14 • **San Antonio, Texas**   April 18, 1994   87
15 • **San Antonio, Texas**   April 24, 1994   97
16 • **Over the North Atlantic Ocean**   June 11, 1994   111
17 • **San Antonio, Texas**   July 1, 1994   122
18 • **San Antonio, Texas**   August 1, 1994   136
19 • **Zakhu, Northern Iraq**   August 13, 1994   143
20 • **San Antonio, Texas**   August 26, 1994   147
21 • **Washington, D.C.**   September 8, 1994   151
22 • **San Antonio, Texas**   September 8, 1994   152
23 • **San Antonio, Texas**   October 1, 1994   159
24 • **Oklahoma City**   October 18, 1994   165
25 • **San Antonio, Texas**   October 22, 1994   173
26 • **Sembach Air Force Base, Germany**   November 7, 1994   179
27 • **San Antonio, Texas**   December 1, 1994   186
28 • **San Antonio, Texas**   January 1, 1995   190
29 • **San Antonio, Texas**   April 1, 1995   196

30 • San Antonio, Texas   May 1995   200
31 • Tinker Air Force Base, Oklahoma City   June 3, 1995   205
32 • San Antonio, Texas   June 20, 1995   219
33 • San Antonio, Texas   July 1995   226
34 • San Antonio, Texas   August 1, 1995   233
35 • The Pentagon   August 10, 1995   239
36 • San Antonio, Texas   September 1995   241
37 • Zakhu, Northern Iraq   August 1996   245
38 • San Antonio, Texas   September 1996   247
39 • Washington, D.C.   October 30, 1996   253
40 • The Pentagon   January 1, 1997   258
41 • San Antonio, Texas   August 23, 1998   260
      Epilogue   268
      Bibliography   271
      Index   277

Preface

On Thursday morning, April 14, 1994, over the clear skies of northern Iraq, two U.S. Army Black Hawk helicopters were shot down by two U.S. Air Force F-15s. There were no survivors: twenty-six were killed, fifteen the sons and daughters of America. The Black Hawk shoot down is one of the worst and most perplexing friendly fire incidents in U.S. military history.

My daughter, Lt. Laura Piper, was one of the casualties. My husband had just retired from an Air Force career that spanned twenty-six years. Laura and her brother, raised in the military, followed in his footsteps, graduating from the United States Air Force Academy and beginning their own careers. At the time of her death we were the loyal, true-blue Air Force family.

After Laura's funeral, the twenty-one-gun salute, the military flyby, and the soulful playing of taps, our family would begin to uncover the events that took twenty-six lives. The Air Force and the country we love would betray us as they covered up the truth. The Black Hawk shoot down is not the first time a branch of the armed services has manipulated evidence and the military justice system to save careers and maintain "integrity," and it won't be the last, but it is one of the worst examples. Parents who lose a child in the service of their country have sacrificed their most precious possession. Our country at least owes them the dignity and respect that comes with truth.

As time passed and the story became buried and forgotten, I came to the realization that if I didn't record this story, no one would. This book is my effort to record the chain of events that led to this horrific shoot down and the events that followed. This is the true story of how events in Washington, D.C., and how decisions of high-ranking individuals do affect the lives of ordinary citizens. The events in this book are complex; they are embedded with technicalities and legalities. To make this book interesting and understandable, I have woven the story of my personal journey through this chain of events that followed Laura's death. Because I am by nature a very private person, this was very difficult for me, but I knew this was something I had to do to tell this story in its entirety. If I had just reported these events in an impersonal manner, this book would be just another government report. Thus, I have revealed many thoughts and actions that will be surprising even to my immediate family.

These personal episodes should not discount the accuracy of this story. I have been scrupulous in my research. Every event and conversation, and even the thoughts of those involved, are documented. At times this story becomes gruesome, but I felt a necessity to be honest. In our sound-bite culture, within which we are entertained by a succession of tragedies, the public is oblivious to what happens to families like ours when the television cameras stop and the reporters leave.

This is a story told from the heart, and my intent is not vengeance. I wanted to tell this story not only for myself, but for the other families around the world who also lost a family member on those two Black Hawk helicopters. In the depths of their loss some have never been exactly sure of what happened on April 14, 1994. Again, to the best of my ability, I have made every effort and spent untold hours researching the Black Hawk shoot down to recreate the tragedy as accurately as possible and as accurately as anyone could have who wasn't there that day.

Lastly, this is also the story of how the Black Hawk family members came together and unselfishly accomplished more than even they expected. I want to make it absolutely clear that they made the larger effort. I was always the researcher, the recorder, and more often than not the observer. In the name of our family my husband, Danny, spoke for both of us, as I was consumed with keeping our personal lives intact and continuing to work and raise a young child. Perhaps this book is my destiny and will also be my contribution to the larger effort of the Black Hawk families.

Acknowledgments

I t is an act of faith to spend untold hours writing a book without any publisher's commitment or interest. I am indebted to Don McKeon, Brassey's publisher, who believed in this story and my ability to tell it. My sincere appreciation to Julie Kuzneski, managing editor, and Cindy Nixon, copyeditor, for their excellent work editing this manuscript filled with airplanes, military and legal terms, and so many acronyms. Thank you to everyone at Brassey's who has had a hand in this project.

Also, my son Sean deserves praise for being my technology adviser. His expertise saved me and many of my written words on several occasions.

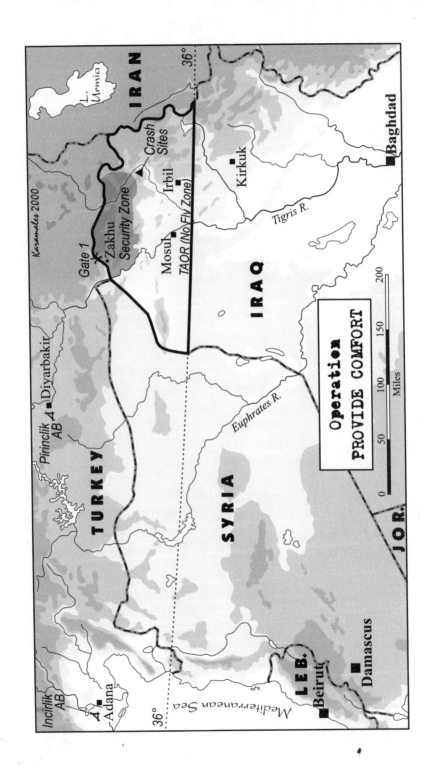

Operation
PROVIDE COMFORT

1

San Antonio, Texas
April 10, 1994
Sunday, 4:00 P.M.

I've heard it said, April is the cruelest month, something I could never understand because April has always been my favorite month of the year. The return of warm weather, beautiful flowers, Easter, and a son who was born on my birthday in April have given me reason to look forward to this time of year. But today as we drive through the Texas countryside, the lush green landscape bursting with wildflowers barely holds my attention. Lost in my own thoughts, I feign an interest in the conversation between my husband, Danny, and our ten-year-old son, Sean. While they chatter about the details of Sean's birthday party we have just hosted this afternoon, I can only stare out the window and nervously twist the gold bracelet on my left wrist.

I am anxious to get home. My daughter, Laura, and her fiancé, Dan Murray, have been vacationing in Egypt this week. This spring there have been numerous terrorist attacks against tourists, and although it is out of character for me to worry, I've been unable to explain this uneasy feeling I've had all week. They are scheduled to return today, and Laura had said before she left that she'd call on Sunday. I just want to hear Laura's voice, be reassured she is safe, and hear of her most recent adventure.

Laura, who just turned twenty-five last month, is my oldest child and my only daughter. I have always been proud of her, and in many ways over the years, she has become my role model. I've admired the courage and determination it took for her to graduate from the United States Air Force Academy almost two years ago. She had set this goal for herself in fourth grade, when she had read in the newspaper that Congress had voted to allow women to attend military academies. This goal was not surprising because Laura was no stranger to military life. Her father had graduated from the Academy in 1967 and just last year had retired from an Air Force flying career that lasted twenty-six years.

These past twelve months have been a year of transition for Danny and me, but we have succeeded in carving out a civilian life in San Antonio. After retirement Danny had immediately taken a position with a large insurance company, and I began teaching school. Last week, on Easter Sunday, we had given thanks for the blessings life had bestowed upon us and looked forward to a bright future. Most of all, we knew we had been blessed with wonderful children, and Danny and I took enormous pride in their accomplishments.

Laura had graduated from the Academy in 1992 pilot qualified. However, because of the oversupply of Air Force pilots, her start date for pilot training had been delayed. It had been a natural choice for her to bide her time going through intelligence school because she was fluent in German and Russian. Last summer she had been assigned to Ramstein Air Force Base, in Germany. She was thrilled to finally have her own apartment and felt privileged to have the opportunity to serve in the Air Force. Her fiancé, Dan, who had been her classmate at the Academy, was also stationed in Germany but at Spangdahlem Air Force Base, where he served as an intelligence officer for the F-15 Fighter Squadron. Coincidentally, last December both Laura and Dan had been sent to Turkey on temporary duty status. Sometimes it was difficult to keep track of which person we were speaking about when we said the name "Dan." My husband, older son, and Laura's fiancé all have the same first name. On occasions when we were all together, we just referred to them as "The Three Dans."

Our son Dan is continuing this family military tradition of attending the Air Force Academy. He is finishing his senior year and is scheduled to graduate in about six weeks. However, Sean, influenced by the movie *Top Gun*, keeps insisting he is going to attend the U.S. Naval Academy. Even with Sean's current naval aspirations, we could have been the Air Force poster family.

Finally we pull into our driveway. Immediately I push the garage door opener and jump out of the truck. As I race in the house I hear the telephone ringing. Picking up the receiver, I hear Laura's distant voice. She is mildly upset. "This is the third time I have tried to reach you, and this was going to be the last time. It is after midnight here in Turkey, and I have to get up early in the morning." First she asks to speak to Sean. She is eager to find out if he received the puzzle box she sent him for his birthday and to ask him if he was able to open it. Sean, a very clever child, had only taken a few minutes to find the secret compartment with the key. Unlocking the intricately carved box, he had found a gold cartouche pendant. Laura had planned this gift several months before. I had told her it was too expensive for a ten-year-old, but she would not be dissuaded. Sean was thrilled with the unusual box and the cartouche. Laura was right; it was a gift he would always remember. Because Laura is scheduled to leave Turkey this week, she had also included a lovely gold bracelet for my birthday, which is later this month. Both gifts were extravagant, but that was Laura, always thoughtful and always early with birthday gifts.

Sean finally hands me the receiver. Laura's voice is filled with happiness and excitement. Before leaving for her vacation in Egypt, she had completed her assignment at Incirlik Air Force Base and had shipped her possessions back to Germany. She tells me how anxious she is to return and decorate her apartment with the brass objects and rugs she has purchased. During the past few months, over the course of long telephone conversations, we have had such fun discussing these treasures. Many years before, her father had bought rugs and trinkets from the very same merchants when he was flying into Turkey.

However, before she can return to Germany Laura has one more task to accomplish. During this temporary assignment she had served as a night watch intelligence officer. Most of the personnel stationed at Incirlik are part of Operation Provide Comfort. OPC is a coalition of American-led Turkish, French, and British forces established after the Persian Gulf War. Their mission is to provide protection and humanitarian aid to the Kurdish refugees in northern Iraq. As a reward for a job well done, Laura is being sent into this protected area of northern Iraq. She is excited because it is a unique opportunity to witness the end result of the mission she has helped to support these past three months.

"Mom, we can't talk very long. I have to get up early to find out when they are sending me into Iraq. I don't even know what day I am going, but I think it will be the middle of this week. Although I want to go, I'm anxious to return to Germany. I have a new job that is going to require a lot of training, and I just want to get back to my apartment. If they send me into Iraq on Wednesday, I'll have time to catch the Friday flight to Germany. I had my telephone disconnected before I left, so as soon as I get back to Ramstein Air Force Base, I'll call you."

3

I end our conversation with the familiar phrase I have used since she was a child: "I love you, babe."

Hanging up the telephone, I felt content after hearing the happiness in Laura's voice and knowing she had safely returned from another adventure, but I didn't know these would be the last words I would ever speak to her.

2

Incirlik Air Force Base, Turkey
April 13, 1994
Wednesday, 6:00 A.M.

This Wednesday morning the sun is slowly rising over the flight line of Incirlik Air Force Base, promising another day of perfect, clear flying weather. Incirlik, in southern Turkey, is not a beautiful military installation, but it is more than functional. Its location makes it critical to America's peacekeeping mission in the Middle East. Incirlik AFB spiraled into global importance during the 1990–1991 Gulf War, when it became the key base for allied aircraft flying into Iraq. After the Gulf War ended, President George Bush established the Iraqi area north of the 36th parallel as a safe area for the Kurdish population that Saddam Hussein seemed intent on decimating. The sky over this Kurdish safe haven is called the "No Fly Zone," and almost every air operation from Incirlik AFB still acts as a deterrent to Iraqi encroachment and also monitors Iraqi compliance with the United Nations Security Resolutions. Gradually over the past three years the pace and excitement of Operation Provide Comfort has slowed to a more relaxed and often boring atmosphere. Pilots commonly refer to their peacekeeping flights over this No Fly Zone in northern Iraq as "burning holes in the sky."

Because of Incirlik's remote location, most of the personnel are here on a temporary basis. They rotate from military bases around the world, usually for a three-month deployment. Although the United States provides the command leadership, Turkey controls the base installation and places many restrictions on the various missions conducted on a daily basis. The United States allows Turkey this oversight because it must continue its military presence in this crucial location.

For many, it is a pleasant assignment. Away from family responsibilities and the additional duties at their home bases, the crews have more free time than they are accustomed to, time to explore the traveler's and shopper's paradise that characterizes Turkey. The nearest city, Adana, has streets lined with small shops selling gold, rugs, and brassware; it is commonly referred to as "The Alley." Many personnel spend their after hours shopping and sharing a meal in the various restaurants that cater to the tastes of Americans. The three months of temporary duty go quickly unless you have been unlucky enough to deploy more than once a year. With the downsizing of the American armed forces, many military members have been picking up additional and longer temporary duty assignments. Some of the crew and support members are on their second assignment this year, which makes them vulnerable to boredom and complacency.

As the sun moves above the horizon, it begins to glint on the inventory of the aircraft needed to provide air support for Operation Provide Comfort. The largest and most visible are the AWACS—the airborne warning and control system aircraft. A modified Boeing 707, with a saucer-shaped radar dome on the top, each is equipped inside with powerful radar and computers that scan the sky for enemy aircraft and simultaneously direct friendly aircraft. They have the capability to track approximately 1,000 enemy aircraft at once while directing 100 friendly ones.

Grouped into family-like clusters, in front of the long gray hangars, are the other planes that will be flying today. Most noticeable are the KC-135s, the refueling aircraft, and the F-15s, F-16s, F-4Gs, F-111s, Jaguars, and Harriers, the fighter aircraft.

Also prominent are the Black Hawk helicopters (UH-60s). Painted in a dark black and green camouflage color scheme, not only are they the backbone of Army aviation, these dependable nine-ton helicopters have been integral in every military mission the United States has been involved in since the Vietnam War. But these Air Force Black Hawks are charged with a critical and sometimes somber mission. They transport the search and rescue teams that deploy when an emergency situation occurs. The Army Black Hawks are based at Pirinclik AFB in southeastern Turkey, where they have flown humanitarian and support missions since Operation Provide Comfort's inception in 1991. They fly almost every day and are a familiar sight over the northern No Fly Zone.

The sky is cloudless and the day promises to be warm. At this early hour crew chiefs and support personnel are readying the aircraft for another day of almost constant takeoffs and landings. Each flight of aircraft has a designated takeoff time. One after another they will fly southeast, parallel to the border of Syria, and enter the No Fly Zone to perform their necessary missions. One mechanical glitch in a single aircraft can delay all the flights behind it.

The activity and noise level on the flight line escalate. Some aircraft are taxiing for takeoff while others are being preflighted. Laura and her fiancé, Dan Murray, arrive at the passenger terminal. Laura, wearing her BDUs (battle dress uniform), blends in with the other military personnel. She has managed to pull back her long, curly hair into a thick braid and at this time of morning wears a minimum of makeup. Despite the austere uniform, her natural beauty still radiates. She carries a small black canvas bag that contains a camera, books, and just enough necessities for an overnight stay. Grateful and even excited about this opportunity to travel into Iraq, she hopes it will be worth the ordeal of the past two days. Because her temporary duty orders to remain in Turkey had expired, she had to go through the aggravation of requesting a special gate pass from the Turkish officials. Then there was the matter of contacting her superior officer, who had arranged this trip, to hammer out the details required for this "reward mission." In fact, the inconveniences and stumbling blocks that preceded this morning have consumed almost all of her waking hours since she returned from her vacation in Egypt. But she is not complaining. She is proud her job performance has merited this trip into Iraq, and now she can finally feel the excitement of this new adventure.

Walking through the terminal, Laura and Dan make a striking couple. Their physical appearance is similar enough for them to be mistaken for brother and sister. Both have a strong athletic build, light brown hair with golden highlights, and mercurial green eyes. First they were friends and classmates at the Air Force Academy, but by their senior year their relationship had become serious. As graduation approached both had been disappointed to receive a delayed start for pilot training. But they were appeased when they were both sent to intelligence school at Goodfellow AFB in Texas. Not only did it give them the opportunity to be together, but on the weekends it was an easy drive to San Antonio. After being away from home during the long Academy years, it had been wonderful for them to spend time at home with us. Upon completion of intel school they couldn't believe their luck when they both received orders for Germany. During the past few months their relationship has deepened, and recently they have begun to plan their wedding and future together.

Although Laura will be returning to Germany at the end of the week, Dan has extended his tour and still has two months of remaining duty in Turkey. He is the intelligence officer for the 53rd Fighter Squadron. Working with the F-15 pilots in his squadron has been a unique opportunity to participate in the flying mission and utilize his intelligence training. His job entails giving daily intelligence briefs and threat briefs to the F-15 pilots before they step to the aircraft to fly. After returning from their mission he debriefs them on what they've seen and what unusual events they may have encountered over the No Fly Zone. Dan takes pride in the camaraderie he has established with the pilots. Often pilots treat a "ground pounder" with indifference, but Dan's outgoing, exuberant personality has made him many close friends in the squadron.

Laura and Dan notice that the C-12 on which Laura is scheduled to depart has pulled up to the terminal. This Army twin-engine aircraft is used basically for staff support, but mostly it is used to transport people, mail, and perishables from Incirlik to Pirinclik AFB, where the U.S. Army Black Hawk detachment is based. The C-12 is an important first link for people and things getting to the Army Command Center, "MCC (Mission Command Center) Forward" in Zakhu, northern Iraq.

Zakhu will be Laura's final destination today. First the C-12 will land at Pirinclik, then Laura will board an Army Black Hawk helicopter for the one-hour trip to MCC Forward. Laura's schedule includes taking a ground excursion with the Army troops at Zakhu and spending the night there. Tomorrow she anticipates flying on an early Black Hawk mission, which will allow her to return to Incirlik on Thursday evening, April 14. Friday morning she plans on catching the morning flight back to Germany.

These last moments together before her departure are precious to Laura and Dan. The past three months have been eventful and wonderful. At this moment in time she and Dan look forward to a future filled with happiness and unlimited potential.

Dan walks Laura out to the flight line. Approaching the C-12, they notice a few of the passengers have already boarded. Laura gets in line and in a matter of moments is ready to board the aircraft. Dan gives her a big hug, kisses her good-bye, and passes her the black canvas bag. He stands by as the doors are secured, the plane makes a turn, and then starts down the runway. After he gives a final wave Dan turns away and begins to walk back to the terminal. This assignment has been the happiest period of his life, but now, after watching the C-12 lift off from the runway, he can already feel the emptiness. He knows it's because this trip signals the end of Laura's time in Turkey. But he has no way of knowing this idyllic period of his life is about to come to a tragic end and that he has just kissed Laura good-bye for the final time.

3
Incirlik Air Force Base, Turkey
April 14, 1994
Thursday, 7:36 A.M.

I t is early Thursday morning; another routine day is unfolding at Incirlik AFB, with no indication that in less than three hours one of the grimmest chapters in Air Force history will occur. In fact, today is going smoother than many of the previous days in the three-year history of Operation Provide Comfort. The weather is crystal clear, and the AWACS radar plane, the first flight of the day, reports no mechanical problems and is scheduled to depart earlier than planned.

At 6:30 A.M. the aircrew attended a preflight briefing. The AWACS staff intelligence representative briefed escape and evasion procedures, the previous day's Iraqi air activity, and threat capabilities. He also briefed a United Nations support mission scheduled to take place today, April 14.

Mission Crew Commander Maj. Lawrence Tracy then briefed the plan for this mission to his officers and technicians. AWACS briefings have a reputation for being short on tactical considerations and long on discussions about box lunches, but Tracy did spend time going over the activity flow sheet, which lists all the friendly aircraft flying in OPC today, their call signs, and the times they are scheduled to enter the No Fly Zone. Major Tracy failed to make note of the helicopters, even though their call signs (EE 01 and EE 02) and their IFF (identification, friend or foe) information had been written in the margin. Although this crew had just arrived in country from Oklahoma earlier this week and this is their first mission on this rotation, Major Tracy finished the briefing quickly. This will allow the crew to board the aircraft ahead of schedule and give them, once airborne, extra time to get on task before the first flight from Incirlik enters Iraq.

All systems are go, and precisely at 7:36 A.M. the AWACS roars down the runway and lifts into the cloudless blue sky. It is the first player of the day, and it will set the stage for the remainder of the missions or

10

packages scheduled to fly over the No Fly Zone. Every event leading to takeoff had gone as planned.

While the AWACS is approaching its initial orbit, the U.S. Army Black Hawk helicopters are preparing to take off from Pirinclik AFB in southeastern Turkey. The crew has preflighted the choppers with excruciating detail. The gunners have secured the weapons: M-60 machine guns, M-16s, and the nine-millimeter side arms each crewmember carries.

Today is definitely not a routine day for the Black Hawks. They have been tasked to fly a high-profile, two-ship mission into northern Iraq. Earlier this week a change of command had taken place at the U.S. Army Command Center in Zakhu. Today the outgoing commander, Col. Jerry Thompson, will escort his replacement into the far reaches of the No Fly Zone for the explicit purpose of introducing him to the two Kurdish leaders who exert control over this volatile political area. In addition to providing humanitarian relief and protection to the Kurds, another important function of the Army detachment is to establish an ongoing American presence in the Kurdish towns and villages by showing the U.S. flag, the other main objective of today's mission.

All the crewmembers have been briefed on the sequence of the flight. First, they will fly the routine leg of their mission into Zakhu. It is at this point that their mission will pick up importance. From Zakhu their mission is to fly the two Army colonels and the other passengers to the towns of Irbil and Salah ad Din, Iraq. Although the flight plan takes the mission deep into the No Fly Zone, the two-ship will remain north of the 36th parallel. It is not uncommon for the Black Hawks to fly this far into the No Fly Zone. They have done it countless times before during the preceding years of Operation Provide Comfort.

The distance and time of this mission require the Black Hawks to be fitted with sponsons. These pontoon-shaped fuel tanks, mounted below the side doors, each hold 230 gallons of extra fuel. Additionally, each of the sponsons is painted with a large American flag, a measure that became necessary when the Black Hawks had been the target of small arms ground fire several months ago. At the last moment mechanical malfunctions force the crew to switch out one of the helicopters, which necessitates removing the sponsons from the disabled chopper and reattaching them on the replacement.

Today the lead helicopter will be flown by Capt. Patrick McKenna, the Black Hawk detachment commander. McKenna is renowned as one of the best Black Hawk pilots in the Army, and his quiet, competent manner has earned him the admiration and respect of everyone in the detachment. After a recheck the pilots turn on the engines, and the rotor blades begin to spin. The Black Hawks depart, on time, at 8:22 A.M.

At 8:45 AWACS is now on station. The mission systems are powered up, and, most importantly, the crewmembers were able to establish their JTIDS (Joint Tactical Information Distribution System) communication and data link with the Turkish ground radar sites on their first attempt. This satellite data system allows AWACS and the ground stations to exchange information, which results in a radar air picture. The huge radome, sitting on top of the aircraft, begins its first rotation. Crewmembers begin monitoring information on everything that moves on the ground or in the air within a 250–nautical mile radius. The pilot noses the aircraft up to 32,000 feet and puts it in a direct heading for the orbit in southern Turkey, where it will fly for the remainder of the eleven-hour mission. This morning has gone perfectly: the flight is on time, there have been no mechanical problems, and the communication link was established with ease. But that is to be expected. This crew has logged many flying hours. Together they have participated in other missions around the globe, and most have flown in Operation Provide Comfort previously. The crew believes it will be a good day, and perhaps they also believe it will be an easy mission.

As the mission crew commander, Major Tracy is responsible for supervising the entire AWACS mission crew. He is the number one guy, overseeing everyone to make sure they all work as a team. On this mission he has additional help. Maj. James Saylor, a mission crew commander instructor, is on board because this is the crew's first sortie for this temporary duty assignment. Saylor's explicit job is to assist Tracy with the crew's transition to this operating theater. He will help Tracy if any unforeseen problems develop.

Tracy sits with the other two key supervisors toward the front of the aircraft in a three-seat arrangement named "the Pit," where each has his own radarscope. Seated to Tracy's left is Capt. Jim Wang, the senior director. Wang, an Air Force Academy graduate, is an experienced AWACS officer. He is a soft-spoken man, secure in his competence as a senior director. And he has reason to be, because today is his sixtieth mission over OPC. Wang's job is critical to the mission. He supervises the Weapons and Surveillance Sections. In Weapons three officers work under Wang controlling all friendly aircraft, regulating air traffic, conducting radio checks, providing threat warnings, and managing air-refueling operations. Seated in the rear, Surveillance is responsible for the detection, tracking, and identification of any unknown aircraft north of the 36th parallel.

It is because the potential exists for Iraqi threats that AWACS carries an officer from Incirlik AFB, who is an Airborne Command Element. The aircrews and support personnel refer to this officer by his radio call sign, "Duke." His most important jobs are ensuring that the engagement mandates are adhered to and executed as written and responding to any situations that may require judgment. Should there be a combat threat, the Duke will act as the eyes and ears of OPC's commander, General Jeffrey Pilkington. This is why the Duke is always a highly experienced individual with fighter experience. And today one of the Air Force's most experienced and knowledgeable Dukes, Maj. Doug Martin, sits in that position, to the left of Wang. His credentials are more than impressive. He has 2,000 hours of flying time as a navigator, mostly in F-111s. Hand-picked as a crewmember in the Libyan air raid named "Eldorado Canyon" and a participant in twenty-seven combat missions during Operation Desert Storm, Martin has earned a Distinguished Flying Cross and two Air Medals for heroism. He is perfectly suited to coordinate with authorities on the ground in Incirlik for the execution of any combat operations that might occur over the No Fly Zone today.

There are guidelines in place that dictate, in detail, how hostile aircraft or military threats will be treated. These succinct guidelines are called the "rules of engagement," or ROE. Although the No Fly Zone is a presidentially designated combat zone, its rules of engagement are peacetime ROE that have been modified for Operation Provide Comfort. Many of the aircrews new to the OPC environment have questioned the need for these less aggressive rules of engagement. The answer is always the same: "The No Fly Zone has too many multinational players for aggressive combat." These peacetime ROE are in place for the sole purpose of slowing down any military confrontation, thus preventing a "friendly fire" situation that was all too common during Operation Desert Storm.

The three supervisors—Tracy, Wang, and Martin—sit together and act as a team to coordinate all operations and unexpected military incidents that might occur during this flight. However, violations of the No Fly

Zone have been rare and threats have been few during the past three years, so today's flight is expected to be an average one and the supervisors in the Pit anticipate just another routine mission.

Senior Director Jim Wang glances over his shoulder and checks the Weapons and Surveillance Sections. The controllers are sitting at their scopes, prepared for the aircraft they will control and direct during this mission. At 9:21 A.M. Lt. Joseph Halcli receives the first radio call of the day, what's called a "check-in" call on the enroute UHF (ultrahigh frequency) radio from the Army Black Hawk helicopters. They give their call sign and altitude as they prepare to enter Iraq through Gate One. Halcli acknowledges their entry into the No Fly Zone and checks to see if they are squawking the correct Mode I and Mode II IFF codes. Wang changes the Black Hawk "friendly general" symbology on the scopes to a "friendly helicopter" symbology. Halcli changes that designator to "EE 01," the call sign for the lead helicopter. The Black Hawk symbology tracks across the scope for three more minutes, then begins to fade. The helicopters have landed at MCC Forward, Zakhu. Halcli knows they have landed at Zakhu from his previous experience in OPC, thus he suspends or freezes their symbology. As Halcli and the rest of the directors and controllers wait for the other aircraft to enter Iraq, the glowing screens of their radarscopes are empty, with the exception of the suspended helicopter symbology. This AWACS crew, fully qualified to handle any situation, continues to prepare for the long, routine mission.

4

Incirlik Air Force Base, Turkey
April 14, 1994
Thursday, 8:45 A.M.

Everything at Incirlik AFB this Thursday morning has continued to proceed smoothly. In fact, there hasn't been the slightest indication that the U.S. Air Force is less than two hours away from tragedy. Events continue to run like clockwork at 8:45 A.M., when the AWACS crewmen notify the Incirlik Command Post that they are on station. The Incirlik Ground Mission Director, whose call sign is "Mad Dog," makes note that AWACS is up and on station early today. He takes this as a good sign, for none of the flights can take off until AWACS is able to provide air control. He thinks, "Perfect, no weather or mechanical delays, the aircraft are going to make their flying windows. Today we'll run on time!" The first flight scheduled for takeoff, in forty-five minutes, is a two-ship of F-15s.

Earlier this morning the two F-15 pilots had met to catch a ride over to their squadron on the base flight line. At 7:20 A.M., after eating a breakfast of cereal and washing it down with juice, Capt. Eric Wickson had walked out of the BOQ (bachelor officers' quarters) to meet his wingman for this mission, Lt. Col. Randy May. Wickson and May are not your average F-15 jocks. Their qualifications and experience rank them as two of the Air Force's finest.

Both are on temporary duty from Spangdahlem Air Force Base in Germany. May, short, stocky, and balding, with a droopy left eye, does not fit the image of the recruiting poster fighter pilot. But appearances can be deceiving. He has over 3,000 flying hours and first started flying F-15s in 1983. This is his second tour at OPC, but he had flown sorties out of Incirlik during Operations Proven Flight and Desert Storm. Most important, Lieutenant Colonel May is a decorated combat pilot and has even racked up a combat kill. This accomplishment is so rare in today's modern Air Force that it commands the highest form of respect from his

15

fighter pilot contemporaries. On February 7, 1991, during Desert Storm, May shot down an Iraqi Hind helicopter over northern Iraq near the city of Kirkuk. During a preflight sweep he had picked up the enemy chopper on radar and made a BVR (beyond visual range) shot using two AIM-7 Sparrows, a radar-guided air-to-air missile. After the kill was confirmed May changed his call sign to "Rotor" and one year later was awarded the Distinguished Flying Cross. Lieutenant Colonel May is highly qualified, among other things, to be an instructor pilot, flight lead, and supervisor of flying. Presently he is the commander of the 53rd Fighter Squadron.

In contrast to May, Captain Wickson looks like the real-life image of Steve Canyon enhanced by the bearing and posture of an Air Force Academy graduate. His blond, good looks are complimented by a square chin and piercing blue eyes. Prior to flying F-15s he flew OT-37s and OV-10s as a forward air controller, also concurrently doing ground duty with the Army as an Air Liaison Officer. This experience provided him with an extensive knowledge of Army operations and Army helicopters, including Black Hawks. He also has combat experience, but not as an F-15 pilot. In 1990 he was decorated with the Bronze Star for parachuting out of a helicopter and helping to direct the air strike over Panama. Wickson went on to F-15 training and ended up in Europe in 1991. He has over 1,300 total flying hours, with approximately 700 in F-15s. Flying in Europe has provided him the opportunity to participate in many high-level tactical exercises, including missions over Bosnia. He is qualified to be a supervisor of flying plus a two- and four-ship lead. This tour, which began on April 6, is his second deployment to OPC, and today is his eighteenth flight over the No Fly Zone.

The Supervisor of Flying had picked up Wickson and May and driven them to the squadron, where they briefed and prepared for their 9:35 A.M. takeoff time. Their first duty had been to check the weather and NOTAM (notice to airmen). They noted that all the areas they will operate in today were reported to be sky clear. Other than a closed section of a taxiway, no other extenuating factors were listed, which meant their day was also off to an excellent start.

At brief time they had gone into the Intelligence Office for their required intel briefing with Lt. Dan Murray. Dan knows both pilots but is a friend to Captain Wickson. He looks up to Eric and has aspirations himself to become a fighter pilot. Recently Wickson had joined Laura and him for

16

dinner in downtown Adana. However, this morning everyone had operated on a professional level. Dan began with the scripted information passed down to him by the Wing Intelligence Group. He reported the number of sorties flown the previous day by Iraqi fighters, the surface-to-air missile battle order, and the search and rescue codes. He had ended with a seven-minute "threat-of-the-day brief," which included all the reported Iraqi threats, capabilities, and locations. There was no reference to an increase in Iraqi ground or air activity or any violations of the No Fly Zone, because there had been none. The previous day had been an average day, and today was expected to be the same. Neither May nor Wickson had any questions. As Dan shook hands with both of the pilots, he thought of mentioning that today Laura would be out over the No Fly Zone in an Army helicopter. But Dan takes pride in his professionalism, and he decided not to mix his personal life with the purpose of this mission. He wished them well, and both pilots had stepped to the briefing room for their preflight brief.

After taking a seat at one of the long tables in the squadron briefing room, they had begun their briefing for today's mission. Captain Wickson was assigned to be flight lead, with May flying in the wing position. Most of the F-15 pilots deployed to Incirlik are qualified flight leads, thus they rotate to keep up their experience level. Even though May outranks Wickson, there will be no rank once they begin briefing and during their time in the cockpit. First on the agenda was checking the frag, or the Air Tasking Order (ATO), which lists all the players that are going to be flying over the No Fly Zone today during the various time slots. The Black Hawks were listed on the classified ATO as "Eagle Flight" with no times given, just "as required." The ATO will be shrunk down on a copy machine so the pilots can attach it to their kneeboard once they are in the cockpit. Modes and radio codes were briefed, as well as how they will do checks on the aircraft.

Wickson had briefed from the ten-page "53rd Flight Briefing Guide." Back at their home base, in Germany, all of their tactical briefings were geared toward OPC using the same briefing guide. Nonetheless, he covered in extensive detail what types of threats they could expect to see, what ranges they would plan to shoot from, and how they would handle the different situations they could encounter. He had spent some time talking about AWACS blind zones, which are primarily the mountainous areas

17

in northern and eastern Iraq. Every day the first flight in, which usually consists of the F-15s, first sweeps the deep ridges and low valleys because AWACS, with its line-of-sight radar, has difficulty tracking aircraft in this rugged terrain.

The most important part of the entire briefing had been the intercept portion. Wickson, in a serious tone, discussed the three different scenarios that they might encounter today: the high fast flier, the medium or low fast flier, and, lastly, the low slow target. Wickson's voice became more intense as he discussed the electronic identification and visual identification of an unknown aircraft. He'd briefed May:

> We will pass the target along the side and do a visual identification. Then we will have one of three options. If it is a friendly aircraft, we will leave the area. If it is an unidentified aircraft, we will set up a racetrack [which is basically an oval, with the tip of the oval being the target] and will just do ovals around the target at about 10–nautical mile legs. So at all times one of us will be going away from the target, and the other person will be coming towards the target looking at him with the radar. If it is friendly, then it will be identified as friendly— I mean, disregard. If it is hostile, it will be identified as hostile with the VID [visual identification], and we will use the ROE [rules of engagement] as applicable.

The term "cleared to shoot" was discussed in the context of the rules of engagement. The final talking point was the significance of "merge": after the crews engage, shoot down, or miss a target, "merge" implies the necessity of returning to formation after they pass the target. Wickson stressed the need to continue working the radar and looking for additional targets. He had emphasized this point because he says it would be a new experience to pick up a target over the No Fly Zone. This entire briefing usually takes one hour and ten minutes, but today the briefing had been completed in thirty-five minutes. The pilots noted that the clock on the wall had read 8:20 A.M. This left them with just twenty minutes before they would climb into the truck that takes them to the aircraft.

They stood, stretched, and used the bathroom for the last time before the four-hour mission. Several times they passed the squadron's mission board that listed today's Black Hawk mission. Written in green ink were the words "April 14, two ship admin flight." Next, they "sanitized" themselves. They removed everything that would identify them as American F-15 pilots, which meant no patches, no wedding bands, no pictures of their families. Everything was taken out of their pockets except an ID card and a little bit of money in the event that they have to divert to another base.

Their next stop was life support. They had put on a G suit (an aviator's standard gravity suit), survival vest, and harness and picked up their helmets. The supply sergeant issued them a nine-millimeter pistol with two clips of fifteen rounds each and a global positioning receiver system. Should they find themselves, unfortunately, on the ground in Iraq, they would use this system to pinpoint their positions with the search and rescue forces. At the operations desk they signed out a VTR (videotape recorder) tape to do their HUD (heads-up display) filming and both a classified and an unclassified "Pilot's Aide." The final item checked out was an escape and evasion kit, which included a map of Iraq, as well as a "blood chit," a piece of paper that specifies in several languages that whoever captures and returns them safely to the United States government will be financially rewarded.

At 8:40 A.M., "step time," Wickson, call sign "Tiger One," and May, call sign "Tiger Two," climbed into the truck with the duty supervisor and drove out to the aircraft. They checked the forms, reviewed the loaded modes and codes, slipped the VTR tape in its place underneath the jet, and did a walk around their respective aircraft.

Now, with a few minutes to spare, they climb into the cockpits of the F-15Cs and prepare to start their engines. Wickson calls Mad Dog and asks if there are any last-minute changes to the ATO. "Mad Dog, Tiger One is engine start, words?" Mad Dog replies, "The combat divert airfield is Batman, negative words." After one more radio check, they start their engines and taxi out to the runway. Tiger One and Tiger Two take off, precisely on time, at 9:35 A.M. They do separate full afterburner takeoffs, fifteen seconds apart. As they make a left-hand turn to the south, the last thing that can be seen on the ground is the squadron of dark green Black Hawk helicopters. Beginning their continual turn to the east, toward Iraq, both pilots are certain that their high level of experience and attention to detail during this morning's briefing has prepared them for any situation they might encounter over the No Fly Zone during this mission.

5.
MCC Forward, Zakhu, Iraq
April 14, 1994
Thursday, 9:24 A.M.

Tucked just inside the northwest corner of Iraq is the small town of Zakhu. Outside the small, wooden, U.S. Army building known as MCC Forward, Maj. Donald Sanders watches the two Black Hawks touch down on the runway. The spring rains have made the Iraqi landscape lush and green, and the cloudless sky is deep blue. It is a picture-perfect day for the execution of a mission Sanders has been planning for three weeks. He is the operations officer and works directly under Colonel Thompson, the MCC commander. Tomorrow, after his change of command reception, Thompson will depart for the United States, and his replacement, Col. Richard Mulhern, will assume command. On a daily basis MCC coordinates land and helicopter missions that support the Kurdish people. Today's mission is expressly designed to introduce Colonel Mulhern to the United Nations representative and to the two very influential leaders of the opposing Kurdish political parties, Massoud Barzani, and Jalal Talabani, with whom the United States wishes to continue a supportive relationship.

The rotors come to a stop and the engines are shut down before the crew and passengers quickly debark. Usually Sanders briefs the crew and passengers in the mission operations room, but today there isn't enough room. Last night they had used it as a temporary sleeping quarters for some of the passengers scheduled for this trip. Sanders takes the maps out to the hood of a vehicle and begins briefing everyone. Today's mission with crew and passengers will total twenty-six people. Time is critical, so Sanders passes around a seating chart for each person to check while he briefs. The Black Hawks will carry a varied group of American, British, Turkish, and French officers. Also on the list are Barbara Schell, from the U.S. State Department, and four Kurdish guards, two for each chopper.

Laura is excited about this opportunity. She knows she has no real purpose or reason to be on this mission, but everyone has made her feel welcome. Waiting to see her seat assignment, she thinks how she will tell her family, especially Sean, about this adventure. This is a unique chance to see places that few will ever have the opportunity to visit and to meet people who shape the policy and politics of this small corner of the earth. A political science major at the Air Force Academy, she is intrigued by the possibilities today presents. Perhaps this trip will be worth the aggravation of extending her stay at İncırlik.

Finally the seating chart passes to her. She quickly scans the schematic of both choppers and notes that she will be seated on the left side, rear section, of the trail helicopter, tail number 26000. As the passengers and crew gather up their belongings, she makes small talk with Army Specialist Anthony Bass. From earlier conversations they learned the commonalities in their lives. Both have career Air Force fathers and families that live less than ten miles apart in San Antonio. Anthony mentions that he will be crew chief on the trail helicopter today and that the pilot, CWO Michael Hall, and copilot, WO Erik Mounsey, are great guys.

The crew signals readiness for the passengers to board, and everyone climbs into their assigned seats. Laura begins to strap herself in, wishing she had a window seat. She wants to see everything. Just as she thinks this to herself, Sgt. Ricky Robinson, seated next to the left window, offers to trade seats with her. Along today as a backup crew chief, he had flown the same mission on Monday with Colonel Thompson and General Pilkington. Laura, thrilled with her new vantage point, barely has time to strap herself in before the Black Hawk begins to lift.

Major Sanders, on the ground, takes note of the two dark green, camouflaged Black Hawks marked with six two-by-three-foot American flags. There is a flag on each door, on both sponsons, one on the nose, and an even larger one on the belly of each helicopter. Silhouetted against the blue sky and distant mountains, the helicopters gain altitude and make a turn to the southeast. Sanders breathes a sigh of relief; this mission has finally reached fruition, and the weather is, as predicted, perfect. He has every expectation that this mission will also be perfect because of the extensive planning required to pull it off today.

Laura's eyes peer out the small window of the trail helicopter. She is awed by the breathtaking and historic landscape. They are flying over the delta adjacent to the Tigris and Euphrates Rivers known as the Fertile

Crescent, the cradle of civilization. They pass over flat rocky areas, which were once Kurdish villages, a grim reminder of Saddam Hussein's cruel devastation of the Kurds during and after the Gulf War. As the helicopters continue to gain altitude, the temperature inside becomes cool. The copilot, Erik Mounsey, offers Laura his green flight jacket. Laura is grateful, puts it on, and continues to look out the window. It is too much effort to make conversation above the noise of the rotors and engines. The flight continues in a southeasterly direction toward a beautiful green valley between two steep, rugged ridgelines. This mountainous terrain will provide protection from Iraqi air defenses during the one-hour flight to Irbil.

Meanwhile, AWACS has almost approached its final orbit in southeastern Turkey, due north of the No Fly Zone. The Surveillance Section has just finished tracking three special mission packages that have exited Iraq and flown into Turkey. These "special packages" are flights made by the Turkish Air Force before the allied aircraft are allowed to enter the No Fly Zone. The purpose of these special packages is an ironic twist to the OPC mission. Early in the morning the Turks attack Kurdish sites they perceive as a threat to their country. Recently there has been a conflict. They have remained in the No Fly Zone, with more frequency, when the AWACS arrive on station. This crew had been made aware of the problem, and it has attached a video camera to an empty screen to record these missions. The video camera runs as Lieutenant Halcli, the enroute controller in the Weapons Section, starts tracking Wickson and May's F-15s, which are still in Turkish airspace.

Halcli continues to monitor his scope. In the lower left-hand corner, in green, the scope reads 9:54 A.M. when he receives a radio check-in from the Black Hawks. "Eagle 01 enroute Whiskey to Lima." "Whiskey" is the code word for Zakhu, and "Lima" means Irbil. However, these code words mean nothing to Halcli. Although this translation information is readily available, he doesn't bother to look it up. But he does initiate the helicopter's symbology on the screen and notifies the senior director, Captain Wang. The call sign "EE 01," denoting the two-ship of Black Hawks, begins tracking in a southeasterly direction across most of the AWACS radar screens, including those of the three supervisors sitting in the Pit, Major Tracy, Major Martin, and Captain Wang.

Halcli allows the Black Hawks to remain on the enroute frequency because it has been the observed policy on his previous OPC missions.

22

All the other aircraft entering into Iraq today will be required to switch to the AOR (area of responsibility) frequency, the standard frequency used over the No Fly Zone.

Lt. Ricky Wilson in the Weapons Section is responsible for controlling all the aircraft above the 36th parallel. He is inexperienced and has never flown an OPC mission before; however, AWACS guidance suggests that the most inexperienced controller be placed in the AOR position. Wilson monitors two main frequencies: the enroute frequency, alerting him of who will be entering his area, and the AOR frequency, showing him the aircraft under his direct control. On his scope he also sees the EE 01 track leave Zakhu and begin to move. And this Black Hawk track is easy to see, because there are still no other aircraft in the No Fly Zone. Then Wilson erroneously begins to direct his attention below the 36th parallel. He views this as one of his primary responsibilities, although this is actually the task of the Surveillance Section.

Because the possibility does exist for a mistake like Lieutenant Wilson's, AWACS is carrying Capt. Mark Cathy, a staff weapons director/instructor who is permanently assigned to Incirlik. He does all incoming briefings for new AWACS crews rotating into Incirlik, but today he is flying a "shoulder ride" with this crew to assist with their acclimation to the Operation Provide Comfort theater and to help the Weapons Section should it need guidance or have any questions.

At approximately 10:00 A.M., with the AWACS two and one-half hours into its mission and just as the first flights of aircraft are scheduled to begin arriving from Incirlik, Captain Cathy retires to the crew rest area to take a nap. Major Saylor, the mission director/instructor, also goes to the back of the craft for a snack and a bathroom break. The crew has forgotten to turn off the video camera, and it continues to record EE 01 as the only symbology displayed on the scopes of the AWACS crewmembers.

At 10:12 A.M. the Black Hawks, flying at a low altitude, begin to enter the mountainous terrain of southeastern Iraq. Because AWACS coverage is line of sight only, when the helicopters fly below the level of the mountains their radar and IFF coverage begin to fade on the AWACS scopes. This is basic knowledge for anyone in the radar tracking business. One AWACS crewmember does take notice. In the rear of the aircraft Capt. Dierdre ("Dee") Bell, the air surveillance officer, sees the helicopters' last known location and sends an "attention arrow" to Captain Wang. The green arrow continues to blink, signaling trouble, for one minute, and then it automatically stops and drops off the scope. Bell directs the AWACS radar to be adjusted to a low-velocity detection setting, which improves the capability of radar to detect slow-moving targets.

At 10:21 A.M. Lieutenant Halcli, believing the helicopters may have landed again, asks Captain Wang for permission to drop the Black Hawk symbology completely from the radar screens, rather than just suspend it, as he had done previously. Wang gives him an affirmative. Meanwhile, Lieutenant Wilson, the AOR controller, is looking in the wrong direction, Captain Cathy is asleep, and Major Saylor is lunching. Major Tracy, the mission crew commander, later was unable to account adequately for what he was doing during this time period.

6
No Fly Zone, Northern Iraq
April 14, 1994
Thursday, 10:20 A.M.

A t 10:15 A.M. Captain Wickson and Lieutenant Colonel May are still forty miles northwest of Iraq. They pride themselves on arriving at Gate One, the entrance to the No Fly Zone, on time, which today and every day is 10:20 A.M. The 350-mile distance to Iraq has been uneventful and was traversed in precisely forty-five minutes. Although they are only fifteen minutes away from their worst nightmare, this mission has continued to run perfectly. All systems are operating smoothly, and from previous check-in calls to AWACS, they know they are squawking the right codes and modes.

Switching his radio to channel 9, Wickson radios Major Martin, the Duke on AWACS. "Tiger, as fragged, words." Wickson is telling Martin they have two aircraft, as the Air Tasking Order depicts, with no problems, and he's asking him if he has any additional information he and May will need to know before they enter the No Fly Zone. Martin replies, "Batman is combat divert, altimeter is two-nine-nine-four, we're on time and going on time, negative words." He has no information to pass to them that differs from that related at their ground brief.

Wickson and May continue their radio checks, critical for proper communication with all the players out in the No Fly Zone this morning. They automatically switch over to what is called the "Have Quick" frequency, which provides a clear communication voice that is not secure but is difficult to jam. As the pilots speak a computer controls the frequency that hops along the entire UHF spectrum. This is their third time on Have Quick this morning, but it is the first time they check in on the main radio. Next is a talk check on the auxiliary radio, used to communicate only with each other. In addition to these other frequencies, both pilots are monitoring "Guard," a radio frequency every aircraft listens to at all times that is used primarily for communication during emergency situations. These radio checks indicate that all their communications are operable and have no problems.

Wickson radios to May, "Tiger fence in." May immediately replies, "Two." This means they will now turn on all their combat systems, allowing them to dispense chaff and flares and activate the ICS (Integrated Countermeasures Suite), an internal system that jams enemy threats. The only thing they don't do is turn on the master arm, which arms the weapon system. Today they are each carrying a weapon load of four AMRAAMs (advanced medium-range air-to-air missiles), two AIM-7s, and two AIM-9 missiles.

Flying through Gate One at 10:20 A.M., every one of their systems continues to check out perfectly. There hasn't been a hitch all morning. They now switch their radios from code 42, the enroute frequency, to code 52, the AOR frequency, which every friendly aircraft is supposed to use in Iraq.

Wickson next radios AWACS. "Tiger is on station." If there is air-to-air activity anywhere over the No Fly Zone, Lieutenant Wilson, the AOR controller, will give him a picture call to tell the pilots what he sees. Today Wilson responds with a concise and simple "Roger," meaning there is no air activity in the area.

Although the mission of the F-15s is to sweep the No Fly Zone for enemy aircraft, they also provide air cover for AWACS and the tankers that have no weapon systems to protect themselves. Wickson and May begin this mission by heading southeast toward the Iraqi mountains and ridgelines. All the aircrews know this is the first place trouble can start because the mountains mask the radar signals of low-flying aircraft, making this area of the No Fly Zone the most likely hiding place for enemy planes. Tiger One, Wickson, is responsible for sanitizing 25,000 feet and below. Tiger Two, May, is responsible for 20,000 feet and above.

Wickson and May nose their F-15s in the direction of these mountains. Immediately Wickson picks up a green rectangular hit on his radarscope. This tells him there is a contact directly off his nose at forty nautical miles. He feels a shot of adrenaline shoot through his body, for although this is not out of the ordinary, this is totally unexpected on this mission that has progressed so smoothly. Using the auxiliary radio, he informs May, "Hit." May rolls down his radar and also finds a single low target, approximately thirty miles ahead.

May, searching high to ensure that no one can sneak up on them and hide, rolls down his radar for a second time and again confirms that he still has an unknown radar hit. Meanwhile, Wickson locks this contact. He takes his normal radar sweep and puts all the energy onto this one specific area in the sky so that he can get information, such as airspeed and altitude. What his radar now tells him is, yes, there is something flying out there. Its heading is 100 degrees, it's flying at 150 miles per hour, and it's very low. Some of the readings on his radar are negative readings, so he knows the contact is low to the ground in mountainous terrain.

Wickson continues to hold the radar lock and does a radio check for the friendly modes all aircraft should be squawking. The first is Mode I, and he receives no response. Next, he reaches down and changes his switch to auto to check Mode IV. Initially when he presses down on the air-to-air interrogator, he gets a friendly response, but then it disappears. Normally he would hold the button down for five to six seconds, so he is not sure—this could be a radio anomaly. He interrogates one more time and does not receive a friendly response. Now Wickson believes this contact is not squawking friendly modes. Concurrently May is also interrogating Mode I and Mode IV. He also does not get a friendly response.

At 10:22 A.M. Wickson radios the information about this contact and its exact location to AWACS. "Tiger One is hits, bull's-eye 030 for 50." Wilson, the AOR controller, who is looking in the wrong direction, checks his screen and replies, "Clean there," meaning he does not have a radar hit at that location.

Almost at this same moment the Black Hawk helicopters, still flying through the mountains, have reached an area of low terrain, and the AWACS line-of-sight radar begins to pick them up again. An intermittent IFF response appears on the AWACS scopes in the vicinity of the F-15s reported radar contact. At 10:24 an "H" symbol, indicating helicopters, appears, most importantly, on the radarscopes of the three supervisors sitting in the Pit, as well as on the scopes of the other AWACS crewmembers.

This last AWACS radio call, from Lieutenant Wilson, does raise a red flag for the wingman, Lieutenant Colonel May. He thinks, "This is odd. We have somebody out there in the No Fly Zone that AWACS doesn't know about. We're supposed to be the first aircraft in the area; nobody should be ahead of us! If someone did happen to go ahead of us today, then AWACS should be talking to them! And, given the fact that this is the only contact we are running in the area, it shouldn't be an overload for AWACS to figure out if they have radio contact with these folks and to connect the two. It is strange to have a contact in this area that AWACS doesn't know about." May does not express this concern to Wickson, the flight lead.

However, no red flags pop up for Wickson. He breaks his radar lock on the contact and goes back to the sweep mode, looking for any other contacts. Curious, he pulls out his map and checks the area of the unidentified contact. He notices there is a road at ground level in that area. Sometimes his radar locks on to road traffic, but this is not Germany, so no one should be traveling at 150 miles per hour. His high level of flying experience tells him that radar can lie to pilots. Wickson and May discuss this on the auxiliary radio, and May replies, "It looks to me like some kind of low flier." Again Wickson interrogates Mode I and IV, and they both check negative.

Just three minutes have elapsed since Wickson's last call to AWACS. Now, at 10:25 a.m., just as he makes another call to AWACS, the Black Hawk IFF response on the AWACS scopes becomes more frequent. This time Wickson tells Wilson the heading and altitude of his radar hit, "Tiger's contact, bull's-eye 030 for 50, low, slow." Wilson, who still continues to look in the wrong direction, below the 36th parallel, replies, "Hits there." Wilson's two-word radio call tells the F-15 pilots that he now has the unidentified hits on his radarscope. Wilson is sufficiently concerned at this point to call Senior Director Wang on the internal weapons network. "Sir, are you listening to this?"

Wickson, above the noise and confusion, can almost hear his heart pound because now he knows that all three of them—he, May, and Wilson—have acknowledged the unidentified contact. Still not absolutely sure that the activity isn't road traffic, he starts a descent, locking the target again and interrogating on the radio. All responses continue to be negative. Soon he is passing below 10,000 feet and is about 10 nautical miles behind his contact. He looks through his heads-up display, and the HUD radar gives him a target designator (TD) box. The computer calculates where the contact is and displays it in the TD. Wickson looks through the box, and the contact is right on a road. So one more time he thinks the contact may be simply road traffic. He calls to May, "My TD box is on the road!" At about seven nautical miles, behind the contact, the TD box comes off

28

the road—the first positive indication he is not locked on to road traffic. Now he is pretty sure there's an actual aircraft in the TD box, but the ground is green and he still can't see anything. At five nautical miles he finally picks up a helicopter in the target designator box. Under the rules of engagement, as Wickson interprets them, if he can't identify the contact electronically as friendly, his next option is to do a visual identification to prove it as hostile because Air Force policy is "Eyeballs beat machines." At 10:27, only seven minutes into their mission, Wickson radios AWACS and Tiger Two. "Tiger One is tally one helicopter. Stand by VID."

As Wickson makes this last radio call, the Black Hawk IFF symbols have been clearly visible for the last three minutes on the radarscopes of the AWACS controllers. They are at the same location as the radar contacts identified by the F-15 flight. None of the controllers advise the F-15s of this IFF data in the target area. Most incredibly, at this time there are still only four aircraft over the No Fly Zone: the two F-15s and the two Black Hawks. And AWACS has only four radar returns on its scopes.

At 10:27 A.M., the same time Wickson radios his intent to do a visual identification, Capt. Diedre Bell, the AWACS surveillance officer, sends an "unknown, pending, unevaluated" track signal in the area of the helicopters' radar and IFF symbols to the other controllers. She uses a switch action to attempt an IFF identification. During the F-15s' flight intercept of the helicopters, no one else on board the AWACS tries to determine the specific IFF aircraft identification or does a Mode IV check on the helicopters. The "H" characters are still present on the radarscope of Senior Director Wang, Mission Crew Commander Tracy, and Major Martin.

Wickson begins his visual descent, just as he had briefed it earlier this morning. The two biggest enemies of fighter pilots are said to be adrenaline and testosterone, and both are skyrocketing in him at this moment. Wickson has flown below 1,000 feet only two other times, and this rugged terrain adds another difficulty factor to the VID. This neck of northern Iraq is rough country. The mountains rise up to 14,000 feet, and the valleys are more like ravines. During his previous flights he'd noticed that these mountains look like backbones running from northwest to southeast. His pulse is racing, his breathing becomes more rapid, and he can feel the perspiration begin to run down the back of his neck. This is dangerous flying, and getting a good ID is crucial. Compounding all these factors is the threat of Iraqi surface-to-air missiles.

Wickson takes a breath and enters the deep valley. Flying faster than 500 miles per hour, his breathing gets heavier as he uses the idle and speedbreak located on top of the fuselage behind the cockpit to control the sharp descent that brings him below the level of the steep mountains, now on both sides of him. He's coming down fast, and within seconds the helicopter is out in front of his canopy. Wickson passes it on his left at a distance of about 1,000 feet off to the side and about 300 feet higher than the chopper. The helicopter moves across the front to the right, and Wickson looks down through his canopy off to the right. He later testifies he descended to 800 feet AGL (above ground level), and the helicopter is less than 300 feet above the floor of the valley. In four seconds Wickson is barely able to give the helicopter three quick glances. Taking speed and altitude into consideration, it is very much like two cars passing in opposite directions, each going 100 miles per hour.

What he sees is a helicopter with a tapered empennage and a vertical tail that is sloped backward toward the rear. It has sponsons on both sides, and he believes they are carrying some type of ordnance. But, because he is above them, he can see only the tip and the tail of the ordnance, not the actual ordnance coming out from each side of the sponson. Remarkably, Wickson makes an immediate positive identification. What he believes he has just seen is a Soviet-built Hind helicopter.

However, he doesn't get close enough to the chopper to identify any markings, such as tail fin flashes or flags, and the dark green coloration blends in with the green background of the valley. At this moment in time, for whatever reason, Wickson makes the mistake of his lifetime. Even inexperienced fighter jocks know that under the rules of engagement, you must identify an aircraft's national origin. But he ignores those rules. He also makes the false assumption that if he has identified a Hind, then it must be an Iraqi chopper.

Now, flying over the top of the helicopter at a speed of 300 miles per hour while trying to keep his wingtips from hitting the mountains, Wickson surprisingly accomplishes the next two tasks simultaneously. First, he makes a call on the main radio, "VID Hind—no, Hip" (a different Soviet helicopter). He surprises himself with that call and thinks, "I am positive of the aircraft but not sure I am saying the right designation for it." He actually pulls out a guide containing the silhouettes of helicopters and confirms, in his mind, that the helicopter he has just seen is indeed a Hind. Back on the main radio he says, "Disregard Hip, VID Hind." And as if he doesn't have enough to concentrate on, he now spots a shadow that is too far behind this helicopter to be its own shadow. He takes a closer look and identifies a second helicopter about two miles in trail. Instantaneously he transmits on the main radio again, "Tiger One is tally two Hind helicopters."

The time is 10:28 A.M., and the AWACS track symbology for the F-15s and the Black Hawks' radar are too close together for the AWACS crew to identify the Black Hawk helicopters. When Lieutenant Wilson hears Wickson's most recent radio call, "Tiger One is tally two Hind helicopters," he responds with, "Copy Hinds" and again makes a call on the weapons net to Captain Wang. "Sir, are you listening to this?" This time Wang replies, "Affirmative," but he offers no guidance to Wilson or to the F-15 pilots.

Wickson is flying low to the ground, something he is unaccustomed to doing. The valley is narrowing, and Wickson's plane is pointing straight at the mountains. Employing his afterburners, he pulls the fighter up at a sharp angle, feeling the G suit tighten around his thighs. Leveling off, Wickson pauses to reflect and wonders if his radio calls have been confusing. To clarify, he calls May again: "Tiger One has tallied two Hinds, confirm."

Lieutenant Colonel May immediately replies, "Stand by" and begins his own VID to confirm Wickson's last radio call. He continues to interrogate Mode I, code 52, and gets one friendly response followed by two unfriendly returns. Preparing for his descent, he is leery about getting down level with the trail helicopter, the only one his radar is cuing. He is well aware that the lower you fly, the more your situational awareness begins to deteriorate because more energy goes outside the cockpit. The closer to the ground the aircraft gets the less time the pilot has to react. Therefore his eyes must focus outside the aircraft a greater percentage of the time to keep his aircraft from hitting the ground. Deliberately staying high, he tries to slow down the speed of the intercept so he can get a good look at the trail helicopter while at the same time trying to locate the lead. Almost immediately he descends to an altitude that is 500 feet above the trail helicopter with 2,000 feet of slant range. May thinks to himself, "I

31

know a Hind is a gunship, so although I have to fly slow enough to ID, I'll have to keep my airspeed above 450 knots because I don't want to become a target."

He dips his left wing low to look down at the trail helicopter, which restricts his view to only the top part of the helicopter's side. May sees high engines, sloping wings, a blunt nose, a slanted tail, sponsons, and a dark camouflaged body. Incredibly, May, like Wickson, also ignores the ROE when he fails to make even a meager attempt to get close enough to see fin flashes, markings, or flags that would depict national origin and that are required on all aircraft. May cannot identify the chopper as a Hind, but he can identify it as negative friendly. Believing he has seen all that is necessary, he maneuvers to the left, kicks in the afterburners, and pulls off to the north. He radios Wickson, "Affirmative VID." Immediately he sees the lead helicopter. Now May has also seen two helicopters! Just before he begins his rollout to resume his racetrack position, he radios to Wickson, "Tally two." The time is 10:28:30. Wickson and May are only eight minutes and thirty seconds into this mission.

Captain Wickson is ten nautical miles behind the helicopters, flying in the opposite direction, northwest. He calls on the main radio to AWACS, "Tiger Two [Max] has tallied two Hinds, engaged." This one ambiguous radio call, "Tiger Two has tallied two Hinds, engaged," will haunt Wickson and May for eternity, and later it will be used as the only evidence to determine one of the pilot's guilt or innocence. However, this call does have an impact on the AWACS controllers, who immediately understand that the word "engaged" means the pilots are going to employ ordnance. The F-15s are going to shoot down the targets.

Although the low, slow-flying helicopters have traveled less than fourteen miles since Wickson and May first picked them up on radar, although they are not flying in a threatening manner, although they are flying southeast, away from the No Fly Zone, Wickson decides to take immediate action. At 10:29 A.M. he makes a second radio call to May, "Tiger, arm hot." This call not only tells May to turn on his master arm, but more importantly, it tells him he is cleared to shoot.

In the excitement of the moment Wickson fails to make the required radio call to Tiger Two requesting the turn-on of the HUD tape, and he also forgets to turn on his own tape. May too neglects to turn on his tape, although it is standard procedure. Additionally, both pilots fail to take into consideration the possibility of aircraft that are lost or in distress. They also neglect the requirement, according to the rules of engagement, giving consideration to aircraft that may be on a medical mission or are possibly being flown by pilots who are defecting.

At 10:30 A.M., scarcely ten minutes after entering the No Fly Zone, Wickson "pickles." He presses the button that expends ordnance, then radios, "Tiger One, Fox." This call informs May and AWACS that he has fired a Fox-3, an AMRAAM costing $1 million per copy.

Wickson is acutely aware he has just made military history. He is the first F-15 pilot to fire an AMRAAM in a combat environment. The missile climbs until the booster motor burns out, and seven seconds later an explosion occurs that is so immense, it is recorded on a satellite photograph of the Mideast taken at precisely 10:30 A.M. Wickson continues to watch as fire breaks out behind the rotor mast, on top of the chopper, and inside the cabin. The Black Hawk begins to break up in the air and impacts the valley floor at seventy-two knots of airspeed.

On the main radio Wickson reports, "Splash one," then, "Two, you're cleared in." Feeling that maybe he has not been descriptive enough, he calls May again. "Tiger Two, second helicopter is east of the fireball two nautical miles." Now he quickly pulls off to the left to get out of Tiger Two's way when he notices the remaining lead helicopter is making a hard left-hand turn.

The lead helicopter had been violently rocked by the explosion of the trail helicopter. Automatically its pilot, Capt. Patrick McKenna, had remembered the three words drilled into helicopter pilots if they should ever encounter a fighter threat: "Deploy to cover." He reacts by making an aggressive left-hand turn to mask terrain. But a Black Hawk is no match for an F-15.

May sees the helicopter move toward the high terrain on the north side. It is obvious the chopper is trying to hide, and May knows if it gets into a dark area, he'll never be able to pick it out of the ground clutter. He does have a small window of opportunity to employ ordnance, and he doesn't rush. His interest isn't in shooting fast, but in shooting accurately. May's weapon of choice is an AIM-9 heat-seeker missile because it is the most discriminatory of all the weapons available to him. Closing in at a two-mile range, he uncages the seeker head and fires the AIM-9. Immediately the missile comes off the left shoulder station. Initially there's a slight dip toward the nose, but then it pulls a large amount of left lead before it gradually corrects back and closes in on the helicopter. A fireball engulfs the lead Black Hawk, and it begins to break apart before it impacts a steep mountain slope at a forty-five-degree angle. May radios, "Splash the second bandit."

Now Wickson's main concern, as flight lead, is additional threats, either an aircraft coming up to shoot or a ground threat. At the same time he is trying to calm himself from the overload of adrenaline that has pushed him through the past five minutes. He radios, "Tigers blow out to the south, push it up." He wants both F-15s to point south and get out as fast as they can to try to deny further threats. But May has other ideas and radios, "Recommend a recce [reconnaissance] pass." Wickson agrees with this call. They fall in lead-trail formation, turning back into the same valley to overview the crash site. May now remembers to turn on his HUD tape.

Flying low over the crash site, they freeze the coordinates of 36°46' north and 44°05' east and call them in to the AWACS. Excited and pumped up about shooting down an enemy helicopter, May looks at the wreckage and films simultaneously. He sees masses of black oily smoke, fire and debris everywhere. It is obvious no one could have survived the holocaust he sees below him. Just before he pulls up to blow out of the area, he makes one last call on the main radio, to which all the aircraft listen. Breathing hard from the excitement and difficult flying, May makes the unforgettable comment, "Stick a fork in them, they're done!"

7

No Fly Zone, Northern Iraq
April 14, 1994
Thursday, 10:30 A.M.

Just minutes before the shoot down of the two Black Hawks, Capt. Gregory Herbin, the pilot of the AWACS plane, had radioed Mission Crew Commander Tracy on the internal network to report the weather and his craft's position. But before he could give this information, Tracy had responded with, "Stand by. The F-15s are engaged!"—evidence that the three supervisors, sitting together in the Pit, were aware that the shoot down was in progress, although they failed to take any action to prevent it.

But one of the controllers had responded to the early warning signs of disaster. Capt. Chris Fuller, the weapons officer who controls the tankers, had been eating lunch and casually watching the scope, waiting for his guys to arrive through Gate One. At 10:27 A.M. he'd heard the F-15s radio that they were going to visually ID the targets. Then he heard Wickson call again with, "VID Hind." This was the call that had immediately piqued Fuller's attention, and he'd yelled over the weapons network, "Turn on the video recorder. Something's happening down there!" It seemed as if just seconds had passed when he heard them call, "engaged." Fuller had known what this call meant, and he knew his tankers were very close to entering the No Fly Zone. Knowing the F-15s were too occupied to provide protection, he'd radioed the tankers, "Hey, let's start working back to the west. Left turn, let's get back to the west!"

Now, immediately after the shoot down, everyone is yelling at once, and there is utter confusion among the entire AWACS crew. Captain Cathy, the weapons instructor, sleeping in the back of the aircraft, returns from his nap. Fuller tells him, "I think we've just shot down a couple of helicopters; it should be on the videotape, and you can probably watch it!" As Cathy is watching the tape Fuller is listening and still talking to his tankers. His scope begins to light up with radar, and he thinks, "We've just shot down two helicopters. Maybe the Iraqis are going to come for our guys." He yells across the console once again. "Turn on the recorder, something else is happening here!" Captain Cathy, still drowsy, turns the tape on and tapes over the previously recorded shoot down. Fuller's concern turns out to be a false alarm.

Concurrently Major Martin is frantically trying to get through on the satellite communication to Lt. Col. Richard Cole, Mad Dog, his counterpart on the ground in Incirlik, to inform him of the shoot down. Martin remembers seeing the Black Hawk nomenclature on the scope leaving Zakhu. Although he wasn't paying strict attention, he did notice that the track stopped, but he had no idea where it was supposed to be going. He's not an expert at reading the green dots on the scopes. In fact, he says, "I'm like a pig looking at a watch" because his job is not controlling aircraft. He represents the commander of OPC, helping the crew and aircraft deal with the unusual or the combat situation and interpreting the rules of engagement. As he was listening to the F-15s' radio calls, he had been trying to determine exactly what was going on and what was going to develop. More concerned about an Iraqi trap or setup, he had thought, "Don't be lured into anything." In his mind, he was trying to come up with a plan, confident he was not going to let the situation get out of control.

He continues trying to relay the information to Mad Dog at Incirlik, but there seems to be some difficulty with the satellite communications. After ten minutes of constant attempts he finally makes contact. Martin relays the pertinent information about the type of aircraft shot down, the time, and the coordinates. Mad Dog, almost in disbelief, gives a brief reply, "Affirmative."

Meanwhile, among the AWACS crew the pandemonium escalates because this all happened so quickly: just eight minutes from the time the initial contacts were picked up until missiles were fired and only two minutes from the visual identification until splashdown!

Thirty minutes later Mad Dog, in Incirlik, calls Martin back. In a serious voice he says, "Do you know where Eagle Flight is?" Sternly he orders, "Get a valid track on them." After completing this brief call Duke yells to the AWACS crew, "There may be a problem!"

Bedlam erupts among the controllers as they try to recreate some of the events leading to the shoot down. Halcli, the enroute controller, is dispatched to look for the card that gives the locations for the Delta Points—

the same Delta Points given by the Black Hawks after they left Zakhu. This Delta Point system, used since the inception of OPC, provides standard code names for real locations. These code names prevent the enemy, who might be listening to radio transmissions, from knowing the Black Hawks' intended flight plan. Then they were deemed too insignificant to look up, but now, with smoldering, burnt bodies lying on the valley floor, this information takes on a new importance. First he looks in the weapons kit, and after five minutes he finally locates the card over in the Surveillance Section: "Whiskey" denotes Zakhu and "Lima" stands for the town of Irbil. Looking at a map, using dead-reckoning procedures, it is clear that the Black Hawks' last tracks on the AWACS scopes were twenty miles from the site of the shoot down.

The controllers call the F-15s on Have Quick and ask them to reconfirm that their targets were Hind helicopters and not Black Hawks. Tiger Flight replies that they saw two pods, one on each side of both helicopters, but they didn't see any ordnance being dispensed. Everyone on AWACS discusses whether the pods were fuel tanks or weapons pods. However, most of the crewmembers are still trying to disprove it was the Black Hawks that were shot down. Someone mentions that the Black Hawks may have landed in a small village enroute to Irbil, but the possibility is just too much of a coincidence. Eagle Flight is missing, and two helicopters have been shot down. In reality, everyone suspects what has happened, but it seems impossible that the F-15s could have made such a deadly error.

Major Martin leaves his position to take a short break in the rear of the aircraft. He leans against the radar console and remarks to another crewmember, "I hope we haven't shot down our own helicopters. I can't believe anyone could make that dumb of a mistake!"

The time is approximately 11:45 A.M., one hour and fifteen minutes after the shoot down. The first calls on the Guard frequency have begun and will continue until the Black Hawks are found. Incirlik has dispatched Harrier jets to take aerial photos of the crash site. Other fighter aircraft are beginning the futile search for parked helicopters on the ground.

The AWACS crew now comes to the realization that they face another serious dilemma. The controllers are very much aware that the magnetic tape recorded their switch actions and the radar information during the flight. All of them now know that from 10:23 to 10:28 A.M. there were intermittent IFF responses on their scopes from the Black Hawks. If an accident investigation is conducted, investigators will be able to use a simple switch action called a "Request SIF" (selected identification feature for five codes, modes I–IV and mode Charlie-altitude) to interrogate the IFF responses. They will be able to identify the target as a Mode I, code 42—a friendly aircraft on the enroute radio code. The big question will be: What was going on during this time to have four minutes of IFF information on the target with no one attaching symbology or starting the identification process? It's going to be a stretch to explain this situation, because the mission crew commander (Major Tracy), the weapons director (Captain Wang), the Duke (Major Martin), and the AOR controller (Lieutenant Wilson) were all at their scopes at the time. How is it possible, with only four aircraft to account for over the entire No Fly Zone, that none of these four individuals were able to see this continuing intermittent IFF signal? How will they explain this oversight? What they do know is that their answers better be consistent and believable. Captain Bell and Major Tracy strongly recommend everyone take notes. AWACS is only four hours into this eleven-hour mission, so the crew will have ample time to continue their discussion and corroborate the details and facts.

Initially after the shoot down Wickson had radioed AWACS to report that he and May would need to get gas ten minutes earlier than scheduled. They were low on fuel due to the extensive use of afterburners during the intercept and engagement. He knew the F-16s were due in Gate One, and he had just heard their radio call. The F-16s protected the area while the F-15s took on a full load of gas. Wickson and May remained in the area for one more hour as they continued their search for enemy activity.

They now prepare to exit the No Fly Zone and continue with the standard procedure of a contact call to Duke, Major Martin. Duke gives the weather at "home plate," Incirlik AFB, and adds, "Negative additional words." Then he surprises Wickson and May by saying, "Good job today, Tiger. Expect to be met at the aircraft." They begin flying back to home plate using the same route they took out to the area.

It is about 11:45 A.M. as the F-15s approach their second checkpoint, called "Derick," in Turkey. Wickson hears two radio calls, one on Guard and one on channel 8, the enroute frequency. "Eagle Flight, Cougar, signal check." Cougar indicates the AWACS, and Wickson knows Eagle Flight is the helicopters. Although there have been previous indications of disaster during the past hour, now he wonders why the Black Hawks need to do a radio check with AWACS. A chill engulfs Wickson's body, and he feels sick to his stomach as he considers the possibility that he and May have just shot down two U.S. helicopters.

8
Incirlik Air Force Base, Turkey
April 14, 1994
Thursday, 10:40 A.M.

A t the Incirlik Air Force Base Command Post, Lieutenant Colonel Cole has been sitting in the position of Ground Mission Director, call sign Mad Dog, since 6:20 A.M. He had arrived at the Command Post about one hour before AWACS departure, fully expecting it to be another ordinary, routine day conducting the business of Operation Provide Comfort. In fact, today's mission was almost the exception because everything had been running so well. AWACS had gotten on station early, there were no major mechanical problems with any of the aircraft, and the weather was clear.

But when problems do occur Lieutenant Colonel Cole can handle them. With eighteen years in the Air Force, 1,000 flying hours in the F-4, and another 1,000 hours in the F-15 under his belt, he has been the supervisor of the Mission Director Program at Incirlik since his arrival here in February. He's the one the pilots would want to speak to when they're having a problem in the air or on the ground because he also acts as a conduit to the command structure at Incirlik. He informs the OPC commanders immediately if anything happens over the No Fly Zone that might require a decision on their part or their approval. In fact, his most critical function as Mad Dog is to be there for Duke, the Airborne Command Element aboard the AWACS. Should Duke run into any situation over the No Fly Zone that would involve committing U.S. or coalition forces, Mad Dog will communicate with him to provide command guidance. Making weather decisions, implementing safety procedures, scheduling aircraft, and ensuring that the ATO is executed smoothly are all secondary functions. This huge responsibility begins when Mad Dog steps in the door each morning and ends when the last aircraft is down.

Lieutenant Colonel Cole tries to talk to Duke about once an hour, even if nothing unusual is happening. He is just thinking he has not spoken to

Major Martin, today's Duke, or any crewmember on the AWACS in a significant period of time. Precisely at that moment he receives a radio call from Martin stating, "We have just shot down two Hind helicopters," and then Martin gives the coordinates of the crash site. Cole is so stunned, he can manage only an "Affirmative" in reply because he has had no forewarning that an engagement was in process. Shooting down an enemy aircraft over the No Fly Zone is an extremely rare event. He pauses a few moments to let the severity of the situation sink in and calls Duke back to confirm the information.

Almost immediately Cole suspects a problem. A recent incident he was involved in when he was flying as a Duke flashes through his mind. On board the AWACS he was overseeing a flight of two F-16s conducting an early morning sweep of the No Fly Zone. They had locked two helicopters down low, fifty miles south of Zakhu, and had radioed, "We've got low fliers down here." On the AWACS scope Cole could see IFF paints, but it still took him ten minutes to figure out they were from Eagle Flight. He had radioed back to the F-16s, "We know who they are; leave them alone." This is the sequence of events Cole would expect anyone in the same situation to follow, because since he has been at OPC this is how it has worked on a daily basis. The F-15s—or whatever plane was investigating aircraft—would ask for feedback from Duke. Duke and the AWACS crew would then try to rummage around and find out whose aircraft it was and identify it specifically. If they were unsuccessful, Duke would then ask the pilots for a visual identification.

Because Cole is a pilot, he is very much aware of some pilots' sensitivity about asking for guidance or taking orders from the Duke. Most Dukes are not pilots like him, but are navigators or WSOs (weapon system operators). Cole frequently tells the other controllers, "Pilots don't like taking suggestions or orders from guys who aren't pilots. On a regular basis, down here at OPC, we have to hammer it into the flying squadrons, 'Duke's word is final!' " Even then, the squadrons sometimes whine about the authority of Duke.

Cole is also thinking about Hind helicopters. Yes, Iraq has Hinds, but so do Turkey and Syria. In his mind, a Hind helicopter is not much of a threat even to the most inept F-15 pilot. "Yep, we've got a problem, a very serious problem."

Now on automatic pilot he begins making the necessary calls to his superiors. The first commander Cole notifies this morning is Lt. Col. Mark Dougherty, the acting CFAC DO (Combined Forces Air Component Deputy of Operations). He briefly tells him what happened, and Dougherty replies, "I'm coming in!" Ten minutes later, as Dougherty rushes through the door of the Command Post, he says, "Confirm you have a valid track on Eagle Flight and find out where they are." Cole radios Duke, "Find Eagle Flight!"

Lieutenant Colonel Dougherty had thought from the moment he had been notified that this was a very strange incident. Not only is Dougherty a commander, he is also a current F-16 pilot who flies over the No Fly Zone on a regular basis. He knows the flying game well and understands a shoot down is a big deal anywhere. But here, at Operation Provide Comfort, this shoot down of helicopters is really turning him for a loop because helicopters had never been a threat in this theater.

Meanwhile, Mad Dog has been busy notifying others in the command structure, and they immediately begin arriving as well. There is silence as they wait to hear what Dougherty has to say. A sergeant is brought in to begin taking notes and keep track of any details that might have later significance. A few of the commanders huddle together, and all quietly concur that this is a very bizarre situation. In the three-year history of this operation, they've never experienced a helicopter encroaching over the 36th parallel. In their minds, it would be just about impossible and extremely risky for Iraqis to be that far north.

The next logical step is to contact Col. James O'Brien, the commander of Operations, Plans, and Policy for OPC. Flight plans for the Black Hawks get passed to his shop. It becomes apparent that his office is more aware of the exact nature of the Black Hawks' agenda for today than are the officers currently at Command Post. Quickly Dougherty ascertains that today's Black Hawk mission was a big deal. A meeting had been planned with Mr. Barzani and Mr. Talabani, two prominent Kurdish leaders with whom he is familiar. The Army commanders and other officials had been sent to discuss security and charity relief for the Kurds. In fact, two days earlier the commander of OPC, General Pilkington, had signed an authorization letter, dated April 12, permitting the Black Hawks to travel outside the Security Zone, a secure area inside the No Fly Zone. Dougherty also learns Col. Jerry Thompson, the Army commander in Zakhu, had called O'Brien last night. Thompson had asked to be able to fly the mission without AWACS coverage. He'd said, "We have this important mission, outside the Security Zone, and we would like to get an early start. It would be best if we could leave before AWACS has spun up." O'Brien had replied, "No, Jerry, you must have AWACS coverage. I don't even have to ask General Pilkington, you and I both know what the guidance is."

Dougherty learns that Colonel O'Brien doesn't pass on the Black Hawks' flight plans or any of this information to the flying squadrons because it has never been standard procedure to do so. He has a demanding job and finds it difficult to attend to each and every detail. Therefore, O'Brien has come to believe the Delta Point system, used by the AWACS to track Eagle Flight, is sufficient for these unusual missions outside the Security Zone.

Colonel Dougherty thinks, "Now everything is happening so quickly, and it's all turning out wrong!" This is the worst thing he can imagine, something he had never envisioned or anticipated. The OPC commanders build scenarios all the time, particularly with the Mad Dogs and Dukes, playing "what if." But this one had never even entered their thought process.

Across the base, at the BOQ, Capt. Steven Neuser is dressed in his Nomex flight suit, in preparation for his scheduled afternoon mission over the No Fly Zone. He has been flying the F-15 since July 1992 and at this point has only 380 hours of experience in the jet. But he has a total of 2,400 hours flying military aircraft. He was an Army aviator, having flown as a chief warrant officer with the 3rd Infantry. His helicopter experience is extensive, with time in the UH-1 Huey, Scouts, Bell Jet Rangers, and Cobras. He has no special qualifications as an F-15 pilot, but he has flown in Operation Provide Comfort before. The first time was in December 1993 to February 1994. He has been in Turkey, on this rotation, for three weeks. Today will be his nineteenth mission over northern Iraq. Back in Germany he is assigned to the 53rd Fighter Squadron with Lieutenant Murray, Captain Wickson, and Lieutenant Colonel May. May is his squadron commander.

Before he deployed to Incirlik his schedule mainly entailed getting the squadron moved from Bitburg AFB to Spangdahlem AFB. Very little flying was going on, and everyone was doing a lot of physical labor. Pilots worked as carpenters building facilities and doing self-help projects. The move had become so intense at one point, he hadn't been able to fly for three weeks. This had caused him some concern because flying is a perishable skill. Since he has been down here he has made a point of getting back into the books because, before arriving at OPC, there were few opportunities to keep current. Mostly he has been spending his time studying the aircraft operating handbooks, tactics, the ATO, SPINS (special instructions), and threat knowledge.

Shortly before noon the phone rings in Neuser's room. He answers it and is surprised to find the F-15 squadron duty supervisor on the other end. "You might want to come into the squadron early, prior to your brief time." Neuser, concerned he may have done something wrong, asks why. The duty supervisor comes back with, "Well, I just can't tell you." Dressed and ready, he hitches a ride to the squadron, apprehensive about why he has been requested to arrive early. He is met at the door. "Why do you think we told you to come in early?" Neuser really is not sure at all. "We've just shot down two helicopters over Iraq. We got two Hinds!" Almost speechless, Neuser replies, "Wow, cool! Who was it?" The duty supervisor answers, "Tiger Flight, Wickson and May." Neuser asks where it happened—because he is next on deck to fly, he needs to know. The schedule indicates he will fly tail number 84-0025, the aircraft Wickson is about to land.

They walk back into the Intelligence Section and look at the map. Checking the coordinates and plotting them on the map, Neuser says, "Those guys were pretty far north." Around this time Dan Murray retrieves a message from the intel net about the shoot down. He has an eerie feeling something is not right, and he can't help thinking about Laura because he knows she is flying with the Army today, somewhere near Zakhu. He doesn't share these thoughts with the others in the room but briefs the message, just received, in a restrained manner. Although few facts are known about the shoot down, the entire squadron is subdued. Neuser notes the almost somber atmosphere. He thinks, "We should be jubilant, but this is too shocking, too unexpected. We all must be in a subtle state of shock."

The guys in the squadron don't discuss it or even give it a lot of speculation because they're waiting for Wickson and May to land. They decide, "Okay, when they land we need to go out to the jet, meet them, and find out more information." Just as they make this decision personnel from Wing Intelligence arrive, announcing, "Eagle Flight is overdue, and there is some concern about where they are supposed to be flying today.

Many of the colonels are concerned. There may be more implications than just a directed shoot down."

Neuser and Dan give the briefing board a quick study. It shows Eagle Flight was supposed to be at Zakhu around 9:30 A.M. local time. The time is now close to noon. Eagle Flight is missing, and two Hinds have been shot down. Shadows of doubt begin descending on the crowded briefing room. Neuser says to Dan, "Were the Black Hawks equipped with sponsons?" Dan doesn't know, but asks, "Why?" Neuser replies, "Because they look a lot like attack helicopters with those things on. From my previous experiences, and I've seen them a lot, outside of a mile you really can't tell the difference." The intelligence officers become silent, and Neuser takes this as a bad sign. He strongly believes something is really wrong now based on his helicopter expertise, but he doesn't voice any more concerns because he knows that's how rumors start. Neuser remains silent and waits with the rest of the group for more information to come in and the pilots to land.

Wickson and May are on final approach to Incirlik Air Force Base. Over Turkish airspace, on their way back home, they had discussed in detail the day's events on the auxiliary radio. Wickson had radioed maintenance at Incirlik that they'd fired munitions. Consequently, the crew chief had done the appropriate planning to have the aircraft reconfigured to replace the missing missile. He'd also told his technicians not to discuss anything with anyone here or off station. As Wickson prepares to touch down on the tarmac, he still feels uneasy because of the calls he has heard on the Guard frequency trying to locate Eagle Flight.

Their landing is uneventful, and the first thing Wickson notices as he rolls the aircraft into the chocks is a group of officers out on the flight line to meet him. He thinks that's to be expected, for it isn't every day that an aircraft lands with expended ordnance. The crew chief gives him the signal to chop the engines, and once they are shut down he brings over the boarding ladder and helps him out with his gear. Wickson reports, "This aircraft is shit hot, code one, there are no defects or problems other than the missing AMRAAM". He also tells the crew chief, "It was just another day at the office, but it is a good feeling, to finally do something, to shoot down an aircraft." The crew chief replies, "That's what we've been waiting for."

Lieutenant Colonel May is also upbeat as he climbs out of his jet and greets his crew chief. "You need to make this aircraft code three." He says this jokingly because several of the aircraft at OPC have Iraqi flags painted on the side, which indicate kills during the Gulf War. The chief knows this means he has to put an Iraqi flag on the plane, because it was involved in the shoot down. "Not a problem, sir. We'll put it on tonight." May pops out the HUD tape and walks over to meet the welcoming group.

Dan Murray had led the group of six officers out to greet Wickson and May. He doesn't usually go out to the flight line to meet the crew, but today he knows the Wing Intelligence officers will be out there. These are his crewmembers, and he feels a loyalty to the pilots to be there and to lead the debrief. The mood is still somber as they approach the shutdown F-15s. For a few moments there is some lighthearted discussion. "Hey, it must have been pretty exciting up there? We noticed you landed with a missile missing." Neuser walks over and shakes Wickson's hand and says, "Hey, good job!" He resists the urge to ask questions because he knows Intel is waiting to debrief them. Dan doesn't join in with the congratulatory atmosphere. Impatiently he waits for this moment to pass, trying to maintain his professional and personal composure.

Dan mainly debriefs Wickson and then just confirms Wickson's information with May. He asks what happened prior to the contact, where they were, what they were seeing on their scopes, who they talked to, if they were in contact with AWACS, and the details of the visual identification. One of the officers pulls out a large map of northern Iraq, and Wickson points to the location of the crash site. Lastly, Dan briefs the shooting pass and asks for a description of exactly what they saw after they splashed the choppers. Wickson mentions only that he saw a huge fireball when the missile engaged the helicopter. Both pilots are asked if this was an AWACS-cleared shot. Wickson replies, "Yes, this was, according to the ROE. It was an ROE shot." One of the bystanders yells, "What was the range of the shot?" Wickson says, "Somewhere around five or six miles." Dan concludes the pilots are nothing less than 100 percent sure they had shot down two Iraqi Hinds, and they convince him they have done everything by the book. Dan has all the information he needs to write the mission report.

May walks over to the group of pilots and asks one of them to take some pictures of Wickson and him standing by the aircraft. After they finish Neuser says to both of them, "I've got one question. Did you see two canopies? Did you see a double bubble canopy?" Wickson says, "It was hard to tell, it could have been." Neuser wonders if they got close enough to the helicopters to get a good visual identification. He doesn't want to put a damper on everything by saying, "Hey, I don't think it was a Hind." He remembers how shocked he was, during his first rotation, last December, to find out you could shoot down helicopters here at OPC. All of his past experiences flying choppers and F-15s had put all helicopters off-limits. He had even had discussions with his flight leads about this. "I can't believe they're going to let us shoot helicopters. They don't pose any big threat; if I'm smart, they can't shoot me."

Lieutenant Colonel Cole, Mad Dog, picks up May and drives over to get Wickson. Wickson shakes hands with May before he climbs into the vehicle. As Mad Dog drives them over to the squadron, he says, "You probably noticed I don't have a very happy face. There is a helicopter missing, and they're still searching for it." Wickson thinks, "This is the second time I've heard something about friendly helicopters." The uneasiness that has again pervaded his body leads him to ask Mad Dog some questions. "How many aircraft were in Eagle Flight, and where were they going?" Mad Dog erroneously says, "One helicopter, and they were going to Zakhu." Wickson begins to feel more comfortable because he and May had shot down two helicopters and they weren't anywhere near Zakhu.

They arrive at the squadron, drop off their life-support gear, and secure their weapons. After a bathroom break they climb back into the vehicle with Mad Dog and drive to the Command Post. Once inside, they do another quick debrief with Dan Murray and several of the OPC commanders. During the briefing Wing Intelligence people are everywhere, walking in and out with messages. A request is made for information on Iraqi Hinds' paint scheme. One of the commanders tells the pilots, "Just explain to us what happened out there." Again Wickson and May go over the details of their mission that morning. At the end of the debrief they are told, "The reason we are asking you these questions is there are two helicopters missing, and they've been missing for two hours. We're a bit uneasy about what happened." The mood in the room and the serious tone of the last statement leads Wickson to believe that they think he has shot down friendly helicopters. Wickson asks a colonel, "Who was Eagle Flight, why were they out there, why didn't I know about it, and what was their flight plan?" Dan has remained concerned yet silent up to now. But the circumstances are giving him strong reason to believe Laura was on one of those helicopters.

They finish the briefing at a little after 1:00 P.M. and adjourn to the next room to review the heads-up display tape. There is only one. Wickson explains to the group that he had forgotten to turn on his tape. However, May, who had also forgotten to turn on his tape during the shoot down, had turned his tape on during the recce pass when he and Wickson had flown over the crash site. The group of commanders and intelligence officers, including Dan, gather together to look at those two minutes of tape, which show wreckage in flames. More intelligence officers enter the room. "Sir, we have the information you requested. All Iraqi Hinds are desert camouflage; in other words brown, not green."

Dan is now certain Laura is dead. He can picture her lying on the canyon floor in Iraq, her body somewhere in that burning wreckage. He excuses himself, runs to the bathroom, and vomits.

Wickson can't believe what he has just heard. Since last December, on his last rotation, this is the first time he has heard that Iraqi helicopters are painted in desert camouflage. He says to himself, "This is looking bad. They're already asking these questions this soon after the incident, when we haven't even finished debriefing." His thought process is interrupted when another officer enters the room and reports, "Turkey has several Hind helicopters; we're trying to find out if they were flying this morning."

Both pilots are brought across the street and ensconced in the office of the commander of the Operations Support Squadron. They are told the commander will watch them while they prepare a statement. The commander instructs them to write a statement in longhand and then type it. There is a television on in the small room, tuned to CNN. Several hours pass, they finish their statements, then spend their time drinking sodas and watching the news. They are shocked when CNN breaks into its regular broadcast with a special news bulletin. The reporter announces, "Two U.S. Army Black Hawk helicopters have been shot down over northern Iraq by two U.S. Air Force F-15s. It is reported there are twenty-six casualties." This is their first real confirmation they had shot down friendlies. Shortly afterward a military attorney and the chaplain pay the two pilots a visit.

During the time Wickson and May are detained, the fallout from the shoot down begins to escalate. At 1:15 P.M. Kurdish civilians notify MCC Forward in Zakhu that two American Black Hawks were shot down. They counted twelve bodies near one crash site. General Pilkington authorizes

48

the launch of a search and rescue land-based team from Zakhu to the crash site. The Harrier jets land at Incirlik with the aerial photographs. The helicopters, although badly burned and mangled, are conclusively identified as U.S. Army Black Hawks, based on an engine cowling in one of the photos.

Although the Incirlik Search and Rescue Squadron has been on alert status since the first report of a shoot down, its departure is awaiting Turkish approval. Turkish officials continue to insist the Army Black Hawks from Pirinclik AFB take on this mission. It takes several hours to convince them this is a task that can be accomplished only by the designated search and rescue helicopters at Incirlik. They are configured for the express purpose of search and recovery, and it already is evident there will be many bodies to recover. Finally at 3:00 P.M. the Search and Rescue Squadron departs Incirlik Air Force Base.

Friendly fire, fratricide, is the curse of warfare. For a commander responsible for the safety and well-being of his troops, there can be nothing worse. Friendly fire is often associated with smoke-filled skies, lightning-quick life-or-death combat decisions, and a hostile environment. But today the weather was picture-perfect, the No Fly Zone was a relatively safe flying environment, and the sky was not filled with hostile aircraft. There was no "fog of war." Nevertheless, in a short time the U.S. Army and Air Force will have to personally notify each victim's family and try to explain the circumstances of their loved one's death. In addition, the print and electronic media will demand answers or hire experts to create their own.

General Pilkington has contacted his superior officer in Europe. Immediately the news goes radioactive and the information travels up the chain of command. This is the stuff that takes a general's breath away as each considers the interservice and international nightmare that will follow. The generals go into a freeze mode and do not talk to anyone else until they are sure how and at what level this incident will be handled.

General Pilkington's next step is to convene an Interim Safety Board, which will assemble all the information necessary for the professional investigators who will arrive tomorrow to conduct the official investigation. He assigns a colonel, the base safety officer, and a lawyer to start collecting records and securing evidence. He has already asked his superior officer for guidance because this investigation will be a high-profile event and many people will be asking questions about this incident.

The other immediate priority is obtaining an accurate and complete crew and passenger list from MCC Forward in Zakhu. In this age of instant news and information, every family who has a Black Hawk crewmember stationed anywhere on the globe will be calling the nearest military installation to confirm the safety of their loved one.

Time Line for Shoot Down

Time* (in Turkey)	AWACS (Cougar Flight)	F-15s (Tiger Flight)	Black Hawks (Eagle Flight)
7:36 A.M.	Takeoff from Incirlik AFB		
8:22 A.M.			Takeoff from Pirinclik AFB
8:45 A.M.	"On station"; begin tracking aircraft		
9:16 A.M.	"H" character programmed to appear on Senior Director Wang's radarscope when Eagle Flight's IFF, Mode I, code 42, is detected		
9:21 A.M.	AWACS acknowledges Black Hawks' radio call and annotates their radar track as "EE 01"		Black Hawks call AWACS on the enroute frequency at "Gate One" (entrance to AOR)
9:24 A.M.	Black Hawks' radar and IFF returns fade		Black Hawks land at Zakhu
9:35 A.M.		Takeoff from Incirlik	
9:36 A.M.	Enroute Controller Halcli interrogates F-15s' IFF, Mode IV		
9:54 A.M.	AWACS receives Black Hawks' radio call; Enroute Controller Halcli reinitiates "EE 01" symbology to resume tracking		Black Hawks call AWACS to report enroute from "Whiskey" (Zakhu) to "Lima" (Irbil)
9:55 A.M.	"H" begins to be regularly displayed on Senior Director Wang's radarscope (IFF, Mode I, code 42)		
10:05 A.M.		Check in with AWACS on enroute frequency	

*Iraq is one hour later than Turkey. To simplify the events before and after the shoot down, all times that occur in Iraq are given in Turkish time.

Time (in Turkey)	AWACS (Cougar Flight)	F-15s (Tiger Flight)	Black Hawks (Eagle Flight)
10:11 A.M.	"H" ceases to be displayed on Senior Director Wang's radarscope		
10:12 A.M.	Black Hawks' radar and IFF contacts fade; computer symbology continues to move at last known speed and direction		Black Hawks enter mountainous terrain
10:13 A.M.	Air Surveillance Officer Bell places arrow on Senior Director Wang's scope in vicinity of Black Hawks' last known position		
10:15 A.M.	Maj. Martin ("Duke") replies to F-15s, ". . . negative words"; radar adjusted to low velocity	Check in with Duke	
10:20 A.M.		Enter AOR and call AWACS at Gate One on AOR radio frequency	
10:21 A.M.	"EE 01" (Black Hawk symbology) dropped by AWACS		
10:22 A.M.	AOR Weapons Director Wilson responds, "Clean there"	Flight Lead Wickson reports radar contact at 40 nautical miles	
10:23 A.M.	Intermittent IFF response appears in vicinity of F-15s' reported radar contact		
10:24 A.M.	"H" symbol reappears on Senior Director Wang's scope		
10:25 A.M.	Black Hawk IFF response becomes more frequent; AOR Controller Wilson responds to F-15s with, "Hits there"	Flight Lead Wickson calls, ". . . Contact"; radar return approximately 20 nautical miles	

Time (in Turkey)	AWACS (Cougar Flight)	F-15s (Tiger Flight)	Black Hawks (Eagle Flight)
10:26 A.M.	Black Hawk IFF response continuous; radar response intermittent		
10:27 A.M.	Surveillance Officer Deidre Bell initiates "unknown, pending, unevaluated" symbol in vicinity of Black Hawks' IFF radar returns; attempts IFF interrogation		
10:28 A.M.	Black Hawk IFF and radar responses fade	Flight Lead Wickson visually identifies a helicopter at 5 nautical miles	
10:28+ A.M.	AWACS replies, "Copy Hinds"	Flight Lead Wickson conducts VID pass and calls, ". . . Tally two Hinds"	
10:28:30 A.M.		Wingman May conducts VID pass and calls, "Tally two"	
10:29 A.M.		Flight Lead Wickson instructs Wingman May to "arm hot" and gives instruction for independent targeting	
10:30 A.M.		Flight Lead Wickson fires Fox-3 at trail helicopter	Trail Black Hawk hit by missile
10:30+ A.M.		Wingman May fires AIM-9 at lead helicopter	Lead Black Hawk hit by missile
10:30+ A.M.		May reports, "Splash the second bandit"	

9
Washington, D.C.
April 14, 1994
Thursday, 8:00 A.M.

It is 8:00 in the morning in Washington, D.C. Gen. Merrill McPeak, chief of staff of the Air Force, is having a breakfast meeting at the Pentagon with Representative Steve Buyer from Indiana and Representative Sam Johnson from Texas. Their breakfast is interrupted when an officer approaches the table and slips McPeak a note. Without excusing himself, without saying a word, he gets up and leaves the room. A few minutes later he returns to the table, slowly sits down, and pauses before he speaks. It is obvious to the congressmen he is extremely upset. McPeak finally says, "We've shot down two of our own." Looking at the two shocked lawmakers, he remarks that he doesn't have much information, but he tells them what he knows. Johnson, a former Vietnam prisoner of war and Thunderbird pilot, asks, "What about AWACS? Couldn't AWACS pick up those helicopters on radar?" McPeak has no answers, but he is thinking, by damned, he'll find out! He knows the buck stops at his office. Too upset to finish his breakfast, McPeak leaves the dining room. He has the responsibility of notifying his superiors: the secretary of the Air Force, Dr. Sheila Widnall; the secretary of defense, Dr. William Perry; the chairman of the Joint Chiefs of Staff, Gen. John Shalikashvili; and, ultimately, the commander in chief, President Bill Clinton.

President Clinton is not having one of his most stellar weeks. Campaigning for office in 1992, he portrayed himself as an internationalist, in favor of committing U.S. troops and resources to bring order and democracy to the world. Since taking office this has not been a successful objective. First, there was the fiasco in Somalia, when eighteen Americans were killed in a firefight. Next, he intervened in Haiti to make that small country safe for democracy. Haiti's leaders defied his attempts, and Haiti simmers in the Caribbean waiting to erupt into another crisis.

In the modern world television and the media play a critical role in

Washington's military decisions. The American public is not interested in being the planet's peacekeepers if the price they pay is sacrificing their own sons and daughters. Who can forget the graphic television footage of dead American soldiers being dragged through the dusty streets of Mogadishu? Clinton's newest strategy is the use of strategic airpower. It looks clean on television, and it doesn't expend as many lives as the use of ground troops. But this week that strategy failed. Earlier in the week, for the first time, F-16s and F/A-18s bombed Serbian ground troops in an effort to stop a Serbian attack on the town of Gorazde. The bombing raids only made the Serbs more determined to retaliate. They placed 200 United Nations soldiers under house arrest, renewed their attack on Gorazde, and shot down a British Harrier jet.

This morning President Clinton is in the Oval Office briefing congressional leaders on his newest international peacekeeping policies. Later this week he is planning to sign a presidential directive that will clearly make international peacekeeping an explicit U.S. objective. In the midst of the briefing he is approached by a White House aide. Clinton stops the briefing, and he and the aide retreat to a private room. Clinton listens intently as he is told about the shoot down of the two Black Hawks by American Air Force fighter jets. "How did this happen?" he demands. The aide replies that the Pentagon is at a loss to explain what had gone wrong. The president is savvy enough to know that just as he is planning to step up America's commitment in Bosnia, this shoot down might undercut the public's willingness to undertake another peacekeeping mission. Military mistakes are more difficult to cover up during modern times. CNN reported the news of the shoot down just hours after it happened. The military will need to develop a plausible strategy to prevent bad press, answer the public's questions, and preserve international relations and the integrity of the U.S. government.

There's also the problem that many of the tragedy's victims were citizens of American allies. Clinton immediately calls British Prime Minister John Major and French President François Mitterrand to express his regrets and sympathies for their compatriots who also lost their lives today.

Clinton appears a few hours later in a televised news conference. He expresses his deep sorrow at the downing of the two Army Black Hawk helicopters. He tells the reporters that he is seeking an investigation and that he has already instructed Defense Secretary Perry and General Shalikashvili to lead an inquiry into the accident. "We will get the facts, and we will make them available to the American people and to the people of Britain, France, and Turkey, our partners in Operation Provide Comfort."

A few hours later, in an interview with the Associated Press, Perry appears pale and clearly shaken by the shoot down. He says, "I take full responsibility for today's tragedy. The fault could not lie with the equipment alone. There were errors, human errors probably, and there might be process or system errors as well." Perry tells the reporters he has postponed a trip to Japan and South Korea to make sure two separate investigations of the incident begin immediately. The first one, by General Shalikashvili, will review the flight procedures in the three No Fly Zones where U.S. aircraft fly: northern Iraq, southern Iraq, and Bosnia. "We need to ascertain whether any action needs to be taken to minimize the chance of any recurrence of this kind again." In addition, a formal investigation will be conducted, and Perry expects this report within weeks. "This investigation will be more complicated than an accident of this type might normally warrant because of the involvement of foreign nationals."

Others in Washington also express their initial reactions. The chief representative of the Kurdish Democratic Party says he is mystified about how the U.S. pilots could have blundered so badly. Turkish Prime Minister Tansu Ciller offers her sympathies to the families of those who died: "The nation of Turkey has lost three officers, and what we need to do now is look at it and investigate further what happened." Iraq's ambassador to the United Nations says the incident should tell the West that it's time to reevaluate the operation in the northern part of his country. "It puzzles me why such a jumpy type of people are flying in the No Fly Zone. Without warning, they just shoot down helicopters. At least you start with a warning. That's a simple rule of engagement."

Only hours after the shoot down House Speaker Newt Gingrich says the Clinton administration should shoulder some of the blame for overextending U.S. armed forces in regional conflicts after cutting the military budget too much. "I think that we are very close to a significant mismatch between our defense budget and our foreign policy. As the force shrinks you've got to be more careful about where you use it." The White House responds immediately: "Attempts to politicize this tragedy are inappropriate."

Lawmakers from both the Republican and the Democratic Party demand explanations from the Pentagon. During the next few days a series of closed-door meetings hastily convened by the military and administration to answer lawmakers' questions and concerns will end in heated discussions.

Senator Sam Nunn, chairman of the Senate Armed Services Committee, says, "Somebody is going to have to sort out how much of the accident was human, how much of it was technical, and how much of it was mechanical." Senator James Exon from Nebraska, the second ranking Democrat on the Senate Armed Services Committee, is visibly shaken and angry leaving one of these sessions. "This tragedy was doubly stunning because the shooting apparently happened in broad daylight. It wasn't like they were dodging clouds. It's unbelievable, our command and control is so bad that an F-15 pilot can't identify a Black Hawk helicopter." Pausing to get control of his thoughts, Exon makes one last statement: "I have to think this is something that's going to cause some heads to roll. I'm not going to be satisfied with just blaming these two pilots. I'm very upset and a lot of tough questions are going to be asked."

10 San Antonio, Texas
April 14, 1994
Thursday, 12:00 Noon

Halfway around the globe from Iraq and across nine time zones from where Laura is stationed, my husband, Danny, is returning to his office building from his lunchtime run. It is a perfect April day in south Texas. The cool spring weather has allowed the wildflowers to remain abundant along the hilly running trail.

It was only one year ago, this month, that he retired from a twenty-six-year Air Force career. With remarkable ease he traded in his blue uniform for a gray business suit and began a second career. He had hoped we could remain in San Antonio. Aptly nicknamed "Military City, U.S.A.," it had been an anchor for us during those twenty-six years. His first assignment in San Antonio had been immediately after the Vietnam War, when he had been assigned to Randolph Air Force Base as a flying instructor. Through the years, like many Air Force families, we had bounced back and forth between San Antonio and other distant places around the world. Shortly before Danny retired he had been commander of the Officer Training School at Lackland Air Force Base on the south side of San Antonio. Our children had always thought of San Antonio as their hometown, and for Sean, it is really the only home he has ever known because he has lived here since the age of three.

It was the fulfillment of a long-set goal when, immediately after retirement, Danny was hired by a San Antonio company. That same week I was offered a teaching position here. Unlike most of our contemporaries, we still had a young child to raise, and we sensed the importance of establishing roots to help us guide Sean through his teenage years. But perhaps it was Danny and I who longed for those community connections, the one thing we missed during his Air Force career. Every family has some trepidation about life after military retirement, but for us, it was everything we had hoped for.

Danny pushes open the door to the gym that is part of the complex of buildings where he is employed and pauses for a drink of water before he heads to the showers. On the big-screen televisions in front of the treadmills and stationary bicycles, he notices CNN is breaking for a special news bulletin. Before he can turn away he sees two helicopters and two fighter planes superimposed over a map of Iraq. Immediately he is drawn to the screen and moves closer so he can hear above the undertone of conversation and exercise machinery. Although little detail is known, he learns two American F-15s have shot down two Black Hawk helicopters over the No Fly Zone in northern Iraq today. That's all he needs to know. Instantly recalling in detail the conversation he had with Laura last Sunday when she'd told him she was going into Iraq this week before returning to Germany, he is certain she was a passenger on one of those helicopters.

Danny feels as if he has been slammed in the chest. He looks around the busy gym and wonders how others can continue their workout when his daughter has just been killed. Somehow he manages to shower, change clothes, and get to his desk. A retired colonel, Danny doesn't even pause to consider how he can confirm if Laura was on one of those helicopters. Quickly he looks up the telephone number for the Military Personnel Center, known in the Air Force as "MPC," at Randolph AFB. MPC's main function is maintaining Air Force personnel records and assignment planning. But Danny is well aware of one of its secondary functions: casualty affairs. The center will be the first to be notified if there were any Air Force members on those helicopters today. In turn, MPC will be responsible for notifying the families of the victims. He knows it is standard procedure never to give notification of a death over the telephone. MPC will send a chaplain and an officer to tell the families in person. As Danny dials the number he remembers that a captain who used to work for him is now assigned at MPC. Danny has the presence of mind to know the captain can help cut through the layers of gatekeepers and office personnel who will guard the information he needs.

With trembling hands he dials the number, and the operator transfers the call. Danny quickly explains his certainty that Laura was a passenger on one of the helicopters. "I have to verify if Laura's name is on the passenger manifest. I know they won't want to release the information over the telephone, they will want to notify us in person. Right now there is no one home, and I am positive Laura was on one of those helicopters.

I need Casualty Affairs to confirm what I am already certain of!" The captain replies, "Sir, I'll call you back as soon as I find out anything, anything at all."

Danny does not call me at work because he knows there is no point in worrying me until Laura's name is confirmed. Just minutes after he hangs up, his telephone rings, and his heart skips a beat. It's our son Dan, who rarely calls his dad at work, but today he needs some advice. His graduation from the Air Force Academy is only six weeks away, and he asks Danny about an assignment he is considering. Danny tells him about the shoot down and his certainty that Laura is one of the victims. He tells Dan to stand by and that he will call him at his squadron as soon as he knows something. Dan can't even begin to believe this could be a remote possibility. He puts it in the back of his mind and decides to go to the library to finish working on a paper due Monday.

It is now close to 1:30 P.M., and Danny has heard nothing from MPC. He decides to attend a meeting scheduled to begin in a few minutes because there is nothing else he can do except carry on as usual. Leaving his desk, he tells his coworkers to interrupt him if he should receive any calls. Once in the meeting, his eyes are glued to the clock. At any moment he expects someone to break in with a message. Finally the meeting is adjourned, and Danny returns to his desk. He doesn't want to leave, go home, and miss MPC's call, so he decides to stay. It is now 3:00 P.M. Sean should be arriving home from school any minute now. Dialing our home number, Danny makes an effort to keep his voice calm as Sean answers the telephone. He routinely asks Sean about his day. After Sean finishes Danny says, "It is very important you tell Mom to call me as soon as she gets home."

Looking back, I had no warning signs that in a few hours my life would change forever. It still astounds me that throughout the day I had such a sense of well-being despite the fact that Laura had been killed before I woke up that morning. It was just one of those ordinary Thursdays. A day you wake to the alarm, eat Cheerios for breakfast, and attend to the preestablished morning routine. I love teaching and can truthfully say I look forward to each day. By mid-April we are preparing the students for the state-mandated assessment test that's scheduled in less than two weeks. In addition to reviewing test-taking skills, my lesson plan book tells me, I also taught decimals and the outer planets that day.

The dismissal bell rings at 2:45, and my students race out the door to enjoy the beautiful spring day. I plan to use the remainder of the afternoon to compile some test statistics on individual student performance due tomorrow. I become frustrated, as I am unable to locate the paperwork I need to complete this report. Teachers are masters at misplacing papers, but I am usually a very organized person. I do one more search and conclude they must be at home on my desk. "O.K., I'll just finish it at home tonight." Then I leave early because Sean has soccer practice and it's my turn to carpool.

By 3:15 I am in my car and driving home, listening to an all-news radio station. Stopping at a traffic light, I hear a report about two American helicopters shot down over Iraq. I listen to the short news brief with interest, but I'm not concerned because today is Thursday and Laura is on her way back to Germany. I remember our Sunday conversation and think, "Monday, Tuesday, Wednesday—three days; that's enough time to fly into Iraq, ride around in a tank or something, and catch a plane back to Germany." Ten minutes later I pull into our driveway, and Sean runs out to greet me. Before I can give him a hug he says, "Dad called and he wants you to call him right back."

Danny answers on the first ring. He tells me about the shoot down and says he is sure Laura was on one of the helicopters. I am not surprised he is thinking the worst. In our relationship he is the pessimist and I am the eternal optimist. We have provided a balance for each other that has allowed our marriage to last twenty-seven years. "Danny, don't worry. I'm certain Laura is back in Germany. Remember, she said she would probably fly into Iraq on Tuesday or Wednesday. I just know she is fine." Danny remains unconvinced. He says he is waiting for MPC to confirm the passenger manifest and will call me back as soon as he hears something.

Sean, who had been standing close by, has heard the entire conversation. I can see he is worried. "Sean, everything is going to be fine. Laura was not on those helicopters." He seems relieved, but I still sense concern. Laura is fifteen years older, but she and Sean share a very close and special relationship. Laura has never allowed distance to separate the two of them. A benefit of her temporary duty assignment in Turkey was the availability of free telephone calls to the United States. Sean had grown accustomed to talking to Laura every day. We both looked forward to those conversations, and we will miss them now that Laura is back in Germany.

Sean and I have planned a trip to Europe this summer. Laura is so excited. She can't wait to show Sean all the places she visited as a child, when we lived there for three years. She has been sending Sean picture postcards of the places she plans to take him. Sean has taped all of them to the side of the refrigerator so he can look at them while he eats breakfast. I remind Sean there is soccer practice this afternoon. "We will have to leave at five o'clock. Make sure you have eaten a snack and are dressed."

As usual, I am a woman with an agenda. Yesterday Dan's graduation pictures had arrived, and they were handsome. Two years ago I had Laura's graduation pictures framed. The large frame includes two military photographs and her graduation announcement double-matted in blue and silver. One picture is a profile shot with Laura holding a saber, and the other is a smiling, full-faced view. Laura was embarrassed when she first saw it hanging prominently in our den. She didn't feel the pictures were flattering because she had broken her nose playing in the National Intercollegiate Rugby Championship a few days before the pictures were taken. Her team had won the championship, and I thought her nose looked fine. She looked confident, beautiful, and I was so proud of all her accomplishments. I take the picture off the wall and place it in the trunk of my car. While Sean is practicing soccer, I will bring it to the frame shop so they can frame Dan's picture identically. For two years I have been anticipating having both their pictures hanging on the same wall with my husband's graduation photo.

It's almost 4:00 and I'm tired. I check on Sean and find him decompressing and watching cartoons. I slip into my bedroom, turn on CNN, and lie down. CNN begins with the news of the shoot down. They show a film clip of a crashed, smoldering helicopter. Listening to the details, I am shocked to learn American F-15s had shot down the two Army Black Hawk helicopters. President Clinton flashes on the screen expressing his sorrow and condolences to the victims' families. "Well," I think sarcastically, "this is a premature gesture. Probably none of the families of the crash victims have even been notified at this point in time." Still I make no personal connection to the event or to Laura. While watching the remaining news, I even fall asleep.

Sean wakes me up and I check the clock: 4:22 P.M. I feel as if I've slept hours. "Mom, Dad is on the telephone and needs to talk to you." Disoriented, rather than pick up the extension in the bedroom, I walk into the kitchen, where Sean has left the phone off the hook. Danny says, "I have just spoken to MPC at Randolph Air Force Base, and I'm coming right home." Now I am fully awake and take this news at face value. "Does this mean Laura was on one of those helicopters? Does this mean Laura is dead?" He replies with a barely audible, "Yes." I say, "No, no, this couldn't be!" Slowly I replace the receiver in its cradle.

My world has just slipped off its axis. Everything is blurry and moving in slow motion. There are no tears, just disbelief. I hear Sean give a low moan and turn to see him standing there, a stunned look on his face. He knows. We cling to each other as I repeat what Danny has told me. Both of us are speechless. There are no words to transcend this unimaginable situation.

Holding Sean, I glance out the front window and see my neighbor and close friend, Renee Ojeda. Her son, Hill, is the same age as Sean. During the seven years we have lived in this house, they have grown up together. I feel a need to repeat what Danny has told me, I guess, so I can begin to start believing it myself. I walk across the street. "Renee, Laura has been killed. She was on a helicopter that was shot down today over Iraq." Renee gasps. "No, Joan, this can't be true." I confess I don't believe it either. I'm sure this is all a mistake. I say what I want to believe: "Well, maybe it isn't true. Laura could be in a Kurdish village. I bet they'll find her."

As the words exit my mouth I glimpse a dark blue sedan coming slowly up our street. In all those many years of being married to an Air Force pilot, I know exactly what military protocol dictates in the event of death, and I've dreaded this exact situation for twenty-six years. I just never imagined this dark angel of death would come for my daughter, Laura. I watch in horror as it approaches our house and soon I am able to see that the passengers are wearing blue Air Force uniforms. It becomes apparent that Laura is not misplaced in a Kurdish village.

Renee and I are frozen as the car stops in front of my house. As the front door opens I recognize a colonel who used to work for Danny. Both back doors open, and the first thing I see is the gold chaplain's cross on the chest of the male passenger. The female passenger is wearing an Air Force nurse's uniform. This is it, this is really true! I meet them at the car and shock even myself with the greeting I give them. All my emotions are replaced by anger. This isn't my Air Force that has killed Laura, this is now their Air Force. "I know why you are here. Can you explain to me how this could have happened? Were these two young, inexperienced pilots out to win an Air Medal at any expense?"

Of course they are now aware I know the circumstances of Laura's death, and they have no answers for me. I see Sean hovering by the front door. I think about him and the need for me to get myself under control. I feel light-headed and sick to my stomach as I struggle to begin breathing in a regular pattern.

Sean and I become part of the entourage that files into the house to await Danny's arrival. Renee, her husband, Richard, and their children also take seats in the living room. Tension fills the room. Everyone feels awkward, and no one is sure how to break the silence. Sean sits close to me, and I wonder how a child can grasp this terrible situation when I can't even begin to understand it myself. I remember the framed picture of Laura I had put into the trunk of my car just one hour ago. I leave the room and go out to the garage to get it. As I reenter the living room I prop the picture up in full view of everyone. "I want you to see the person those pilots have killed today."

We all hear a car door slam and know Danny is home. He rushes through the door, his face ashen as he assesses the small group assembled in our living room. Automatically he shifts into his military mode as he recognizes the colonel. Introductions, firm handshakes, and greetings out of the way, we are left to confront the situation. In a somber, controlled voice the colonel says, "Laura was a passenger on one of two Army Black Hawk helicopters flying in the No Fly Zone over northern Iraq. Two U.S. Air Force F-15s mistakenly identified them as enemy targets and shot them down." I hear him say the words "friendly fire." This takes me by complete surprise, because although I am familiar with the term, I just never would have thought to associate it with the scenario of Laura's death. Friendly fire seems to be a situation reserved for wars and battles. What happened to Laura doesn't seem to fit my mental image of friendly fire. It seems more like a huge, dumb mistake. How could an event that results in death be deemed "friendly"? As my mind races with these thoughts, this impossible, unbelievable scenario fuels the anger in my soul.

The colonel tells us there are no survivors, but a search and rescue team has been deployed to the crash site for the purpose of recovering the remains of the victims. A Casualty Affairs officer, who will be assigned to work with our family, will keep us apprised of the situation. Most likely because of Danny's tenacity, we are the first family to be notified. The Army, State Department, and the U.S. government have yet to officially notify the other twenty-five families who reside in the United States, Europe, Turkey, and Iraq.

Just as the colonel gets up to lead the rest of the Air Force members out the door, I realize he probably volunteered for this duty out of loyalty to Danny. I know this has been a difficult situation for him. He probably had as many questions as we did. How do you tell a family the U.S. Air Force has killed their loved one? There is no feasible explanation, there are no answers; for now, just the facts will have to suffice.

We are left alone, but there is no time to reflect or grieve. Our next thought is to notify our families. We know Laura's name is now in the public domain, and we don't want any of them to learn about this tragedy from a news broadcast. It is a race against time. Immediately I think of my mother. In her late seventies, she has had two heart bypass surgeries, a pacemaker, and takes medication for a congestive heart condition. Her perseverance and strong will have allowed her to continue living independently in Venice, Florida, where Danny and I met and went to junior and senior high school. Impulsively I dial her number, and she answers right away. "Mom, I have some very sad news. Laura has been killed." Quickly I tell her what I know. "Mom, don't have a heart attack and die on me now!" My mother, a New England stoic, has little to say, and I don't prod her because I know she, like myself, is struggling to stay in control. We talk for only a few more minutes—there are so many others to call.

Finally we're able to get a call through to Dan's squadron at the Academy. He knows why we have called, and I can hear the disbelief in his voice. He and Laura had a close and deep relationship. They had more commonalities than differences. Laura was the trailblazer, the first one to test the waters of independence. Now he will walk that path alone. He wants to come home on the next flight and I agree. I have an immediate need to hold my family close to my heart through the difficult days that lie ahead. We make plans to get him on the first flight in the morning. Then I say the words that bring stark reality to this still abstract idea of my only daughter's death. "Dan, bring home a blue uniform. You will need it for Laura's funeral."

My thoughts turn to Dan Murray, who is like family to us. I find it odd that we haven't heard from him, and I wonder if he was on the helicopter with Laura. I call his mother in Arizona. When she answers I sense a hesitation in her voice. Carefully I try to ascertain what she knows. Finally I just say, "Sherry, Laura is dead. She was killed in a shoot down over northern Iraq today. What do you know? Have you heard from Dan?" In a weary voice she tells me Dan had called with the news late this morning. He had told her not to call us because the Air Force had to officially notify us first. Sherry also mentions Dan is under orders not to call us until he has permission. Lastly, she says the pilots who killed Laura were from Dan's squadron. This early into the tragedy I find this connection unimportant, perhaps ironic. I'm just relieved Dan is safe.

We continue making calls long into the night. At last it becomes too late to do anything else constructive. Emotionally spent, we go to bed— but never to sleep. I'm too numb to grieve or cry. I stare into the darkness and try to understand how this could have happened. I have so many questions, but my practical side takes over and I tell myself to put all these questions and concerns aside. It will take all my energy and concentration to get through tomorrow, the next few days, the rest of my life.

11

Incirlik Air Force Base, Turkey
April 14, 1994
Thursday, 7:00 P.M.

By early evening the news of the Black Hawk shoot down has enveloped Incirlik Air Force Base. Reports on CNN have been embellished by rumor and professed inside information. With shock and speculations, the mood has become somber, as almost everyone here knows someone who was a victim or is involved in either a major or minor way in this military catastrophe. In every office, every enlisted and officers' quarters, in the dining halls, everyone speaks in hushed tones. During the last three years the coalition forces had flown more than 50,000 combat operational hours. The flying safety record was near spotless, the flying environment safe—almost routine for a designated combat zone. What occurred out over the No Fly Zone today that had precipitated this tragic event? What happened today that had not happened in the past three years?

This afternoon General Shalikashvili, chairman of the Joint Chiefs of Staff, and Dr. William Perry, U.S. secretary of defense, had held a news conference on television. They promised the families of the victims a complete investigation and accountability of those responsible for this shoot down. General Pilkington had already been notified to cancel the safety mishap investigation and begin an AFR (Air Force Regulation) 110-14 investigation. Unlike a safety investigation, where testimony is confidential and given with the understanding that it can be used only for mishap prevention purposes, the testimony and records in an AFR 110-14 investigation may be used for any purpose deemed appropriate. Most importantly, the findings can be used for criminal proceedings, and the complete investigation, minus the classified portions, is releasable to the public.

At Ramstein Air Force Base, in Germany, Gen. Robert Oaks, commander in chief of the U.S. Air Forces in Europe, had immediately started appointing the Accident Investigation Board, composed of a board president, eleven board members from the U.S. Army and Air Force, three associate board members representing France, Turkey, and the United Kingdom, four legal advisers, and thirteen technical advisers. For those selected, this was extremely short notice because they are scheduled to depart for Incirlik AFB tomorrow morning, April 15.

It is 7:00 P.M., and the AWACS plane is nearing its final approach to Incirlik. Immediately after the shoot down the crew knew their actions would be investigated and judged. During the remainder of their mission they had worked together to get their facts consistent and believable. Therefore, the key mission crewmembers have made copious personal notes.

After they land there is just enough light left in the day to see the small group of Air Force officers assembled on the flight line. As the AWACS crewmembers exit the aircraft, they are escorted off the flight line, and the mission part of the crew is directed to the Operations Center conference room, where they are met by the Incirlik staff judge advocate and an Air Force attorney. The videotape is secured as evidence and rushed over to a combat camera. Over 100 pages of personal notes are confiscated and secured in a safe. The crew is advised that an AFR 110-14 Investigation Board is currently being assembled in Europe, and then the attorney explains that everything that is going to be said or written tonight has the potential of being used as evidence in a criminal case. Tomorrow additional military attorneys will begin arriving at Incirlik to provide individual legal counsel. The crew is advised of their legal rights, and most decline to make a written statement until they receive legal counsel.

The commander of the Operations Support Squadron presides over the group gathered around the conference table. He has a list of initial questions concerning the procedures the crew followed today because he needs to get some answers back up the chain of command in Europe and finally back to Washington. The crewmembers, who had worked so diligently all afternoon to arrive at a consistent story, are easily able to give an abbreviated verbal statement. Essentially they all say the entire incident had happened very quickly. Initially they didn't think they had any radar or IFF at the locality where the F-15s had called out unknown targets. Then they did see something and started tracking it. By the time they were able to interrogate the radar hits, the F-15s had made their visual passes, misidentifying the helicopters. Minutes later the shoot down occurred. They didn't have time to direct anything, and they hadn't had time to conclude anything. One of the AWACS crewmembers says, "We're a good crew. I don't think there are any problems with this AWACS crew. I don't know what you'll find with the F-15 pilots. I imagine they're probably a good crew too. The problem was most likely within the procedures and the way that they were perceived. That's where you'll find the problems."

Earlier the F-15 pilots had been persuaded to consent to urine tests to determine the presence of drugs or alcohol. In the wake of the confusion following the shoot down, the Incirlik Legal Office had decided to make this urine test a choice. When twenty-six lives are lost a urine test for drugs or alcohol should be standard procedure, not a choice. This is one factor the 110 investigators will scrutinize. Almost the entire AWACS crew decline the test, with the exception of the staff mission crew instructor, Major Saylor, and the AOR controller, Lieutenant Wilson.

The AWACS crew is released from the debrief. Major Martin, the Duke on the AWACS today, walks silently down the hall, alone. Lieutenant Colonel Cole, the Mad Dog on the ground during the shoot down, follows him, sensing something is wrong. Cole puts his hand on Martin's shoulder and ushers him into a small, empty room. It is clear Martin is upset. He tells Cole, "I have done something terrible. Twenty-six people have been killed today, and I had an opportunity to stop it!" Cole tells him it wasn't his fault: "Hey, man, I'm an F-15 pilot, and I can speak with some authority about this situation. This isn't the reaction you would expect from F-15 pilots sweeping the No Fly Zone. In fact, it is just the opposite of what anyone would expect. If I had been up there flying today as a Duke, I would have expected the F-15 pilots to query me on their next course of action. The last thing I would have expected is they would call 'engaged' and shoot down the helicopters." Major Martin confides, "I really didn't know what the radio call 'engaged' meant until this morning. I didn't think the pilots were going to pull the trigger and kill those guys! As a previous right seater in an F-111, I thought 'engaged' meant the pilots were going down to do a visual intercept."

Cole senses Martin is still very troubled and says in a serious tone, "If I had to choose to put anyone up there today in that situation, it would have been you. You have more combat time than anybody I know under the age of forty-five in the current Air Force. So of all the guys I have working for me at this particular time, I would trust your judgment the most in that kind of situation." Cole looks Martin in the eye one last time. "We can all look back and say, 'I think I could have stopped it,' but that's not the reaction we were expecting from the F-15s. We were expecting them to do what every pilot has done for the last three years when they've intercepted an unknown aircraft. We would expect a radio call saying, 'What do you want us to do with these guys?'"

It is after 10:30 P.M., and lights are burning in several commanders' offices throughout the base. In building 362, on the flight line, the commander of the Operations Support Squadron finally has a few brief moments to reflect on today's events. He is used to long days because that's what it takes to supervise 121 people and get the job done down here. He has some anger and a lot of questions about the shoot down this morning. It's one of his jobs to run the weekly detachment meetings where every flying squadron is represented and they go over sorties flown that week, morale issues, and safety. For as long as he's been down here, he has reiterated to the squadrons, "Be very cautious about misidentifying aircraft over the No Fly Zone." It's an important issue, with so many nations and so many different aircraft. For instance, the French F-1s are identical to the Iraqi F-1s. Weekly, he brought up the issue and most recently had said, "Anytime F-15s or anybody else out there picks up a helicopter on radar, it is probably a U.S., Turkish, or a United Nations chopper. They're numerous and they are out there often." He has always emphasized to the squadron leaders, "Check with AWACS and then do a visual identification." Then he would follow up with, "Anytime you intercept a helicopter as an unknown, there is always a question of procedures, equipment failure, and high terrain masking the line-of-sight radar. There are numerous reasons why you would not be able to electronically identify a helicopter. Use discipline. It is better to miss a shot than be wrong." Sometimes he would say, "It is better to let a bad guy through than to shoot a friendly."

Across the base the light burns in the office of Brig. Gen. Jeffrey Scott Pilkington. In his early fifties, Pilkington has distinguished good looks and still maintains the build of an athlete. A 1968 Air Force Academy graduate, with over 3,000 flying hours, he is an anomaly in today's Air Force. For he is a "flying general"—a general officer who still flies on a regular basis and keeps current in his aircraft. Well thought of by his colleagues and superiors, his close friends call him "Scotty." It is his responsibility to ensure that rules and procedures are in place to provide for safe operations and that they are followed. He takes this responsibility very seriously and makes it a point to fly at least twice a week as an F-16 flight lead to monitor the flying operations. In addition, he flies at least two missions each month with Eagle Flight and on occasion flies on the tankers and the AWACS to learn of any problems or shortcomings that might need his attention.

Over the course of the past nine months, he has made changes to make the operation safer and to improve the integration of all the forces. When he noticed any violations of the rules, he dealt with the cases quickly. This had resulted in sending numerous pilots, the majority being F-15 pilots, and at least one AWACS crewmember home for violation of rules or procedures or for lack of good judgment.

Now he must sit down and write a letter to his commanding general and explain what he believes happened today. He writes:

> It is my firm conviction that there were rules and procedures in place which should have and would have prevented the tragedy, had those rules and procedures been followed. There had been unknown aircraft in the area of responsibility numerous times before. Each AWACS had done the job we expected. The Rules of Engagement had been followed. Identification friend or foe, the IFF, had worked as expected. And if a visual identification was required, that visual identification had been done correctly and had worked. Some of the rules and procedures, like the Rules of Engagement, have been in place for three years and six commanders before my arrival. In some cases, I imposed stricter rules than had been in place before. I believe that I had every reason to expect that the safeguards, which were in place, were adequate. Why they, in fact, were not adequate was not due to a lack of clear guidance or procedures, but due to guidance and procedures not being followed or a lack of adequate training or a lack of attention or mistakes.

The letter written, Pilkington moves on to the business of continuing his command at Operation Provide Comfort. When General Oaks had called from Germany and announced they were changing the plans for the investigation, Pilkington had offered to resign his command. Oaks had said, "No, I still have the utmost confidence in your leadership. It would look like an immediate admission of guilt if we remove you now." General Oaks had thrown in a caveat before he terminated the conversation. "Scotty, you are under orders not to speak with anyone involved in this incident, not the pilots or AWACS crew or anyone else, and they are not to speak with each other. Also, none of you in the chain of command can discuss this incident, and this will last until the investigation is completed." Now, after their conversation, Pilkington worries about how he can continue his command in an effective manner without addressing the shoot down. To him, it seems it should be a matter of open discussion among the command structure down here. They have an immediate need to understand what happened today and make an instantaneous effort to change any procedures that failed. But that is not to be, and he must press on doing the best he can under these unusual circumstances.

Tomorrow, due to the shoot down, will be a down flying day. He knows the atmosphere on base will be strained, particularly among the commanders, because they do not know conclusively how the shoot down happened and they aren't allowed to talk about it. It's crucial this atmosphere doesn't filter down to the crewmembers and affect their missions. Pilkington makes plans to gather all the pilots and every crewmember that flies: helicopter crewmembers, AWACS crewmembers, tanker crewmembers, and pilot crewmembers. At midmorning they'll meet in the base auditorium, where he will go over the procedures and clarify the rules of engagement. Most importantly, he is changing one rule. No one will be allowed to shoot at a helicopter without his personal permission. On Saturday, April 16, Operation Provide Comfort will be up in the air, business as usual.

It is now past midnight. April 14, 1994—the worst day of his military career—is finally over. Pilkington dims the lights in his office and returns to the comfortable leather chair behind his desk. He leans back and thinks, "April fourteenth will never really be over. It will all be there, every minute detail, stored in the recesses of my memory. I will relive yesterday over and over for the rest of my life."

He is exhausted but not ready to go home just yet. As commander, responsible for everything that walks or flies down here, he feels not only a deep sadness, but also enormous frustration about this friendly fire tragedy. He closes his eyes, leans back in his chair, and ponders again. "There had often been unknown aircraft out in the No Fly Zone. Some of those had been transports, some had been helicopters. They had occasionally come across the border from Iran into northern Iraq north of the 36th parallel. Others had come from Syria and Turkey, and a few were high-altitude reconnaissance aircraft. Some were United Nations helicopters. Some were helicopters whose origins were never quite determined. So the situation had occurred numerous times before, probably every few months or so, maybe more. They had never even once come close to having shot one down or close enough that it drove them to make a change to the rules of engagement, because the procedure had always worked!"

The normal procedure was for the fighter pilots to communicate to AWACS that something they did not expect was in the area. AWACS then would energize the chain of command and normally get back to them. Quite often they would find out that Southern Watch, the U.S. operation going on south of the 32nd parallel, would be aware of something about which they had failed to inform him or the Command Post. But in three years of flying, they never even once had a close call. There had never been a reason to change the rules of engagement. "Everything had always worked before!"

12.

Black Hawk Crash Site
Latitude 36°46′ North, Longitude 44°05′
East, Iraq
April 15, 1994
Friday, 12:15 A.M.

The commander of the Air Force Special Operation Forces, Lt. Col. John Wagner Zahrt, exhausted and emotionally drained, leans against his Black Hawk helicopter parked above the crash sites and pauses to catch his breath. His flight suit is covered with oily black soot, and the smell of death and destruction is everywhere. He glances at his watch and thinks, "It is just past midnight, thank God. April fourteenth is finally over. This has been a day I'll never forget."

The chain of events that brought him to this point in time was too preposterous for him to have ever considered. Just fourteen short hours ago he had been sitting at his desk when he'd gotten a call, over a secure line, saying two Hind helicopters had been shot down. Although he was no stranger to military mishaps—he had been a combat helicopter pilot for most of his career—this news had raised the hair on the back of his neck for two reasons. First, shoot downs were a very unusual, an almost unheard-of event at Operation Provide Comfort. Second, Zahrt knew Eagle Flight was out today, flying on a mission that would take its choppers deep into the No Fly Zone.

He had put these concerns aside to focus on his responsibility, the preparation and launching of a Mass Casualty Response Team out to the crash site. Immediately he became aware this mission was not routine. In fact, looking back, it was not like any he had ever executed. Normally they would take two choppers, but quickly he was informed that two commanders and extra personnel from Incirlik would be accompanying his team, necessitating a third helicopter. He had become very frustrated when he received word that the Turkish officials were delaying his team's departure. "We know two helicopters are down, and we know Eagle Flight is missing. Let's get this show on the road!" At that point he had only one concern: rescuing possible survivors.

Finally at 3:00 this afternoon, the Turks had given permission for his helicopters to launch. Three and one-half hours later his chopper, call sign "Ghost," reached the Iraqi border. During the flight the crew had discussed the possibility of survivors. The obvious problem was that eight hours had passed since the shoot down—and time is everything in the rescue business. However, they'd learned from other situations that you never give up hope.

There had still been plenty of light as they entered Iraq, but it began to fade during the forty-minute flight to the crash site. Once they arrived the choppers split and circled several times, making an aerial survey of the area. The first site was in a flat field by a stream close to a small village. From the air the debris had seemed confined to a small, very burnt area. He was able to land close by. The second site was farther up a hill in very uneven terrain. The debris was more scattered and the ground not as scorched. The other helicopters couldn't find a place to land that was close enough to this site. Eventually they landed 1,000 meters farther up the hill.

The rescue team members steeled themselves for the arduous and gruesome tasks that lay ahead. Although they were prepared for the mission's tedious and exhausting physical work, even experience doesn't make the emotional aspect easier. The circumstances of this crash made it all the more difficult.

As the rotors of Zahrt's chopper slowed to a halt, armed Kurds approached them. This had caused some alarm, but these Kurds were part of a Peshmerga patrol group, the military arm of the Kurdish people. Even though his team had made it clear they were friendly forces, they maintained a nonaggressive posture as the Peshmergas led them down to the sites. After being introduced to their leader they noticed the large number of local people gathered around the perimeter of the wreckage. Zahrt sensed there had been even more Kurds who fled after his team had landed. This thought caused him to consider the possibility that some had already sifted through the debris because it had now been almost nine hours since the shoot down, but it was too difficult to find any specific evidence of tampering because an aircraft crash site is just a splatter of miscellaneous.

Some of the trees were still burning, and a small ground fire continued to smolder near the main wreckage of site one. The air was permeated with the odor of burnt metal, fuel, and flesh. Dismembered bodies were strewn around the molten heap of what once had been the fuselage of a Black Hawk. It appeared the helicopter had broken in half, because the tail section was displaced several feet away from the main chopper body. Nothing else was distinguishable other than two large areas of scorched metal. There were no survivors.

Fortunately the Kurds had marked the position of each set of remains earlier that afternoon. As the team continued to walk the area, one of the crewmen expressed in a reverent voice, "I wish the guys who pushed the button could walk in my shoes. Perhaps those F-15 jocks would have exercised more caution, wouldn't have been as trigger-happy, if they could walk through the aftermath of an AMRAAM and a Sidewinder."

They continued taking a survey of both crash sites. Site one, on the flat terrain, was identified as the trail Black Hawk hit by the AMRAAM. They counted twelve bodies, all in close proximity, except for one lying farther away in a patch of tall grass. It had taken ten minutes to ford a stream and walk down to the second crash site. Site two contained the lead helicopter downed by the heat seeker. Apparently, after the missile hit it, the chopper had slammed into the side of the steep hill and rolled over. There was just enough light left for the Kurds to point out fourteen bodies. Twenty-six sets of remains; it all checked out. The remaining question was how to proceed with this nightmare.

As they hiked back to the main area, the sun dropped behind the mountains, and almost instantaneously it became dark. A group of six Special Forces troops, launched overland from Zakhu, had arrived. The rescue team welcomed the manpower and, most of all, the assistance with security because there were still about 200 Kurds gathered farther up on the road.

Although they weren't considered an immediate threat, the Kurds were extremely upset. No strangers to death and destruction, these people had survived the Persian Gulf War, when Saddam Hussein had destroyed entire villages of men, women, and children. But even to them, this act was unspeakable and incomprehensible. Worse, several of them had witnessed the shoot down. This morning the F-15s, passing at high speeds and low altitudes near the flight of the Black Hawks, had caught the attention of the villagers and farmers in the fields below. None of them had ever seen anything like it. One of the Kurdish farmers had run inside to get his video camera. Standing on the roof of his small house, situated high on the side of a hill, he had videotaped the lead F-15 releasing the AMRAAM. After the helicopters had been blown up in midair, he had then run down to the crash site and continued videotaping. Tonight, as they stood in the darkness on the adjacent road, these usually stoic Kurds were unable to hide their grief because five of their own had been on board these Black Hawks—four guards and one interpreter.

After much consideration Lieutenant Colonel Zahrt made a command decision. He told his crew, "The task of removing the bodies has to be done in an orderly manner. We'll wait until daybreak when there is sufficient light." Using satellite communication, he called the Command Post at Incirlik and relayed his intentions. Immediately it became clear by their terse reply that the Command Post had other intentions: "Retrieve all the remains tonight." He was so taken aback by this order, he asked Incirlik to reiterate the directions. Then he said to his team, "Let's do it."

Quickly he decided to evacuate the remains from one site at a time, beginning with site one. Instead of using lights, which might attract unwanted attention, the team members donned night-vision goggles. Their first and foremost concern was an accurate accounting of the remains, making sure they had all the body parts. They began putting the remains in bags, collecting them at a designated point near the landing zone. Eventually they would be loaded on the parked helicopter and flown to Zakhu.

This process had taken over three hours. Because of limited space on the helicopters, the teams had had to transport nine sets of remains from crash site one to Zakhu, off-load them, and return for the other three remains.

Now Zahrt's watch tells him it is past midnight, the beginning of a new day. But this grim recovery mission is only half completed, the most difficult part still lying ahead, because crash site two presents several challenges. The steep, rocky terrain makes it too difficult to move the bodies up the hill, yet it is not practical to carry the bodies over a steep ridge and across several streams down to the road. The only alternative is to use the hydraulic hoist installed on the search and rescue helicopters. The hoist is designed to lift one or more individuals up to the door of the helicopter, where they can then be pulled in. The team decides to give it a try because there seems to be no other choice.

The first set of remains they will attempt to remove belongs to Colonel Thompson, whose body is set apart from the other victims. He lies in a grassy patch, on his back, and almost appears to be sleeping. The only physical evidence on him of the horrible explosion is his scorched eyebrows. The team's first attempt takes thirty minutes, but it works.

In the dark of the night, with no lights, the team works relentlessly to evacuate the remains of their fallen comrades. The helicopters, as needed, fly over to the refueling tanker, refuel, and return, while another helicopter comes in to get another litter. Soon the rescue team develops a system. By the break of the morning twilight, they have evacuated all the remains and are off the ground. An American civilian worker who normally works deep inside northern Iraq is left at the site to provide an American presence for the following day.

The three helicopters and the exhausted rescue team fly back to Zakhu. The remains of the victims had been placed here temporarily throughout the night until they could be flown to Pirinclik Air Base in Diyarbakir, Turkey. The staff at Zakhu had tried to sort the remains by nationality as they arrived in several helicopter lifts. By 6:30 A.M. on Friday, April 15, all the remains have been flown to Pirinclik.

The Mortuary Affairs Team that has been flown into Pirinclik is trying to identify the bodies as they arrive. Soon it becomes apparent that not all the remains are complete. The commanders know they have limited time to go back out to the crash site and do another search for remains before a C-141 from Ramstein Air Force Base arrives to take the bodies back to Germany tonight. Once at Ramstein, autopsies will be performed and positive identifications made.

At 11:30 Friday morning two Black Hawks and some of the team members who had worked through the night doing the initial recovery are launched back to the crash area. By the light of day they are aghast at the magnitude of the devastation and how far some of the debris is scattered. They locate a door to the lead helicopter 500 feet from the crash site. It is more difficult to locate human remains today. Charred bits of everything are strewn everywhere. The acrid smells of last night have developed into a stench. The workers coat their noses with Vicks to block the odor. They spend hours sifting through the debris for body parts and scraps of human remains. Most of the time they are able to recognize the pieces of human remains only by flies that have already swarmed to the decaying flesh. In the afternoon a judgment call is made to stop the process and return to Pirinclik.

When they return with the remainder of the body parts, the team sees the large C-141 parked on the tarmac. Caskets are being off-loaded, and this adds to the already somber atmosphere. All the American Army personnel stationed at Pirinclik, in support of the Black Hawk mission, are like family. They live together, eat together, and fly together. Most are stationed here on a temporary assignment from Giebelstadt Army Air Field in Germany. Soon all the bodies will be placed in caskets and flown back to Germany.

By late in the day of April 15, all the families, on three different continents, have been notified. They will now have to wait for the positive identification of their loved ones' remains. Some of the families will wait at least a week to receive this notification and the release of the body for burial. It will be the longest week of their lives.

The caskets have been reloaded on the C-141. As the plane turns and taxis down the runway, the ground crew stands at attention and gives their fallen friends a last salute. Fellow Black Hawk pilots find these circumstances too tragic to believe. It could have been any one of them. Three years of a near-perfect safety record down here at Operation Provide Comfort . . . what went so terribly wrong yesterday morning? Everyone has questions. No one has the answers.

13.
San Antonio, Texas
April 15, 1994
Friday Morning

I awake early, and as I drift into consciousness the events of yesterday quickly become today's reality. Late last evening, after conferring with my principal, I had made a decision to go to school this morning and personally tell my students the circumstances of my absence. Even last night I knew this was not an ordinary military accident because after twenty-seven years of keeping up with military news, I couldn't remember any incident even remotely like this one. I also sensed that the repercussions would be long lasting and that as long as the public was interested it would remain a major news story. San Antonio has a population of over one million, but the atmosphere is more small town than large metropolis. Military news makes the headlines in our city on a regular basis, so I was certain this latest military disaster would filter down to my fourth graders. I knew it was in their best interests to hear the truth from me rather than try to understand it in their own way through the television news and secondhand sources.

Getting dressed, I listen to the news. There are no new details, but I hear all flags will be flown at half-mast for two weeks in honor of those killed. Looking at my reflection in the mirror, I take stock of my mental condition. I'm subdued, sad, still unbelieving, and, most likely, I decide, in a state of shock. I look the same as I did yesterday morning preparing for school, but I'm clearly a different person.

The sun is just rising as I drive through the quiet streets. It's surprising that everything outside my immediate realm appears so normal. In the parking lot of my elementary school, I sit for a few moments to compose my thoughts and to bring a perspective to the task that currently faces me. Before the students arrive I prepare the lessons for the next week. I remain composed until colleagues start arriving. Their shock and dismay brings a reality to Laura's death. "Dear God, just let me get through this immediate task." And I do. The principal, guidance counselor, and I gather the two classes of students I teach every day. As the forty students sit attentively on the floor, I explain the incident in the simplest of terms. Their reactions differ, but experience tells me that children deal best with the truth and that they are most concerned about how this tragedy will affect them. Therefore, I assure them I am fine and will be back teaching them as soon as possible. It is a relief to walk out into the morning sunlight feeling some satisfaction that I had handled it well.

When I arrive home Danny is standing in the kitchen talking on the telephone. This would become his normal position during the week that follows. He tells me the officer from Casualty Affairs will be coming this morning. Sean, whom we have kept home from school, wanders aimlessly around the house, nothing, not even television, holding his attention very long. I spend some time with him, but he is distant, detached, and just waiting for his brother to come home this afternoon.

Midmorning the Casualty Affairs officer arrives. She gives us the standard benefits and burial briefing, and we sign the obligatory paperwork to set all this in motion. Formalities out of the way, it is now time to address the more difficult issues. Casualty Affairs has not been officially notified as to whether there are recoverable remains, but we discuss our options. If only a few remains are recovered, they will be cremated and placed in an urn. More recoverable remains warrant a sealed metal casket. Lastly, if a complete body is recovered, we will have our choice of a wood or a metal casket. I think to myself, "Expect the worst," for I'd already seen the crashed, burned helicopter on the latest television news report. This all doesn't seem too important because I know Laura has left this earth, and what she has left behind is more important than a recoverable body.

The officer also tells us the Air Force is trying to secure a key to Laura's apartment in Germany. They need to locate Laura's will and insurance documents. She assures us the Air Force will close her apartment and ship her household goods and personal possessions back to us. I can see the look of disappointment on Sean's face. He had been looking forward to our trip to Europe for so long. As we sit at the table I think back on this past year. Sean and I had a ritual most Friday evenings: we would celebrate the end of the week, because each concluded week brought us that much closer to our planned trip to see Laura, by driving to the neighborhood shopping center for ice cream. Usually we would have the car's sunroof

81

open, and a George Strait song would be playing softly in the background. I always said to Sean, "How was your week?" He would always reply, "Great, except for one thing: I miss Laura." Immediately we all make a decision to fly to Germany after Dan's graduation from the Air Force Academy at the end of May. We will personally close her apartment. Perhaps the trip and seeing her apartment will bring closure and healing to each of us.

For now, we are in a holding pattern. Until we are apprised of when Laura's remains will be shipped back to the United States, we cannot make plans for a funeral or memorial service. Sitting around our kitchen table, we discuss options we might consider for a funeral. This all seems impossible to me. Just twenty-four hours ago I had been thinking that the next milestones for Laura would be a wedding, pilot training, and, later, children.

The only thing I am certain of is I want to deliver the eulogy. I had brought Laura into this world, and my final act of love would be to give her a fitting farewell. I somehow know she would have done the same for me. Danny raises no objections to my request, and I'm not sure if he is placating me or if he is relieved I have taken on this task. It doesn't matter because this is not a request; it is something I feel bound to do. I loved Laura, as I love all my children, more than life. God has always provided me the strength to deal with life's adversities, and I know he will provide the guidance to allow me to give Laura's eulogy with grace, warmth, and dignity.

After the Casualty Affairs officer leaves, Sean yells from the den, where he's been watching television, "Come here quick. Nanny is on CNN." I'm speechless! My mother, who I'd been sure was incapacitated by Laura's death, is doing an interview from her living room. She is sitting in a chair holding a picture of Laura. At first I'm relieved to see she is holding up so well. Laura is still the only victim identified in the news reports, and they list her home of record as Venice, Florida. During Danny's active duty years Florida was our home of record, and Laura had still used that address. After we listen to the news segment, I call my mother. She seems unsure if she has done the right thing. I reply, "Mother, I want everyone to know the extraordinary person those pilots killed yesterday. I don't want Laura to be a 'nameless face.'"

In the days ahead this is the stance we would take. An incident like this is important and unusual enough to be newsworthy. We would rather give an interview and have reporters use our words than have them make up something on their own. In every circumstance the media are respectful—concerned about getting their facts straight and anxious to tell the story of Laura's short life. We make great copy. "A dedicated Air Force family with a remarkable daughter who fulfills her dream of following in her father's footsteps to the Air Force Academy. While on a peacekeeping mission in the skies over northern Iraq, her helicopter is mysteriously shot down by two United States Air Force F-15 pilots." More than once, I think it all sounds too much like the plot of a made-for-television movie.

I am consumed by anger, and my gut feeling is that the pilots are responsible. Fighter pilots have always had a dual reputation. For the most part, they are intelligent professionals who have worked hard and sacrificed greatly to achieve their status. But they also have a reputation of being arrogant, swaggering risk takers. The unofficial mission statement of the Air Force has always been, "Our mission is to fly and fight and don't you forget it." Fighter pilots are at the top of the Air Force food chain, revered by one another and their superiors, who are most often former fighter pilots. General McPeak, Air Force chief of staff, is the consummate fighter pilot. A former member of the Thunderbird performance team, since taking command he has placed his fighter pilot brothers in most of the Air Force's leadership positions.

I express my feelings, in very certain terms, to Danny, but he wisely persuades me to keep my views silent. "Joan, we have been promised by Secretary of Defense Perry that a full investigation will be conducted and those responsible will be held accountable." Always the good soldier, Danny continues, "Let the system work. Now is not the time to place blame and make malicious statements we will later regret." I agree, based on my loyalty to Danny and to the Air Force that had been our life for so long. In the days, weeks, and months ahead, the media will ask us repeatedly where we place the blame, who we hold responsible. Publicly, we remain committed to the integrity of the Air Force and the U.S. government. Still, in my private moments, I wonder because I have so many questions and no answers that make sense to me. But I am consoled by an investigation that, I believe, will answer all my questions. I will have to be patient.

The morning and afternoon wear on. Friends at the door, disbelieving and in shock. This doesn't happen to the ordinary family who lives on your street. The telephone rings continually; Laura's friends from around the world have just heard the news on CNN. They want to come to the funeral, but for now, we don't have a date, time, or place.

Sean and I leave for the airport to pick up Dan. Both of us are glad to escape the confines of our house, where our life has spun out of control. For the twenty-minute drive, we pretend we're just normal people. Dan is among the first passengers off the plane. He runs toward us in an emotional reunion. Sean and I can't hug him long or hard enough. I am comforted by his presence, and Sean clings to him and would continue to do so for the remainder of the horrible week.

Barely twenty-four hours have passed since this nightmare began. I've hardly slept and haven't eaten. Danny and I are constantly on the telephone, everything is in chaos. My voice has been reduced to a hoarse whisper from crying and talking constantly since yesterday. There is little food in the house and no one thinks about dinner. Around 4:00 P.M., PTA members and teachers from my school arrive with an enormous amount of food. They sustain us with nourishment, but most importantly, with compassion and support. I know they are unsure of how to approach us, but we are happy to welcome them in our home. We don't want to be left alone, and we tell them what little we know. They, like us, have so many questions, and we don't have answers for them.

Late in the evening Dan Murray calls from Turkey. I'm relieved to hear his voice, just listening as he talks. He apologizes for not calling us sooner but explains that the Air Force would not allow him to do so until now. He has received permission to accompany Laura's remains back to San Antonio. In a few hours he will be leaving for Germany and will keep us apprised of the time schedule after he knows more. Before ending the conversation he reveals some information that startles me, for although I'd heard this news from his mother yesterday, it sinks in only now: "Joan, the pilots who killed Laura are my guys. I'm their squadron intelligence officer. They are nice people, they knew Laura, and I consider them to be my friends. In fact, Laura and I recently had dinner downtown with one of them. Yesterday I briefed them before they flew. Essentially I was the last person who spoke to them before they took off and the first one they spoke to when they landed. An investigation is being conducted, and I will be called to answer questions; therefore, I am not allowed to discuss what happened in any detail. All I can tell you is there were many extenuating circumstances. We can discuss this when I see you." Just before he hangs up Dan tells me he wants to do the eulogy for Laura. We decide to share the privilege. As we had spoken the sadness in Dan's voice had concerned me. How does a twenty-five-year-old cope with a tragedy of this magnitude?

Later Renee walks over from across the street. It's late, Dan and Sean are upstairs watching television, and Danny is lying down in our bedroom. We sit in the dim living room and talk. I'm too keyed up to sleep, and it's helpful to quietly sit and decompress. She tells me no one can get through because our telephone line has been busy. Friends have been calling her all day wanting to do something but not sure what. It is decided she will be their point of contact because I know our family will need help to get through the long week that lies before us.

My mind is still on the conversation I had with Dan Murray. I confide in Renee what he has just told me. She is shocked and tells me, "I can't believe you are taking this information so calmly."

"Renee, I probably should be shocked by these revelations, but the past two days have numbed my senses. Anyway, at this point in time I am past being shocked. The only thing that really matters is Laura is dead, and I can't entirely get a grip on that." I had no way of knowing this was just the beginning of many strange twists in this never-ending story.

The next day begins, as it will end, with the telephone ringing. The media has made the connection, and we are receptive to interviews. We have become savvy enough in this short time to make it clear we will not indict the Air Force for Laura's death. Our focus for now is Laura. We want people around the nation to know her for who and what she was. I have always loved talking about her. We were secure in our love and support for each other. Our last conversation, less than one week ago, had ended with "I love you." And her very last words to Sean, as they always were, had been "I love you, Pangerhead," a silly nickname she had called him since he was a baby.

In the afternoon we are informed by the Air Force that there is a body, not just recoverable remains. Her body and those of some of the other victims are to be flown from Germany to Dover Air Force Base, Delaware. From that point a civilian carrier will ship them to San Antonio. The time frame is not definite, but the best we can hope for is Tuesday for Laura's final homecoming. We are advised to contact a funeral home and make the plans for the memorial service and burial. After many telephone calls we schedule the memorial service for Thursday at Randolph Air Force Base Chapel, in San Antonio, and the funeral for Saturday morning at the Air Force Academy, in Colorado.

Our family, friends, and Laura's friends begin making plans to attend. Renee sees that we will have a problem. I had forgotten that it was San Antonio's Fiesta Week, the biggest party of the year, and there would be very few hotel rooms available. Over the course of the next few days, Renee organizes our neighborhood, and the entire street plans to provide sleeping accommodations, extra cars, and food for the week. I'm not surprised by their generosity, but I'm so grateful. I don't even know how I can get myself through the next week. How can I take care of family and visitors? I know this Fiesta celebration is a very special one for Renee. Her sister is a duchess in the Fiesta Court, and the entire Ojeda family had been planning to attend every Fiesta function.

As I look through my kitchen window, I see Renee talking on the telephone in her garage. She looks as tired and haggard as I do. I realize, even at this early stage, this tragedy has already taken a toll on all of us. I try not to think of the coming week but just focus on the details that will get me through this weekend.

14.

San Antonio, Texas
April 18, 1994
Monday

In addition to coming to terms with Laura's death—knowing I would never again see her, hear her voice and her infectious laugh, or hold her—I continue to deal with the harsh reality of the official business that comes with death. Monday begins with another visit from Casualty Affairs. It is clear these wonderful, caring people are carefully chosen for their compassion in dealing with broken families.

First, they tell us the Air Force had secured entry to Laura's apartment in Germany and found her official last will and testament. Danny is named as the executor and is informed of his responsibilities. Second, the Air Force has promoted Laura posthumously to the rank of first lieutenant and awarded her the Defense Meritorious Service Medal. Danny asks if Laura is eligible for the Purple Heart and is told no. He doesn't question the decision but wonders specifically why she is not eligible. It's his belief that she was killed in a combat zone. However, he puts these questions on the back burner, focusing instead on the difficult next few days.

The officer also tells us Laura had chosen not to take out government life insurance. I was aware of this decision because she and I had discussed this when she was going through intelligence school the previous year. An instructor in her finance class at the Air Force Academy had advised Laura that money spent on insurance, for a young officer with no dependents, was put to better use in an investment program. And that's what Laura had decided to do. It was fine with me when we had talked about it last year, and it was fine with me now. No amount of money would soften the loss and grief for my family. Bottom line, the death benefits would amount to around $6,000. Out of that sum, we would be required to pay for most of the funeral expenses. Burial at the Air Force Academy would be at government expense.

During these past few days of waiting for word of when Laura's remains would be returned to us, we kept track of the progress via CNN. It is a surreal and sobering experience to watch your daughter's casket being loaded on a large Air Force cargo plane in Germany for a transatlantic flight from the privacy of your living room. Many news broadcasts over the weekend pondered the same question everyone had: "How could this have happened?" I carefully listened to the various experts espousing their theories, looked at their charts, diagrams, and computer-generated recreations, but I was always left with more questions than any definitive answers. Although I had more than a mild curiosity, my focus for this week was on Laura and self-preservation.

Monday evening the late news shows the lumbering C-141, carrying Laura's body, touch down in the darkness on the taxiway at Dover AFB in Delaware, home to the military's largest mortuary. We have been made aware that the caskets would be off-loaded and opened, then folded uniforms with appropriate military decorations would be placed inside with the remains. Not all the bodies of the American victims are on board— some are being held in Germany for a more conclusive identification. My heart goes out to those families who will have to endure a longer wait.

We are in constant contact with Dan Murray. His latest call informs us he will be arriving in San Antonio with Laura's remains late tomorrow night, Tuesday. Somehow, for all of us, having Laura's body return home will be a comfort.

Meanwhile, family, friends, and some of Laura's classmates have begun to arrive. Many of Laura's friends had asked to be pallbearers, and we continue to plan the two services, the one in San Antonio and the other in Colorado. There are so many small but important details that need immediate decisions, such as discussing the services with the chaplains, selecting the music for the services, and writing an obituary, but answering the door and telephone consumes most of our time.

Another sleepless night. Tuesday is here, and Laura will be returning home for the last time. There is little time during the day to dwell on her homecoming. The protocol staff at Randolph AFB call to tell us that Dr. Sheila Widnall, secretary of the Air Force, will be attending Laura's memorial service at Randolph to present the Defense Meritorious Service Medal. My mother is arriving at noon, and other family members call with their arrival times. Dan Murray's entire family is due to come in tomorrow.

But most of all, the eulogy I'm to give in two days is still not written. It is impossible to find the time to gather my thoughts. All night I had lain awake thinking of what I might say or what I should say. These are the most important words I will ever utter in my lifetime. There will be no second chances. I will have to get it right the first time. But I don't regret my decision. I have faith that somehow it will all come together.

We become aware, via local press reports, that there is another family in San Antonio who has also lost a family member, a son, in what is now being termed "The Black Hawk Shoot Down." I don't have a name, an address, or any information about them, but I constantly think about their pain and feel a need to reach out to them. However, I'm continually distracted by other things. Danny still mans the telephone, and I write Laura's obituary. Our doorbell rings constantly, and we have become a regular on the florist's delivery route. As family and friends arrive from out of town, Renee makes sure they know what house in the neighborhood will accommodate them. My mother and mother-in-law arrive, and I can sense they become more comfortable in this hectic environment where there are few free moments to ponder our great loss.

Finally it is evening and time to leave for the airport. We take two cars because Danny will have to go over to the air cargo area to accept Laura's body. Some of us will wait at the main terminal to meet Dan Murray. We watch through the darkness as the Continental jet taxis closer to the terminal. We can see through the huge glass windows Dan Murray and a female Air Force major exit the aircraft, climb down the steps to the tarmac, and stand at attention. The cargo doors are opened, and Laura's casket is removed. Tears stream down the faces of our family and friends as we watch the silver casket loaded on a hearse and taken away.

We meet up with the rest of the family and drive to the funeral home. Mentally I am unprepared to view or touch the casket. Until now I could think of Laura's death in abstract terms. It wasn't real and it wasn't tangible. Standing near the casket, I walk closer and lay my hands on the top. There is no closure, there is no healing. I feel only anger and hopelessness. The sealed casket makes me wonder how much of Laura is left. Every parent worries about the obvious—leukemia, a drunk driver, even an act of terrorism—but this scenario for Laura's death was never a thought. Sean is watching me out of the corner of his eye. I know he fears I will lose control, but I remain composed because I have no choice. I am his rock and his safety net. He takes my hand, and we stand in silence before Laura's casket.

It is late when we all arrive back at the house. Dan Murray seems to be holding up pretty well considering the hell of the past week. We insist the other officer who had accompanied Laura's body from Germany stay with us in the neighborhood. She is from the intelligence group Laura was assigned to in Germany. We are comforted by her glowing stories of Laura and the high opinion she had of Laura in the short time she knew her. After everyone has had time to eat, unwind, and drift off to bed, Dan Murray and I go out to the garage and sit in the quiet darkness. We talk about so many things: how happy Laura had been in the weeks before she was killed, plans for the funeral, the eulogy neither of us has yet written, and his family, who are arriving tomorrow.

Finally I say, "Dan, tell me how this happened." He breathes a low sigh, "Joan, those pilots are good guys. One of them is a close friend. During these past few days I've had time to think, and maybe I don't know every detail, but I believe they did everything right. Many things happened that caused the shoot down. The biggest one is the Army didn't pass their flight plan down to us. I didn't even know Laura was going that far south into the No Fly Zone. You know I can't tell you much more because of the Air Force official investigation that is still being conducted. I was questioned by the investigative team before I left for Germany last Saturday and took an oath not to discuss the shoot down at all."

Dan pauses and then says, "Joan, when I was briefing both pilots before they went out to fly last Thursday, I almost said, 'Be careful, Laura will be flying out there on an Army helicopter today.'"

Maybe Dan is right. Perhaps the pilots did do everything right. Perhaps I'd been too hasty in blaming them. But I know I will have to know every detail of this shoot down if I am ever going to find peace in this life. Although Dan is privy to much of the information I need to know, I will never compromise him by asking for any confidential details. But for the present, this is not the paramount objective in my life. I need to get myself and my family through the next few days.

Wednesday begins much as the other days since April 14. Throughout the day more friends and family arrive until every bed on our street is occupied. The media are a constant presence, but we need them as much as they need an update on their story for the next news broadcast. They keep our local friends informed of the time and place of the memorial service tomorrow afternoon. After lunch, guests are watching television, sitting by the pool, and new people are still arriving. This morning the newspaper had reported the name of the other San Antonio family who had lost a son in the shoot down. They gave a street name but no street number. I grab a basket of flowers and tell my mother to get in the car. We need to get out of the house, and I need to find the other family. My mother says I'll never find the house without the number. "Mother, I just have a feeling I'll be able to tell which house it is."

It is a beautiful day; we roll back the sunroof and drive in silence until we get to the community where the street is located. After a few quick right-hand turns I easily find the street and slow down. On my right I see a house with people standing outside, and I know this is where the Bass family lives. We introduce ourselves and are led inside. I'm confronted by the same things I left at home: grieving parents, shocked relatives comforting one another, and masses of food and flowers. They are surprised to see me and even more surprised to learn our common bond. Cleon Bass is an Air Force captain still on active duty. Cornelius, whom they called by his middle name, Anthony, was their beloved youngest son, and Connie, his mother, is inconsolable. Anthony's remains have not been returned to the United States, but the Basses are hopeful they will arrive by the end of the week and have tentatively scheduled the funeral for Saturday. We hold one another, cry, and talk about Anthony and Laura. We wonder if they were on the same helicopter and if they had time to talk to each other. I invite them to Laura's memorial service tomorrow afternoon and express my regrets that we will be in Colorado burying Laura on Saturday, so we will be unable to attend Anthony's service. Leaving their house, I say to them, "Anthony's and Laura's names are forever linked together. It is important we keep in touch because we will need each other to lean on in the months ahead."

While we have been gone the mood at home has become more jovial. Laura's friends are telling "Laura stories," funny or outrageous things Laura did at the Air Force Academy. Guests are becoming mellower and mingling with others they've never met, discussing what their connection is to Laura. Like many families, there are divorces and people who have not seen one another in decades. Vernitia, my mother-in-law, is playing hostess, and I'm grateful because she has a gift for putting others at ease. I watch, helpless, as she rounds the corner, enters the kitchen, and almost bumps into Ed, her ex-husband and Danny's biological father, whom she has not seen in forty-five years. She introduces herself: "Hello, I'm Vernitia Piper, Laura's grandmother." Ed looks at her in astonishment and replies, "We've met, in fact; we once conceived a child together." They laugh, hug, and continue talking, both genuinely pleased to see each other. That's the tone of the afternoon: everyone putting aside their feelings and differences to honor Laura's memory. We laugh at the Laura stories and hug one another a lot.

Late in the evening Dan Murray and I find a quiet moment to discuss the eulogy. Both of us are exhausted, we have nothing on paper, but we each rehearse what we intend to say. I know it will be another sleepless night exploring the possibilities of this last tribute to my only daughter.

Out of sheer exhaustion I do sleep but wake up at 5:00 A.M. For the first time in the week since Laura has been killed, the house is quiet. I sit down at the computer and begin writing. I am calm and my mind is clear. I feel the strength of a divine presence guide me through the writing process. In a dreamlike state the words flow effortlessly on the screen, and by 7:00 A.M. I'm finished. The first draft is near perfect, and as I wait for the printer to produce the final product, Dan Murray comes downstairs. Guests have begun to wander in for coffee. Dan and I escape to the solitude of the back patio. Still in my pajamas, I sit on the diving board of the swimming pool and read what I have written. Dan announces it is perfect and that he will write a piece that complements mine. We want no redundancies in our words this afternoon. I feel confident Laura would be proud of both of us.

As I get dressed for the service, I begin to feel anxious. By the time the white limousine arrives to transport us to Randolph Air Force Base, the anxiety is replaced by anger. In the past week this anger has made me strong and unafraid of the difficult task that lies before me. Sean sits beside me, and we cling to each other during the thirty-minute drive. Few words are spoken as we are all lost in our own thoughts of Laura. When we arrive our family is seated, and Danny and I are escorted to a small private room in the rear of the chapel. We spend a few moments with Secretary Widnall and her husband. All too soon it is time for the service to begin. As we walk down the aisle to take our seats, I see the chapel is filled to capacity. The Air Force Band of the West, which used to fall under Danny's command, is playing music we have selected. The flag-draped metal casket is flanked by beautiful flowers sent by so many people who loved Laura. Off to the side, in a prominent position, is the large graduation picture that had previously hung in our den, displayed on an easel.

The chaplain begins the service and introduces Dr. Widnall. I know she has put herself in a precarious position by attending this funeral because it was on her "watch" that this horrific event occurred. In the short span of time since the shoot down occurred, I've learned that the words "friendly fire" are difficult to acknowledge even during times of war, and this instance is even more perplexing. She says many kind things about Laura. "Lieutenant Laura Piper was wise beyond her years. In a brief shining life she was, in the words of Walter Lippmann, 'the custodian of a nation's ideals, of the beliefs it cherishes, of its permanent hopes.' Defender, peacemaker, peacekeeper, humanitarian, there is no more meaningful work." As I listen to Dr. Widnall's words, my heart palpitates and my mouth is dry, but it is so important to have this last opportunity to share Laura with family, friends, and strangers. Upon concluding her remarks Dr. Widnall presents us with Laura's Defense Meritorious Service Medal.

The chaplain introduces me, and I begin the walk to the podium. Suddenly I remember I haven't seen Sean since we arrived. His brother sits in the front row with the other pallbearers, but Sean is not there. I begin the eulogy while scanning the audience, searching for Sean. He is not sitting with our immediate family. Finally I see him sitting between Renee and Richard Ojeda, probably the two people in the entire church he feels the most comfortable with at this moment. Relieved, I take a breath and continue.

"This is a labor of love for me. Laura was a rare and special individual, and it has always given me pleasure to talk about her. Laura lived life with a passion and a purpose that give definition to my life and to the people who knew her. She had the courage and conviction to accomplish things I never would have dreamed possible for myself. Her enthusiasm for life was contagious, and it allowed for few missed opportunities." I talk about Laura's connection with each member of our family: she followed in her father's footsteps to the Air Force Academy; she was the trailblazer, pathfinder, and friend to her brother Dan; she had a deep attachment and limitless adoration for Sean. And lastly, I relate the encouragement she gave me to return to college and obtain a teaching certificate. I quote from a letter written by her classmate: " 'I'll always remember Laura as a fighter, who never gave up. The Academy was rough on all of us, but Laura never gave an inch. She never complained, but used humor and laughter to make light of bad situations and before anyone knew it we were all laughing and happy again. Laura's smile, sparkling eyes, laughter and good nature will be with me forever.' "

Dan Murray follows me, and he captures the spirit of Laura in his carefully chosen words. He tells about how Laura could recite the entire Dr. Seuss's *ABC* book because she had read it endlessly to Sean. He reminds me that Laura was a modest person and would have been overwhelmed to see the family and friends who had traveled from so many distant places around the world to honor her today. He ends with a quote from Laura's favorite poem, "The Station," by Robert Hastings. Laura had first read this piece in Ann Landers's column, and it had become an integral part of her personal philosophy. Dan's concluding words are the same words Laura had chosen to have printed under her graduation picture in her Academy senior yearbook:

> Stop pacing the aisles and counting the miles. Instead, climb more mountains, eat more ice cream, go barefoot more often, swim more rivers, watch more sunsets, laugh more, cry less. Life must be lived as we go along. The Station will come soon enough.

As we leave the chapel and Laura's body is gently placed in the hearse, I can still hear the strains of music coming from inside. We all stand and wait as a flight of T-37 jets fly the missing-man formation over the chapel. I remain composed, but on the inside my heart is broken. We leave with Laura's body for Colorado Springs tomorrow and will repeat the service.

A large contingency of friends and family gather at the airport in the morning for our last trip with Laura. We are already emotionally spent from yesterday; the mood is quiet and reserved. At Colorado Springs military protocol dictates all passengers remain on board until the casket is unloaded and placed in the hearse. During the drive to the Air Force Academy, I notice spring has not yet arrived in the Rocky Mountains. The trees are still bare and the air is cool. I think back to the happy memories the Academy has held for all of us: Danny's graduation in 1967, our marriage in the chapel on the evening of his graduation day. He was stationed here for his first assignment after he completed pilot training, returning to become an instructor in the T-41 program that teaches cadets how to fly. Laura was born in the small hospital nestled in the hills behind the chapel in March 1969. As I held her in my arms, I could watch the deer feeding outside the hospital window. In the summer she was baptized in the Academy chapel. We left the Academy in 1970. Danny went to Vietnam, we traveled the world, had two sons, moved more times than I can count, and built memories in other places. In 1982 Danny and I celebrated our fifteenth wedding anniversary by renewing our wedding vows in the Academy chapel. Laura and I returned in June 1987 for her to report for "Beast Summer" training in preparation for her first year at the Academy.

It was cold and rainy that June morning the incoming freshmen were to report. As we approached the Academy a shroud of fog seemed to hang on the spires of the chapel. We hugged and cried, and I told her how proud I was of her and that no matter what happened, I always would be. It was the most difficult thing I had ever done to leave Laura in the cold, wet mist, standing alone, holding a small suitcase. Although I'm not superstitious, I'll always wonder if the fog wasn't an evil omen. Driving down the hill, I had passed the Academy cemetery and made an unplanned turn into the drive. I parked the car and walked among the grave markers, some of them belonging to Danny's classmates who had been killed during the Vietnam War. Silently I had asked those who had "gone before" to look out for my Laura.

Our family returned often for parents' weekends and finally for graduation in June 1992. Now we are returning again, and Laura's life has come full circle. I just didn't think it would end this way.

The Saturday morning service is beautiful, sad, and poignant. The chapel is filled, this time with different faces, and Dan and I repeat our words from Thursday. The casket is carried out of the chapel and down the steps. We drive behind the hearse that will take Laura on her final trip to the Academy cemetery. The sky is deep blue as we watch the puffs of smoke rise from the rifles that pay tribute to Laura with a twenty-one-gun salute. Her brother Dan removes the flag from the coffin, folds it, and hands it to an Air Force officer. Taps play mournfully as he walks over and places it in my arms. I turn and give it to Sean. We hear a roar in the distance, and our eyes lift upward. Soon a formation of F-16 fighters flies over the cemetery in the now familiar missing-man formation. We begin to get into the limousine for the ride over to the Officers' Club, where we have planned a small reception. As we begin to drive away Danny asks the driver to stop. He gets out and picks up some long-stemmed red roses from the top of Laura's casket and returns to the car. A news photographer snaps his picture. Tomorrow it will run on the front page of the *Rocky Mountain News,* and I'll always remember it with such sadness.

We return to the cemetery during the twilight hours of the evening to see where Laura's body is now interred. She has now officially joined the ranks of those who lost their lives on foreign soil. She drew her last breath so far away from this place where she took her first breath. Now she will remain here for eternity, and a bronze marker will stand in vigil of her memory.

15. San Antonio, Texas
April 24, 1994
Sunday

We arrive home from Colorado around midnight to the chaos of a home left in disarray by the events of the past week. There are wilted flowers in every room, heaps of dirty clothes, towels, and bed linens, and empty coolers in the garage that once held food delivered by caring friends. Our living room has become the repository for all the letters and sympathy cards, most unopened, we have received since Laura's death. By the end of the week the postman had begun personally delivering the mail in postal bins. Stacked on the floor are unread magazines and newspapers that contain articles about Laura or the shoot down. I want to open all the mail and read every news clipping, but it will all have to wait until I have time to savor each personal note and have the clarity of mind to comprehend the information in each news report. I lived the past week in a vacuum, attending only to the immediate and the necessary. There is no choice but to begin picking up the pieces of our lives and putting them back together. I long for order, solitude, and rest—all currently lacking.

Our family has been invited to a memorial service scheduled for tomorrow, Monday, at 10:30 A.M., in the chapel at Fort Myer, Virginia. Military officials tell us the chairman of the Joint Chiefs of Staff, the secretary of defense, and the president of the United States will speak to honor the men and women who died in defense of freedom in the helicopter tragedy in Iraq. Our family is pleased this horrific tragedy and Laura's death will be acknowledged and mourned in this public forum, but it is impossible for us to attend. It has taken all our reserve to plan and execute the San Antonio memorial service, the trip to Colorado, and Laura's burial at the

Academy. A trip to Washington would mean leaving on another plane today, and that's just not possible. We know not all of the families who lost loved ones in the shoot down will be attending. Funerals are still being scheduled for some of the victims. In this time of paralyzing grief the government is unwilling to provide arrangements or funding for travel to Washington.

We spend most of Sunday trying to bring some semblance of order to our lives because we have decided to return to work and school tomorrow. My students will be taking the state standardized basic skills test on Tuesday and Wednesday, as will Sean. I have been their teacher, coach, and mentor, and the best place for me this coming week is with these students. It is my belief, emotionally, that it is best for Sean and me to return to our normal routine. Staying home, remote from our social ties, work, and school stress, is tempting, but with just over one month remaining, we need to finish out the school year. I know it will be difficult to return tomorrow, but it will be that much harder if we extend our absence, and I couldn't say to Sean, "You go back to school and do your best on those tests. Mom will be at home in her pajamas too consumed with grief to return to work."

Monday morning comes too early, and I begin to have doubts about my resolve to carry on this business of living so soon after Laura's death. I drive Sean to school and try to give him the courage to make it through the day. We talk about the likely possibilities of unwanted sympathy and attention by teachers and inappropriate questions by classmates. Fighter aircraft shooting down helicopters with "fire-and-forget missiles" is the stuff of which video games are made. Pictures of Sean appeared on television and in the newspaper all last week. The handsome blond boy grieving his sister, holding the flag that draped her coffin, was too poignant for news photographers to resist. Arriving at his school, I give him a long hug. "I'm not going to tell you to have a good day because I know it will be a difficult one for both of us. Remember, Laura would want us to be strong, and today we will have to be."

It is easier to give advice than to take your own, and as I drive the remainder of the way to my school, I steel myself for the long day ahead. I have just about convinced myself I can do this when I drive by the Ojedas' restaurant. On the marquee are the words LAURA, WE WILL ALWAYS

REMEMBER YOU. It takes me by surprise, and I feel the tears welling in my eyes. But after telling Sean he must be strong, I have no choice.

The faculty and the families of my students have given me so much support. I am indebted to all of them and feel that my simple words of gratitude last week were not enough for all they did to help sustain my family. Purposely I stay in my classroom during the morning. I am not comfortable in this new role as a victim, and I do not want anyone to feel sorry for me. I didn't raise my children to be victims, and I never expected myself to be in this position. In addition to becoming instant victims, we have been headline news in San Antonio this past week. My students have watched my family on television and read about us in the newspaper. In the eyes of these children, I am now a celebrity, which gives me additional reasons to feel uncomfortable.

I know it will take time before the spotlight fades and people see me again for what I was and not for what I have become. In the meantime, I find it easier to face the students than adults because children somehow can ask a few questions, deal with the issue, and move on. And that is exactly what happens. My students are not surprised to see me; in fact, they expected I would return today. To put them at ease, I talk with them about some of the events of last week, I answer some of their questions, and then it's back to work. The most important thing to them now is that they have a big test tomorrow. There is much catching up to do and no time to think about anything but my students and the business of running a classroom. The time passes quickly, and by the end of the day I'm beginning to feel comfortable and less like an object of curiosity. Coming back to work was a good decision.

When the bell rings and my students leave, I am right behind them. Today I must be home before Sean in the event his day has not been as uneventful as mine. Before turning in on our street I check the mail. As I turn the key in the mailbox, I can feel the locking mechanism catch on all the envelopes that are crammed into our cubicle. Carefully I remove all the letters and cards, then get back inside the car. Out of habit I flip through the mail until my eyes are drawn to a bright yellow envelope. I stare in disbelief. The card is from Laura and is postmarked April 14, the day she was killed.

I rip open the envelope, and as I open the card two Egyptian coins drop out on the seat. Laura writes,

Thank you so much for all your help while I was in Turkey. I loved being able to talk to you and Sean so often. I'm happy to be returning to Germany in a few days because that means I'll be seeing you soon.

I love you,
Laura

It is so like Laura to thank me with a card but so unlike her to put two coins in the envelope from her most recent trip to Egypt. I pick them up off the seat and put them in a safe place. Sean also has received a postcard dated the same day. Laura must have mailed them the morning she left for Iraq. The cards and coins are a wonderful surprise, and I'm too grateful to be sad.

The house is quiet and empty for the first time in almost two weeks. Suddenly the stress of the day consumes me with exhaustion. I decide to take advantage of the solitude by lying on the couch for a few moments or at least until I hear Sean's bus drive down the street. I turn on the television and see Secretary of Defense Perry giving a speech. It takes a few moments for me to understand it is a rebroadcast of the government memorial service held earlier this morning. Once I had gotten to school the events of the day had clouded out the rest of the world. I had completely forgotten. The first words I hear are, "Lieutenant Laura Piper's mother summed it up with great wisdom. She said, 'People are always wondering where are our role models today. Well, here they are.' " I know he is referring to an interview I gave last week to a reporter from the *Washington Post*. He goes on to say, "Operation Provide Comfort was a very complex operation and no system will ever be one hundred percent perfect. Flying these sorts of missions is a task of immense difficulty—quick judgments, fast reactions, and great skill are constantly required. When something does go wrong, I pledge to you that we will have a full accountability of what happened."

Gen. John Shalikashvili, chairman of the Joint Chiefs of Staff, says a few brief words. He discusses the dangers of the military profession and how tragedy can strike at any moment. He says, "This loss cuts deeper, for this tragedy touches the very fabric of our institution. An institution whose code, whose passion it is to take care of each other and to protect each other from any danger. And when that goes wrong, as it did eleven days ago, our hearts are doubly heavy, and our grief especially deep." He concludes with, "We can't alter the events of April 14th, we can only mourn and we can strengthen our resolve to learn the truth."

President Clinton is the last speaker, and he talks about the American spirit, compassion, courage, and sacrifice. He tells the audience, "We must remember not only those who died for their country, but for [sic] how they were loved." He mentions the wonderful daughter and sister who lifted those around her with her vigor and promise and the Air Force colonel who thought his daughter was a hero. The president says of the victims, "They're all heroes and we owe it to them to honor their lives and to answer the questions of their families, to find the answers which they rightfully seek."

As the camera pans the audience I strain to see what the other families look like. They represent the "Face of America"—people you would expect to see at any ordinary gathering. But these families have had something so extraordinary happen, they'll always be set apart from the crowd. I now wish we could have attended the service, but in my heart I know it was impossible. Most of all, I feel confident for the first time since Laura's death that everything will be handled with honesty and integrity. The chairman of the Joint Chiefs had promised, "We will find the truth." The secretary of defense had said, "I pledge full accountability." Lastly, the president of the United States had pledged, "We will find the answers to the questions the families so rightfully seek." I'm at peace with my concerns about the shoot down. Three of the most powerful men on earth have promised me the truth, answers to my questions, and full accountability. I will have to bide my time until they are able to accomplish these three objectives.

In the evenings, during the rest of the week, I begin reading the hundreds of cards and letters that have arrived since the announcement of Laura's death. Each one means so much. It truly is a comfort to know that so many people remember Laura in such a special way. Some cards contain old photographs of Laura, and others contain amusing stories or special memories. For someone so young, Laura had touched many lives. There are letters of condolence from the president, our congressmen, and General Pilkington. General McPeak sends his via a news release printed in every Air Force newspaper and our local paper:

We scramble, we fly, we patrol to keep the skies above free from danger. That is why we took to the air over Iraq on the 14th of April, as we had done for the previous 1,103 days of Operation Provide Comfort. But that day, something went wrong. We dedicate ourselves and our service to the goal of ensuring that such a thing will never happen again. We mourn the loss of our sister, First Lieutenant Laura Piper.

One of Danny's classmates from the Academy, who is now an Air Force general, writes a telling letter:

> I know there is little we can do to ease the pain in your hearts over the tragic loss of your daughter, Laura. It's all the more personal for me because the pilots fell under my command at Bitburg Air Base until the end of February, when the squadron transferred to nearby Spangdahlem Air Base. I am still at a loss to explain why the tragedy occurred. Hopefully the mishap board will pinpoint the answers.

These remarks make me wonder how such an egregious mistake occurred that even a commanding general can't understand how it could have happened.

I also learn that there have been numerous memorial services held around the world. Especially touching are the words of the Kurdish leaders. "We Kurdish people prefer to die in thousands rather than our guests." At the memorial service held in Turkey, a Kurdish religious leader said, "We mourn the loss of those who sacrificed their lives for the sake of our children and the freedom of our nation. They came to save us and to give us dignity. Their sacrifice will remain in the minds of our children for the rest of their lives. We will teach their names to our children and keep their names in our books of history as heroes who gave their lives for our freedom."

Very late at night, when sleep just doesn't come, I sit in the living room and begin reading the newspapers and magazines from last week. The headlines are ominous: SECRECY SHROUDS DOOMED MISSION, U.S. BACKS DOWN AFTER TRAGEDY, SAFEGUARDS FAILED TO SAVE HELICOPTERS, PILOTS GAVE NO WARNING BEFORE FIRING ON COPTERS, PATROL OVER

Iraq Just Day's Work Until Disaster, Don't Blame the Fighter Jocks, and The Agony of Death Due to Friendly Fire.

This is all it takes to fire my curiosity. Into the early morning hours I begin my quest for my own answers. I can't resist reading each word of every article. Some of what I read perplexes me more because the promises made by President Clinton, Secretary of Defense Perry, and General Shalikashvili still ring in my ears.

I learn there had been over 1,400 helicopter flights since the No Fly Zone was set up in 1991. An F-15 test pilot says to a reporter, "I was surprised that this type of mistake was made." A retired general who used to fly F-15s says, "It's very easy to tell the difference between a Black Hawk and a Hind. Even my old eyes can tell the difference. F-15 pilots worldwide are shaking their heads." Military officials say the Black Hawks were equipped with extra fuel pods, which gives the appearance of Hinds. Pentagon officials are bewildered by the pilots' rush to shoot. One angry official says the F-15 pilots were trigger-happy Nintendo players. "They could have circled those helos and seen the color of the crew's eyes."

A *Newsweek* commentary by David Hackworth defends the pilots: "It's easy for laptop commandos and armchair generals to criticize what happened the morning after. Some will say the pilots had itchy fingers, were reckless Rambos, too eager to kick ass, or that people were asleep at the switch. It is better to defer judgment on what happened until the Pentagon's high powered investigation is over." I believe he is right. Although I have, since the beginning, had an intuition that the pilots were primarily at fault, I'll keep these thoughts to myself until I see the results of the official investigation. I have more than enough to keep me occupied for the next two months. Dan's graduation is less than one month away, and then we're off to Germany to close Laura's apartment.

I continue to be drawn and mesmerized by the stacks of newspapers and magazines. Sean also has an interest, and I tell him I won't hold any information from him. There will be no secrets; he'll always be kept in the loop of information so long as he is interested. He discovers a cartoon in *Newsweek* that depicts a fighter pilot covering his eyes in the cockpit of a jet. Painted on the side of the plane are two helicopters indicating two kills. Sean hides the magazine in his room to protect me. He thinks I will get upset if I see it. However, I've already seen it, and I amaze even myself with the detached attitude I've developed from immersing myself in the stacks of information about the shoot down. This will become a powerful asset for me in the future.

Danny is not drawn to these stacks of articles because he believes they are just speculation. His mind-set has always been, "Just give me the facts. I'll draw my own conclusions." However, they are all I have for now, and although I don't believe everything and I don't agree with every opinion, they provide good background knowledge. I believe this will be helpful to me when the results from the Air Force investigation are released.

During these late nights I learn that some of the connections in the shoot down are almost ironic coincidences. I had read that the State Department employee killed, Barbara Schell, had been cited for heroism for helping Americans evacuate from Iran when U.S. diplomats were being held hostage for 444 days in 1980–1981. During those years our family lived in Germany, and Danny was flying C-9 transports out of Rhein Main Air Force Base near Frankfurt. The C-9s had two missions: medical evacuation of service members from foreign countries and flying distinguished visitors—high-ranking government and military personnel—to foreign countries for official business. In January 1981 it appeared likely the hostages held at the embassy in Tehran would be released. Danny had piloted one of the two C-9s scheduled to meet the hostages in Algeria and bring them back to Germany.

I'll never forget the morning of January 21, 1981. Laura was eleven and Dan was nine years old. We stood in the dark on the runway, along with hundreds of others, waving small American flags and waiting for the C-9s to land. Laura began talking to a man standing close to her. "My dad is one of the pilots flying the hostages back this morning." The man asked her name and she said proudly, "Laura Piper." The man replied, "No kidding, my name is Piper too." He produced a business card to prove it, and we learned he was a reporter for the *Baltimore Sun*. Hal Piper had gone on to write a very nice piece about Laura and even sent her a copy. She had always treasured the memory and saved the article in one of her many scrapbooks.

Now, in 1994, Hal Piper edits the *Baltimore Sun*'s opinion page. Last week he had read about Laura's death and remembered her from that dark, chilly morning in Germany. Realizing this was the same little girl he had written about so many years before, he felt compelled to write about Laura again. "The Girl on the Tarmac" is a composite of his earlier memories of January 1981 and more recent facts he had gathered from other newspapers about Laura. It is one of our family's favorite pieces.

As I was paging through the paper the other day, the name "Piper" leaped off the page at me. Naturally I took a closer look to see what my fellow Pipers were up to.

A photo of a young woman in dress military uniform accompanied the article, and there were some quotes from her father, and I suddenly realized that I knew these people—or had met them once.

In January 1981, I covered the release of the 53 Americans held hostage by Iran for 444 days. The hostages were flown first to Algeria and to Frankfurt, Germany, where a crowd gathered [at] the airport to await them.

During the long, boring wait for the plane's arrival, I started talking to a nearby family. A bubbly girl of about 12 was bouncing around on the tarmac, trying to keep warm in the chilly January dawn, sparkling with energy. They weren't a hostage's family, she said: they were at the airport because her dad was flying the plane from Algeria. She wondered if I would put her in the newspaper story I was going to write. Sure, I said, what's your name? "Laura Piper."

"No kidding? P-i-p-e-r? My name's Piper, too." I showed her my business card to prove it.

Eventually the plane arrived to wild cheers, waving flags and fluttering yellow ribbons. The hostages got off and some of the Air Force flying crew came toward the spectators, including Laura's dad, a trim, dapper major in a cowboy hat.

"Dad, his name's Piper, too," Laura pealed out.

"Is that so?" said Major Piper, not particularly impressed.

I introduced myself and asked about the flight from Algeria, and jotted down his quote that it had been pretty uneventful. We agreed that we probably weren't related, or if so, too far back for anyone to remember. His people were from Texas and mine from Chicago.

I copied down Laura's address and promised to send her a copy of my story if she was in it. She was in it and I'm pretty sure I did remember to send her a copy; at least I hope so.

Last week she was in the newspaper again. Second Lt. Laura A. Piper, 25 years old, was one of the 26 people killed when U.S. fighter pilots mistakenly shot down two helicopters carrying a United Nations relief mission over northern Iraq.

She died doing what she wanted to do, her family said. Laura was born at the Air Force Academy in Colorado Springs. [She returned there to witness her parents' renewal of their wedding vows.] One day when she was 10, Laura's mother told reporters, she read in a newspaper that the Academy was to begin admitting women. "That's where I'm going." The mother recalled Laura saying not "I'll try" or "I'd like to," but "I'm going."

To improve her chances, Laura dropped out of band in junior high school, so that she could devote more time to studies and to athletics: She was a shot-putter and rugby player. And as a high school student in Fairfax County, Virginia, she was elected as the student representative to the school board, where she lobbied for the board to support a drive to raise money for the homeless.

Laura wanted to be a pilot like her father, and at the time of her death she was scheduled to begin pilot training.

Newspaper accounts portray the Piper family as bearing their grief stoically. "They tell you when you start (at the Academy) that there's always a price," said Laura's 23-year-old brother, Danny C. Piper, who will graduate from the Academy next month. "They tell you to look around at your classmates, and that some of them will die in the line of duty, or on the job, in service to their country."

The stories say that in addition to service to country, Laura loved seeing the world. The family refrigerator in San Antonio is festooned with postcards she sent to her 10-year-old brother. She cruised the Nile last summer. And the *Washington Post* account mentioned one of Laura's exciting childhood experiences—waiting for the plane on which her father was bringing the American hostages to Germany.

"It was freezing cold that morning, and we had to get up real early," recalled Laura's brother Danny. "It was amazing to see so many people out there in the dark, waving flags." When the plane landed, the roar of the crowd was "louder than any football game I've been to. That influenced her a lot."

Today, 2nd Lt. Laura A. Piper is to return one last time to the Air Force Academy, for burial.

—Hal Piper, *Baltimore Sun*

I still haven't been able to resume a regular sleep pattern since Laura's death. Every night I go to bed, fall asleep, and then wake up a few hours later. I slip out to the living room and continue reading everything I have and what others have sent me about the shoot down. I continue to be astounded by each new fact uncovered. One source says the pilots were seasoned officers, that in fact, one of the pilots is a lieutenant colonel who commands the F-15 squadron: "This guy was not some young, inexperienced pilot." An unidentified Pentagon source thinks the two pilots may face disciplinary action, possibly a court-martial. Secretary of Defense Perry says, "If the individuals are found culpable we will discipline them." The *Washington Times* reports the Black Hawk helicopters had the switches off in the systems that identify the copters to other aircraft. Perhaps the most important fact I uncover is a small article in the *Atlanta Constitution*. The headline reads COPTER TRAGEDY TAPED: "The mistaken downing of two U.S. helicopters by American fighter planes was captured on videotape. The shooting last Thursday was captured, in its entirety, by Iraqi Kurds who handed the footage to the Military Command Center in Zakhu, the same day, to help them with their investigation." Perhaps someday I can view that tape, because it just might make this easier to understand.

On Tuesday, coming home from school, I pick up the mail. The newest edition of the *Air Force Times* newspaper is in our box. On the cover is a large picture of Laura, with the headline WHY DID SHE DIE? I'm not surprised. I'm beyond that point. We knew they would be doing a follow-up story this week because they had asked us for pictures of Laura and we had cooperated. Danny is taken aback by the headline and writes a letter to the editor saying, "Those words made it appear that we in some way were seeking to place blame for Laura's death." I begin to think Danny is too sensitive, too careful about not blaming his Air Force. But I understand, because twenty-six years of service ingrains that kind of loyalty. Although he probably is right, I'm more questioning. I can't seem to put these doubts aside.

More important to me is that all the articles give me more information or a new perspective. An Air Force general is quoted as saying, "American aircraft flew more than five million combat missions during the Vietnam War, sixty-four thousand combat missions in the Gulf War and forty thousand peacetime missions since 1991 and, until April fourteenth, not one had been lost in a friendly fire incident." Laura was 1 out of 5,104,000? I never win door prizes and have never chosen more than one correct number playing the lottery, but I'm unlucky enough to have a daughter killed with odds of 1 in 5,000,000.

The remainder of the articles rehash the same old technical concerns: transponders, faulty IFF equipment, AWACS failures, radio codes and modes. A general says during a Senate hearing, "The fighter pilots are not a bunch of cowboys, they're disciplined professionals." After the Senate hearing he remarks, "Unfortunately we've got two of America's finest out there who fired missiles and we have twenty-six dead Americans and Allies." In the same newspaper the author of a 1993 report on technology assessment says, "Visual identification is only the last step of many. Pilots who think they have spotted enemy aircraft are likely to try to confirm that theory rather than disprove it." Lastly, one article ends with a quote from a director of the Air Combat Command: "It is very hard for me to believe with all the safeguards we have that we really got to the point where this occurred." He is saying out loud what everyone else is thinking.

It has already been a gruesome year for the Air Force. On March 14 an AC-130H gunship crashed off the coast of Kenya, killing eight crewmembers. On March 23 at Pope Air Force Base near Fayetteville, North Carolina, a horrific midair collision killed twenty-three Army paratroopers and injured more than eighty military members. Three weeks later the Black Hawks were shot down, with twenty-six killed. These tragedies are sobering even to the most battle-hardened combat veterans. One senior Air Force official says, "It was more than I could take watching that family talk about their daughter. It's all so sad." It will take another year for me to learn that military members are much more likely to lose their lives in accidents than in combat.

Two weeks later the repercussions of the "Why Did She Die?" article appear in the May 16 edition of the *Air Force Times*. It contains readers' responses to the story, and as I read them I can feel that old anger climb up my spine. All the letters are written by retired people. Quotes from their letters read: "Other than gender I cannot imagine why Air Force First Lieutenant Laura Piper was singled out. This was symbolism over substance"; "I can't believe you find Lieutenant Piper's life so much more valuable. Did you just want to belittle the thousands of men who have given their lives for this country?" Here's one of my top favorites: "I highly resent you singling out Lieutenant Piper because she was a woman. Your use of the *Air Force Times* to advocate the radical feminist position is not within your purview." The "Letters to the Editor" section usually contains at least one from a cranky retiree who is so incensed about something, he wants to cancel his subscription, and this edition's section is no exception: "You have tried to elevate Lieutenant Piper to the status of a goddess. Your mawkish treatment of this multiple tragedy disgusts me. Cancel my subscription immediately." By the time I finish reading the letters, I find a twisted humor in the remarks of these pathetic people. The editor discusses how his staff agonized over putting Laura's picture on the cover. The reason was simple: she was the only Air Force victim in the April 14 incident. A complete list of the other victims' names was not available when the paper went to press.

On the facing page there is a photograph of the Black Hawk crash site. The title of the article below it is "A Pilot's View of What Went Wrong." Initially I think, "O.K., another opinion piece by one of those laptop commandos who's going to tell the readers that pilots are the most noble men who walk the earth." But my assumptions are wrong. The author, Jerry Cox, is a former fighter pilot and previous F-15 squadron and wing commander. He writes, "As I read and listened to the Pentagon's explanation of what might have happened it was clear to me that officials were praying the incident was an 'act of God' that would absolve everyone of blame." He discusses human error, a breakdown of visual identification, as the primary cause, to which even the Pentagon alludes. Yet Cox takes it another step: "Translated that means that the F-15 pilots could not tell the difference between a Russian Hind and a U.S. Army Black Hawk. The Air Force describes the No Fly Zone as stressful, but it is probably more boring than stressful. Stressful is when the enemy shoots at you everyday. Intercepting a target in an area with few if any threats should be an easy task for a pair of Eagle pilots." He really gets my attention when he says, "I would suggest that flight discipline is an issue in this accident. Flying regulations are guidelines and are not to be confused with good judgment. Flight discipline and good judgment are the main themes of a good commander." Quoting the Pentagon general who said, "we're not dealing with cowboys or trigger-happy people," Cox then asks, "But if that is the case why all the rush to shoot a couple of helicopters wop-wopping around in the desert?" The rest of the article reads:

Did either pilot have the discipline and good judgment to recognize that this intercept was not going as expected? Were there any mental red flags and warning signs? In my view, there is no excuse for failing to recognize the difference between a Hind and a Black Hawk under these intercept conditions. Even if the helicopters were Iraqi there was no rush to shoot because the Iraqi pilots may have been lost, in distress or defecting. If the helicopters were identified as Iraqi and then committed a hostile act, there was still plenty of time to pop them with a couple of missiles.

Cox ends the piece with words that will haunt me during the coming year: "Pentagon investigators may probe the IFF and rules of engagement issues until hell freezes over, but in the final analysis the decision to shoot or not to shoot belongs to the pilot. For fighter pilots who make life and death decisions, there is no substitute for discipline and good judgment because the results of their mistakes usually are catastrophic." In the stacks of information that I have perused during the past month, Cox's words are the first voice of reason.

After reading that last issue of the *Air Force Times*, I decide to stop this pursuit of personally looking for the causes of and reasons for Laura's death. I will wait until the official investigation is completed and released, then I will reach my own conclusions. I admit my mind is clouded with the loss of Laura; the wound is too fresh and my grief is too new to unravel the clues that led to her unnecessary death. All the memorial services and official responses talk about the noble mission that took place on April 14. Because I talked to Laura almost every day before she was killed, I know in my heart there was no good reason for her to be on that helicopter. One of her superiors, in a gesture of largesse and self-importance, arranged the flights as a reward for the young lieutenants who had worked in the Intelligence Section. And who wouldn't jump at the opportunity to see new people and places that have international importance?

Ever since the time of Laura's death, I've been surprised by the number of people who remark, "Everything happens for a reason." I don't contradict their beliefs, but I know everyday random acts occur for no good reason. My mind may be dulled by grief, but I am absolutely sure that Laura was killed for not even one good reason.

16

Over the North Atlantic Ocean
June 11, 1994
Saturday, 2:30 A.M.

We are midpoint over the Atlantic. Next stop, Frankfurt, Germany. Until two months ago we had expected to fly into the arms of Laura and make wonderful memories exploring Europe with Sean. But now Dan Murray will be meeting us and taking us to Laura's apartment in a small German town near Ramstein Air Force Base. Our main goal is to oversee the packing and shipping of Laura's possessions back to our home in San Antonio. We will then close her apartment and arrange for the shipment of her car. I dread all of this, but it has to be done. It seems like a sacrilege to let strangers dismantle the apartment she took such care to find and furnish. It was one of her dreams—after our many moves, the Academy, and years of roommates—to finally have her own personal space with room for all her cherished possessions. Together she and I had spent endless hours shopping for the perfect dishes, linens, and furniture for that long-awaited apartment on her first real Air Force assignment. It was a dream come true when she was selected for a tour in Germany. Not only was Laura fluent in German, it would be a chance to relive her happiest childhood memories.

Our immediate plans include making her apartment our home base and using her car to take Sean on excursions through Europe. We don't have an itinerary; we'll take each day and trip as it comes. Danny has taken two weeks' vacation, and I'm sure we'll be ready to go home by that point. In the news Pentagon leaks speculate the official investigation of the shoot down is expected to be released around the middle of July. I'm trying not to think about it, because for now, I need to make an effort to make this trip as upbeat as possible for Sean. The circumstances could be better for his first trip to Europe, but we all believe this will be an important step in accepting Laura's death. We know we would always regret it if we didn't take the time to view life from Laura's last perspective.

111

The constant drone of the jet engines forces me to relax. Amid the plane full of summer tourists, Sean and Danny sleep. I am melancholy, which is an embellished word for depressed. The past two months have left me physically and emotionally drained, further exacerbated by my inability to sleep. In a short time I've become an expert on grief and the grieving process. After putting aside my search for clues to a complete understanding of the Black Hawk shoot down, I began reading books about grief. I'm well acquainted with all of the stages, and I honestly believe some of them will be unattainable. At this moment I'm trying to move up to acceptance, but at any given time during any particular day, I often slip back to stage one. It is supposed to be helpful to discuss the death of the loved one as often as possible, each time adding more detail. But I'm lacking the detail. And in our American culture of quick fixes, I'm supposed to be on the road to recovery. I have become almost professional at appearing to be fine, and everyone remarks on how well I am doing. Sometimes I almost believe it myself, but I know it is far from the truth. I'm amazed by the number of people who confide in me that they are taking a prescription mood enhancer or an antidepressant. Not for me, at least for right now. I know to reach some level of recovery, I will need to feel the pain and sadness and learn to work through it. And further down the line, if I'm unable to handle all of this sadness and loss, then I'd like to think there is something out there I haven't tried.

From my late night reading I also know I have post-traumatic stress syndrome. Previously I thought this was a condition experienced only by Vietnam veterans. However, research tells me anyone who has lived through a very unexpected trauma can have flashbacks coupled with extreme emotional highs and lows. One moment I'm strong and convinced I will survive this experience, and a few minutes later I am unexpectedly paralyzed with sadness and wonder how I will continue. I agonize about Laura's last moments. Did she realize what was happening? Did she die in pain? In my mind I see images of the crash site and Laura's burning body. A simple thing like the sound of a jet engine from a noisy plane flying too low can make me break out in a sweat. I tell myself, "Don't dwell on it, don't think about it." But I can't make the gruesome pictures go away.

This crowded plane filled with sleeping passengers is the first free moment I have had to myself since April 14 because our life has been one event after another. On Saturday, May 28, the day after school had ended for the year, we drove to Colorado for Dan's graduation. I had always enjoyed the long trip through the farming and ranching areas of central and north Texas. We always drove nonstop, breaking only for food and gas. The anticipation of seeing Laura and later Dan and Laura made the trips fun. Sean would be in charge of the music, his favorite song being "Amarillo by Morning," which he would play almost continually. Usually, with luck, we would be there for breakfast the day after we departed. It was all part of the happy ritual we played out several times a year. But this last trip, almost two weeks ago, had been different for all of us. Dan had worked so long and hard to make this graduation happen. I was so proud of him and so determined not to let Laura's death undermine what should be a joyous occasion. There were reminders. Memorial Day fell on that Monday before graduation, and of course Laura is buried at the Academy cemetery. Dan Murray, on extended leave, had joined us and other family members to make the Wednesday graduation ceremony memorable for our Dan.

But before our extended families began arriving in Colorado Springs, we had some unfinished business to attend to. We met at the Association of Graduates (AOG) building to discuss the Memorial Fund established after Laura's death. While there I asked when Laura's name might be added to the Graduate Memorial Wall. The names of graduates who died in combat are inscribed on this marble monument in the terrazzo area, where cadets form up and march to lunch every day. It had seemed like such a small request, but I wanted to ensure that Laura would receive the recognition she deserved and that her memory would be preserved. And historically it had importance: Laura would be the first female graduate to be included on this wall to honor those who died in service to their country.

The AOG director informed me that Laura might not be eligible for inclusion on the wall because the Air Force was considering listing her death as an aircraft accident. I was stunned. In my mind, anyone killed by an AMRAAM missile over a combat area, regardless of the circumstances, should be listed as a combat death. He said they were waiting for an official ruling.

Then there was the matter of the grave marker. We had to decide on an inscription, and this eternal decision was important to us. Immediately after Laura's burial we couldn't make so final a decision, so we had

113

postponed it. On Memorial Day, as on almost every morning while we were there, we had gone out to the cemetery early. Sean had bought a flag and I brought flowers to mark the occasion. All the graves were decorated with individual flags. It is a beautiful setting, but so sad. A cardboard plaque marked Laura's grave and the ground around it was still raw dirt, her death too recent for the grass to have grown back. I walked around the adjacent graves and read the markers of those whose lives were taken at a young age and speculated about each one. Did they die from a car accident, suicide, illness, the Gulf War, a military accident? It seemed important to know. I wanted everyone who walks through these hallowed grounds to read Laura's name and know how she was killed. As I knelt in the red dirt and said a silent prayer, Laura's death became only more meaningless, more senseless.

The remainder of the week went well. We were just another proud family from out of state, here to celebrate an important milestone. Parents of service academy graduates are among the proudest parents of all at any college graduation ceremony. We had all traveled down the same hard road with our children. First, there was the stringent admission process, then the hardships of the first year, followed by the rigorous academic, psychological, and physical challenges. It's not an easy journey and many drop out. Most of those graduating that week had relied on the understanding, support, and love of their families. It was almost as if the entire families were graduating together. In a sense they were. These young, dedicated individuals could be called to serve in harm's way, and some would pay the ultimate price, like Laura. The lives of their families would be forever changed.

This was the third Academy graduation ceremony I'd sat through in my life, and each successive time doesn't dull the anticipation and excitement. The day was clear, the sky as deep a blue as the cadet uniforms, and the American flag was waving in front of the majestic Rocky Mountains. Air Force Secretary Widnall was the guest speaker, and she spoke about the sacrifice of keeping America free. I wondered if she was thinking about Laura. Even under our circumstances, it was such a proud, happy moment when Dan's name was called and he stepped up to accept his diploma. Now it would be up to him to be the pathfinder, the trailblazer for Sean.

Then it became time to prepare myself for the grand finale. I knew the Air Force Thunderbirds would come screaming up from behind the mountains and burst down low over the graduation ceremony, thrilling the graduates and the packed stadium of onlookers. However, the roar of their engines, the flare of the afterburners had ceased to provide me with a thrill. The announcer had said, "The roar of their engines represents the sound of freedom around the world." But not for me. The roar of their engines will always represent the sound of death.

All my concerns and questions about the shoot down weren't entirely forgotten during the week. It was the topic of discussion at many of the social events. My husband's classmates who were still on active duty or those who had come to celebrate Dan's graduation gathered in corners and talked about topics like ROEs, Guard calls, transponders, and the need for fighter pilots to be aggressive. I had begun to develop more than a casual understanding of those terms, and I unobtrusively eavesdropped on their conversations.

One of Danny's classmates, a previous combat pilot and aviation buff who had followed the events and articles written since April 14, had confided in me, "Joan, I'm mystified how this could have happened." His next statement completely surprised me: "Do you think this thing was a CIA or government setup to kill someone on one of those helicopters?" He was not the first to suggest this possibility, but coming from him it was so unexpected. I'm not sure of so much about Laura's death, but I am positive it wasn't part of a diabolical scheme. It was curious and a small comfort to know that others with more insight into flying and combat were as troubled about the circumstances of the shoot down as I was.

The voice of the flight attendant shocks me into the present. "Please begin preparing for arrival." As the passengers begin to wake up, the trash is collected, seats and tray tables adjusted, I prepare myself mentally for another challenging test of my emotional endurance. Circling the enormous Frankfurt Airport, I point out to Sean Rhein Main Air Force Base across the runway. "That's where Dad used to fly, and that's where we stood the morning he returned with the hostages." Sean isn't as interested in old memories as much as making new ones. That's a good thing. For the next two weeks we'll concentrate on new experiences, not reliving the old ones.

Dan Murray meets us, and we begin the almost two-hour drive to Laura's apartment. I think the entire way, "Let's just get this over with." I know walking into her apartment for the first time will be very difficult.

Already, zooming along the autobahn, the sights and smells of Germany are bringing back too many forgotten and happy memories of that other life I've begun to separate myself from. Dan turns off the highway, and we drive through the German countryside, as beautiful and peaceful as I've always remembered it. We pass through small towns, each so much like the other, I begin to lose track.

Even before I am psychologically ready, the car stops and I recognize Laura's red Honda. We're here. I can sense the tension as we get out of the car, enter the two-story house, and begin walking up the stairs. Dan unlocks the door, stands aside, and we enter. It is very much like entering a previously sealed Egyptian tomb. The essence of Laura is everywhere, and things are just as she had left them last December before she departed for Turkey. Stacked in the living room are unopened boxes and packages that had been shipped from Turkey just two weeks before she was killed. This is harder than I imagined, but I thank God for this last "Laura" experience. She had taken such care in decorating this apartment. I'm not surprised to see a framed print, hanging above the sofa, of a German steam engine pulling into a train station. Laura had purchased this on a previous trip because it symbolized her favorite poem, "The Station." I'd had it professionally framed for her as a surprise. As I would expect, every drawer, every closet is in perfect order. Laura was my neat child—she would alphabetize my spices, sort the canned goods by content and size, and her room was almost always perfect. I miss her so much, but I know Sean is concerned about me. He watches my every move, and I can see he is praying that his mom doesn't lose it. I remain stoic. Grieving is a solitary pastime.

We spend Sunday *"Volksmarsching."* Every weekend and holiday there are organized hikes through Germany that average between six and ten miles. Sean has grown up hearing about Dan's and Laura's experiences hiking through Germany. Laura had promised she would take him. It is wonderful to be outside after the long flight, and Sean just loves all of it. It would have been one of the highlights of Laura's life to be hiking along the trails with Sean, teaching him simple German phrases. At the finish point we sit with Dan Murray, drink wine, and discuss our plans for the next few weeks. Monday, we will drive out to the base, finalize dates for shipping Laura's household goods and car, and attend to more of the paperwork of ending Laura's life.

On Tuesday we point the car toward Munich and begin our whirlwind tour of Europe. Our travels take us as far south as Venice, Italy. We drive like demons, packing each day full of every site and event humanly possible, trying to live in the present and not the past. Sean is a born traveler. He sits in the front passenger seat, reads the maps, figures out each currency and the price of gas by the liter. We climb mountains, visit castles, and ride in a gondola on the Grand Canal. It takes much resolve not to reflect back on the previous trips when Dan and Laura were children. It is a gift to see the world through the eyes of a child, and each time it is different. We drive back to Laura's apartment for the weekend and another round of *Volksmärsche*. It's an unspoken consensus: if we keep busy enough, keep traveling, keep driving, keep hiking, the grief and sadness ever present in our lives will be left behind.

On Monday, June 20, as we prepare for a trip to France, Danny receives a telephone call from Gen. Robert Oaks, the commander of the U.S. Air Forces in Europe stationed at Ramstein AFB. It is under General Oaks's authority that the 110 investigation is being conducted. Danny has known General Oaks for years and last served under him when he was commander of the Officer Training School at Lackland AFB. Once he had even taken him waterfowl hunting in south Texas. The general expresses his condolences concerning Laura's death and tells Danny the 110 investigation is now completed. The report is currently going through the Air Force Legal Department in Europe before being forwarded to the Pentagon next week. He extends an invitation to drop by, but Danny declines because he knows this is an awkward situation for Oaks.

Tuesday we're on to France. Sean figures out the exchange rate for francs and is in charge of getting the money ready to pay the tolls along the French highway to Paris. Paris is still one of my favorite cities, and I notice the many changes that have taken place since my last visit. The buildings have been pressure washed, there's a McDonald's on almost every corner, and English-speaking CNN is available on television sets in each hotel room. And tourists, I just don't remember this many. The number of tour buses, the length of the lines everywhere we go makes Paris feel more like Epcot Center at Disney World. But Sean feels the magic of this beautiful city, and I don't think we miss one landmark or museum.

We had heard about the Nicole Simpson and Ron Goldman murders earlier in the week but had not kept up with the details. Friday morning, as we prepared to check out of our hotel, we watched a replay of O.J.'s latest adventure. As we sat in our hotel room, in Paris, watching the white Bronco drive through the streets of Los Angeles, I drew no connection to my life. But there would be. For the next two years the Simpson/Goldman murder would continually crowd out other important newsworthy events. The public, feigning disinterest, couldn't get enough details and versions of the grisly crime. It contained all the elements of a tabloid tragedy: the fallen hero, beautiful celebrities, abuse, drugs, infidelity, murder, and suspense. If the Pentagon had concocted a plan to distract the public from one of the worst friendly fire incidents in the history of the armed forces, it couldn't have done it better than O.J. In American society the fourth estate, "The Press," can be seen as the unwritten fourth branch of government. Public opinion coupled with the press can force an issue or let it slide. I will come to believe the Pentagon was betting on the latter.

With the Eiffel Tower in our rearview mirror, we have no definite plans except to sleep at Laura's apartment in Germany tonight. Sean sees signs that say "Verdun," and Danny tells him some of the historical significance of this World War I battle site. There is a family connection: Danny's grandfather, a major in the U.S. Marines, had fought in France during the war. Neither Danny nor I have ever been there, so on a whim we turn off the main route and follow the signs. The French countryside is glorious, with acres and acres of vivid red poppies. We spend the remainder of the day touring battlefields and war cemeteries, finishing the tour in Luxembourg, at General Patton's grave. Gazing at the oceans of white headstones amid the green fields of just a few of the war cemeteries, I'm reminded again of the high cost of freedom. It is a solemn ending to our last excursion. Driving back to Laura's apartment, few words are spoken as we think ahead to the coming week and our departure. This last weekend will be spent *Volksmarsching* with Dan Murray and preparing for the movers who are scheduled to come on Monday.

Saturday morning, I'm up too early, and I can't go back to sleep. I get in Laura's car and make the fifteen-minute drive to the base to buy some breakfast items and a newspaper before Danny and Sean wake up. The Ramstein Shoppette is deserted, and the manager is just putting out the morning edition of the *Stars and Stripes* newspaper. When I arrive back at the apartment, Danny and Sean are still asleep. I sit in the living room, read the paper, and savor the quiet solitude. It's been several weeks since I've had the luxury of an American newspaper. I read each article, and when I get to the fifth page, the headline U.S. in Dilemma Over Pilots Who Downed Helicopters jumps out at me. This is so unexpected, my heart begins to race as I continue reading. I can see it is a reprint of an article from the *Los Angeles Times*, dateline Washington. The first paragraph perplexes me: "The Clinton administration is facing a controversial decision over whether to discipline the pilots of the U.S. F-15 jet fighters that shot down a pair of American Black Hawk helicopters over Iraq two months ago." Another red flag pops up. This should be a nonissue. The secretary of defense promised me on television, before millions of people, full accountability. I continue reading to see if my concerns are valid.

Defense Secretary William J. Perry, who most likely will end up making the final decision on the issue, is coming under pressure—both from some U.S. military officers and from the Turkish government—to court-martial the pilot on charges of negligence. The decision is expected to be a difficult one for an administration that has already had its problems with the uniformed services. Insiders say the military itself is split over the issue, and the pilot, whose identity has not been made public, is a Persian Gulf War veteran. Those arguing for instituting court-martial proceedings are said to include a growing number of senior Air Force officers. This senior leadership contends that the pilot's error was so grievous that it amounted to negligence. The helicopters were clearly marked and they were flying at slow speeds, clearly no threat to the fighters. But Air Force Chief of Staff, General Merrill A. McPeak, is said to be strongly opposed to any such action, on grounds that the pilot's mistake was understandable under the rules of war. General [George] Joulwan, head of the U.S. European command, is expected to give the official report a final review this week. Sources familiar with the report say it is expected to reaffirm that the shoot down occurred because the lead F-15 pilot misidentified the helicopter. He did not take extra precautions to confirm their nationality. Any punishment is expected to fall mainly on the pilot of the lead fighter. The pilot of the second F-15 is expected to receive less of the blame, since by practice he follows his leader.

119

This is the first time speculation from the Pentagon puts the blame squarely on the shoulders of the pilots. Preeminently, I have a great deal of concern about the accountability issue. General McPeak is loyal to his fighter pilots, but I can't imagine how he thinks he can let them skate if their negligence was responsible for twenty-six deaths. The encouraging news is the investigation is completed and almost ready to be forwarded to Washington, D.C. After Washington our family can't be too much further down the line of contact. All of these rumors or maybe truths make me even more anxious to read the report.

On Sunday I begin the task of sorting through Laura's belongings. What do we want to ship? What do we do with the things we don't want? I am not in a frame of mind to make any of these decisions, and for the present, I can't bear to part with a single item. It is decided we will let the movers pack and ship everything. Laura kept perfect files of all her legal documents, and we will hand carry those with us on the airplane because her shipment will not reach San Antonio until September.

In the living room, propped up next to a bookcase, I uncover a small black canvas bag covered with dirt. A tag attached to one of the zippers has Laura's name on it. I open it up and look inside; everything is covered with sand. These are toiletries; a book with a folded page, indicating she had not finished reading it; her wallet; and some clothes. I realize Laura must have taken this bag with her into Iraq. Considering its condition, she most probably left it wherever she spent the night on April 13. The Air Force must have sent it back from Iraq to Ramstein, and someone with a key to her apartment had delivered it. Closer scrutiny reveals a copy of orders for her assignment to Germany and another set for the temporary duty to Turkey. I keep looking, but I don't see any for the trip into Iraq. I've been in the military environment long enough to know that orders are cut and issued even for day trips. I mention this to Danny and he agrees. Where are the orders that gave Laura permission to spend the night and travel into a combat zone?

Monday my resolve fractures, I can't help but be sad as I watch the things we bought for Laura's apartment put back in boxes and shipped home. It is never easy to close a life, especially that of someone as young and promising as Laura. There is a hole in my heart that will be there forever and no one will ever be able to fill. Each moment that passes I miss the mother-daughter relationship that had sustained us for the past twenty-five years. Every parent hopes their offspring will be an improved version of themselves, and Laura was. She was also a fighter, a champion of what's right, not what's easiest. I know Laura would want me to learn everything I can about the shoot down and look for the truth.

17

San Antonio, Texas
July 1, 1994
Friday

S ince returning from Germany, this week has been a rare experience. I haven't had to be any place, get ready for the next event, meet any deadlines, or go to work. The best part is I don't have to get dressed each morning and face the world. I've had the opportunity to catch my breath, do normal things, or just do nothing. After unpacking I'd spend most of the time taking care of unfinished tasks that have weighed on my shoulders for months. Before leaving for Germany I had tried to complete all the thank-you notes for the flowers and acts of kindness showered on us during the week of Laura's funeral. The very last bunch of notes just went out in the mail this morning.

The second thing I have postponed is the decision about the inscription on Laura's grave marker. Since Dan's graduation and our last visit to the Academy cemetery, we have gone over the multitude of possibilities for the wording. I'd held firm to my conviction that I want the words to indicate how she had met her early death. Now, after repeated discussions with our family and Dan Murray, we have been able to finalize the wording. It will read:

LAURA ASHLEY PIPER

1st LT US AIR FORCE

CLASS OF 1992

MAR 18 1969   APR 14 1994

KIA FRIENDLY FIRE OVER IRAQ

LOVE MOM 3 DANS & SEAN

The third almost insurmountable task is my living room. The floor is still stacked with piles of newspapers, magazines, saved memorial service programs, photographs, and dried, faded roses from Laura's funeral. The dining room table and every other available surface holds the cards and letters that have arrived over the past two and one-half months. I can't even consider discarding a single item. Yesterday I ventured out to purchase large square plastic containers with tight covers to store everything. While walking down the aisles of the large discount store, I realized it had been almost three months since I'd shopped anyplace other than a grocery store. For now, shopping doesn't hold any entertainment value or allure. There are too many other concerns to contend with.

Some of those concerns are as mundane as clipping the shrubs in our backyard, which, due to inattention, have grown into a jungle. Others are more immediate, like trying to create some semblance of a family atmosphere for Sean. Bless our neighbors, the Ojedas. The know Sean needs to have normal activities this summer, so they've included him on their family trips. He left with them this morning to spend the weekend in Houston, and next week he will join them at their lake house. We both need the breathing room.

There is a sense of anticipation. We are in a holding pattern until the official AFR 110-14 accident report is released. Try as I may, I am unable to put any part of Laura's death aside. It continues to consume every aspect of my life. I need to know more and I need to know everything, because it is easier to reach the acceptance stage of grieving once you know the truth and the details. I'm sure this report will fill in the missing pieces of this continuing nightmare. My sleep pattern is even more disrupted from the jet lag of our Germany trip. When I awake at two in the morning, I go outside, sit on the deck, gaze up at the dark sky, and think about Laura.

Today, as I begin making order out of the chaos of our living room, my efforts are interrupted by the telephone. A friend who lives in New York tells me there is a front-page story about the results of the Black Hawk 110 investigation in today's *New York Times*. Driving to the nearest bookstore, I think it probably doesn't say much. The Pentagon hasn't told us anything about this official 110 report, not a hint of what it contains, not when it will be released, and they have a legal obligation to inform the families of the victims before any information is released to the press. In the bookstore I scan the front-page headline: Copter Deaths: Pentagon

FINDS HUMAN FAILURE. This perplexes me. Turning to the inside page, where the article is continued, I estimate the entire piece is several thousand words. Too long for a reporter's suppositions.

Returning to the privacy of my empty house, I immediately begin reading. I learn Defense Secretary William Perry, along with his top civilian and military aides, was given a three-hour briefing on the report, two days ago, on June 29. The White House has acknowledged that President Clinton is aware of the findings of the report. After Perry makes some determinations about what actions need to be taken and finalizes the report, he will brief the president. The article's source for all the information is "a senior Defense Department official."

This senior official says, "Multiple human error was responsible for this horrible tragedy." He specifically gives detailed examples that lead me to think this is an official Pentagon news leak. While most of the previous speculations about the shoot down had focused on the pilots, this report says there were other serious factors involved. For example, controllers on the AWACS plane knew there were friendly American helicopters in the area, had the information on at least three of their radarscopes, then failed to warn the F-15 pilots. The electronic IFF system on the Black Hawks was emitting an incorrect code for the No Fly Zone. The Black Hawks were equipped with external fuel storage tanks that made them resemble Russian Hind helicopters. It is also noted that there had never been one incident of a Hind sighting during the three-year period the No Fly Zone has been in effect. The report contains no evidence to suggest the Black Hawks were operating in a threatening way. Another contributing factor may have been that the F-15 radar and interrogation systems were designed for fixed-wing aircraft, meaning they could have had difficulty distinguishing helicopters. This senior official concludes with, "It was a chain of events that led to this tragedy."

I am most perplexed by the findings about the pilots, because in the beginning I'd imagined they were young hotshots with very limited combat experience. Soon after the shoot down, I had learned one of them was a lieutenant colonel, the F-15 squadron commander, and a Gulf War veteran. I had expected he was the flight leader on April 14. However, this article reports conclusively that the aircraft flying in the lead was piloted by a captain. The lieutenant colonel had been flying the wing position. It continues to say that the lead pilot shot down the trail helicopter, and twenty seconds later the wingman, after visually identifying the Black Hawks as hostile, fired a missile at the lead helicopter.

Another senior officer is quoted as saying, "The Pentagon will place responsibility for the accident on at least eight people including the pilots. There is the possibility they will be relieved of their duties and could be court-martialed. Secretary Perry will most likely make the decisions about punishment for those found guilty because of the accident's international considerations, its high profile and the gravity of the accident."

I guess this news report about says it all. I wonder if these Pentagon officials and sources lined up in the hallways of the Pentagon to talk to this reporter for the sole purpose of gaining self-importance, but most likely, this was an official leak. How much more information could there possibly be that hasn't already been leaked to the press? When the Pentagon finally gets around to briefing the families and releasing the official report, it will be anticlimactic. Throughout the next week the news leaks will continue, with major articles in the *Washington Times*, *USA Today*, and the *Air Force Times*.

I had first seen a copy of the *Air Force Times* in 1967 at the Base Exchange during our first Air Force assignment. Danny was a brand-new second lieutenant going through pilot training in Arizona. I'll never forget the headline in that edition: 5,000 MORE AIRMEN GOING TO SEA. With my limited military background I couldn't imagine why people in the Air Force were going to sea—they're not sailors. Then I found out SEA is the acronym for Southeast Asia. This was a wake-up call. If I was going to spend the next twenty years married to the military, I better learn this stuff. I immediately subscribed to the publication and over the past twenty-seven years have read almost every weekly edition, gaining a now very valuable military education. After Danny retired I'd almost let the subscription lapse but found it difficult to break old habits, so I'd renewed for what I thought would be one last year. Now I'm finding out the importance of this incremental military knowledge gained over a long period of time. For instance, when the news first reported problems with the AWACS crew, in my mind, I could pull up pictures of the plane and a vague idea of their mission, from back in the 1980s, when the debate about selling AWACS to Saudi Arabia made military headlines.

The *Air Force Times* has been constantly in the information loop since the shoot down, and I can usually rely on the accuracy of this independent paper's articles. This week's edition proves to be no exception. The headline reads, REPORT BLAMES PILOTS, CONTROLLERS IN IRAQ SHOOT DOWN. There is some additional news. First, the report is scheduled to be made public in the middle of July. Boldface bullets under Secretary of Defense Perry's picture list the factors contributing to the shoot down: the pilots were not briefed that Army helicopters would be in the area; the two controllers on the AWACS, tracking the helicopters, and the F-15s didn't communicate with each other; the F-15 pilots made two passes, incorrectly identified the helicopters, and then opened fire. This article goes further than others this week, naming one of the pilots: Lt. Col. Randy May, commander of the 53rd Fighter Squadron at Spangdahlem Air Force Base in Germany. I already knew the lieutenant colonel was flying the wing position. The reporter is unable to name the other pilot, the captain who had been the flight lead. It can't be confirmed if they have been relieved of their duties, but it is known they are both in Germany. The last paragraph says, "Although Perry has taken responsibility for the tragedy, General Robert Oaks, commander of the U.S. Air Forces in Europe, will have to decide whether those involved in the incident should face disciplinary action or whether they acted properly." I hope this is true, because Danny has such confidence in General Oaks.

On Thursday I receive a telephone call from an Air Force officer at the Pentagon. The 110 investigation results will be publicly released on July 13 at 2:00 P.M. Air Force officers will travel to the location of immediate family members and give them a personal briefing on the morning of July 13 at a nearby base. A copy of the investigation will be delivered to our homes that day. I call the Bass family and ask if they would like to arrange for both of our families to be briefed together. It seems unnecessary for two sets of officers to travel to San Antonio and give two separate briefings. They agree and I notify the Pentagon. Also, I wonder why we just can't hand carry this 110 report home from the briefing rather than have the Pentagon go to the trouble and expense of delivering it to our houses, but I don't press the issue. The important thing is that in a little more than one week, I'll be able to read the report and make my own assessment of what happened that morning in Iraq almost three months ago.

Even in stressful times, life goes on. Finally it is July 13. I'm reminded that twenty-six families across the United States and in Turkey, Iraq, France, and England are also anticipating this long-awaited briefing. I don't really understand why I am so apprehensive, because I've read all the press leaks and probably know the meat of the report. Nonetheless, I notice my hands are shaking as I get dressed. It probably has more to do with reaching another milestone along the journey of Laura's death than with the report itself.

Sean has decided he wants to attend this briefing, and that's fine with me and Danny. I continue to be open and frank with him. I reaffirm my belief that it is better for children to know the truth than to create their own fantasy. Sean, from an early age, has had an intense interest in military aircraft. Through the years he has collected a personal library of books about airplanes and is better at identifying military planes than Danny. Last April, the day after the shoot down, I remember sitting on the floor by the bookcase in his bedroom as he pulled a small Scholastic sticker book about helicopters from the shelf. I had purchased it for him at an elementary school book fair. It showed pictures of all the common military helicopters. Sean had pointed out a picture of a Black Hawk on page 12. We both noticed he had never gotten around to placing the corresponding sticker on that page. One might think that if my ten-year-old could identify a Black Hawk, experienced Air Force pilots could do the same. After all, it isn't a rare, exotic aircraft. Before the shoot down Sean had always wanted to become a pilot. Now he says he thinks he will become a doctor.

The guard at the gate gives us a smart salute as we slow down in our car. Randolph is a showcase military installation, and many of the buildings date back to World War II, when this base was used to train pilots. The "Taj Mahal," a tall rococo-style building in the center of the base, is actually a disguised water tower, and this distinguishing landmark can be seen for miles across the rolling Texas countryside. This morning everything is pristine, the white buildings contrasting sharply against the manicured green landscaping. We pass the chapel on the left, with its beautiful Spanish architecture, and the Missing Man Monument on the right, sleek and modern. Somehow it all seems to fit. This base always represented home to us, coming back to San Antonio from distant assignments, but now it brings back too many memories, both happy and sad.

We select a parking space shaded by one of the large oak trees that surround the Officers' Club, where the briefing will be conducted. Walking up the pathway, we are joined by the Bass family, and we all enter the club at the same time. An Air Force colonel introduces himself and leads us to a private room prepared for the briefing. After offers of juice or coffee we sit at a large circular table, and the briefing begins. Each family is handed a black two-inch binder. The cover of ours reads, "Briefing Prepared for the Family of First Lieutenant Laura A. Piper." The colonel begins by reading a summary of the events leading to the shoot down of the helicopters. He follows with what's called a "Statement of Opinion," the opinion of the accident investigators on the major contributing causes of the shoot down.

> The 14 April 1994 shoot down of two US Black Hawk helicopters by two US F-15C aircraft in northern Iraq was caused by a chain of events which began with the breakdown of clear guidance from the Combined Task Force to its component organizations. This resulted in the lack of a clear understanding among the components of their respective responsibilities. Consequently the helicopter activities were not fully integrated with other Operation Provide Comfort air operations in the Tactical Area of Responsibility. Additionally OPC personnel did not receive consistent, comprehensive training to ensure they had a thorough understanding of the rules of engagement. As a result, some aircrews' understanding of how the approved rules of engagement should be applied became over-simplified. . . .

As I listen to him read I realize all of this had been printed, almost verbatim, in the newspaper almost two weeks ago. The colonel now directs us to begin reading the information in the black binder. He and the other officers will stand by to answer any questions we might have. With several military officers hovering over us and Sean playing with his juice and his father's coffee cup, Danny and I preview the binder's contents. Immediately I'm certain I can't read this now. The contents include over 150 pages, 5 tabbed sections, diagrams, charts, and 12 pages of notes that reference 581 tabs from the unabridged report. Clearly this is information overload. I will need an uninterrupted, quiet atmosphere to even begin sorting this out.

I ask the colonel if I can read this information and the 110 report, in its entirety, before I begin asking questions. He replies, "Yes, an officer at the Pentagon will be available this week to answer any of your questions." I write the telephone number in the black binder for safekeeping, because surely I can read the report in a few days. I think it is a better strategy to read the official report in context rather than extruded bits and pieces included in this executive summary. Before leaving we thank the team that has traveled to Randolph AFB solely for the purpose of this one-hour briefing. I knew they were uneasy. Some of the teams briefing today may encounter hostile families who will cast blame on the closest military officer. Not us, not the Basses. We are still part of the Air Force family.

Pulling up in our driveway, we see two large boxes stacked in front of our door. The United Parcel Service label has a return address of Department of Defense, Washington, D.C. I can't believe this is the 110 report. It's huge and heavy! We drag the boxes into our recently cleaned-out dining room and begin unpacking. I stack the white stapled volumes on the table. When they are all unpacked I count twenty-one volumes. Every single concern, question, and answer to any mystery left about the shoot down must lie between these white covers.

I'm glad I had planned for Sean to visit his grandmother and cousins in Florida for all of next week. Late this afternoon I will take him to the airport and immediately come home and start reading. I'm beginning to feel a time constraint. My summer vacation is almost over. I return to school the first week in August, and the students begin the following week. Friends and family have advised me to take a leave of absence this year. When I began my first year of teaching last year, I had taken out wage compensation insurance. Under the unusual circumstances of Laura's death, I'm sure I could qualify for some financial compensation. I've given it a lot of thought and remain undecided. It is tempting to have the next year to recover my mental equilibrium. The other consideration is I've worked hard and long to pursue a teaching certificate. I've already lost one important thing in my life. I'm not sure if I want to give up another.

When I return home from the airport, CNN's lead story of the day is the release of the official report. Cameras pan the two-foot-high, twenty-one-volume accident report stacked on the table in front of Secretary of Defense Perry and General Shalikashvili, chairman of the Joint Chiefs. Perry says he endorses the report and accepts its findings. "It is a full and complete documentation and disclosure of what occurred. It involved thirty-one people who began the investigation the day after the accident occurred. They spent more than twenty thousand hours and interviewed one hundred thirty-seven witnesses. Additionally several thousand hours were spent testing and inspecting the equipment involved in the accident and they conducted more than one hundred separate airborne flying tests with F-15s and Black Hawk helicopters." He pauses. "It's a tragedy that never should have happened." General Shalikashvili remarks, "There were a shocking number of instances where people failed to do their job properly." Lastly, Perry steps to the microphone and says, "Our third promise to the families of the victims was to address accountability, and we have taken the first step today and the only proper step I can take under the Uniform Code of Military Justice. This investigative report is the starting point. I have directed my military commanders to review the testimony and make recommendations."

The July heat envelops San Antonio during the next week. Temperatures exceed the 100-degree mark, and the city scorches in the blazing sun. I'm in training, rising at dawn and walking at a brisk pace for three miles, because exercise combats depression and increases my mental acuity. The remainder of my day is spent in the house with the air conditioner humming and the ceiling fan whirling as I begin examining the 110 report. It is mesmerizing, sometimes compelling, and often tedious and boring, but I persevere, determined to read every page. I begin, I'm sure, where everyone who has read the report begins: with the testimony of the pilots. Even though the Air Force contends the shoot down was a result of a chain of human events, I can't help but wonder what kind of mind-set the pilots had to have to shoot at low, slow helicopters and make a decision to fire so quickly. The pilots and the other individuals most accountable are not listed by name, only by number. The lead pilot is Witness #26, and the wingman is Witness #25, whom I know by name to be Lt. Col. Randy May. During this first reading their testimony seems strong and believable, but this makes it even more difficult to ascertain how they could make the hasty determination to shoot so quickly and still be within the parameters of the rules of engagement.

The AWACS testimony is another story. At least two of the crewmembers, the mission crew commander, Major Tracy, and the AOR controller, Lieutenant Wilson, declined to testify. Often the answers of the testifying crewmembers are vague and very disturbing. Before and during the shoot down a video camera was recording their mission. According to crew testimony, the tape with the recording of the shoot down was accidentally erased. Some of the crew were sleeping or taking a break, and it isn't clear what the rest of them were doing or thinking. The negligence on that aircraft is extremely disturbing. Even more upsetting, this Monday Air Force Secretary Sheila Widnall had traveled to Tinker Air Force Base in Oklahoma City, home base of the AWACS, for the sole purpose of a drop-in visit to boost the morale of the AWACS squadron because this week the press had reported, in detail, the damning evidence in the 110 report about their gross incompetence. Evidently this negative publicity had affected all of the AWACS' crews.

Reading through all the evidence and testimony, I begin to put together some of the events and fill in missing details. I learn Laura was sitting in the back row of the trail helicopter, which means she was killed by the lead pilot, the nameless Witness #26. Also, Widnall had been to Incirlik the Monday before the shoot down and had flown on an AWACS mission over northern Iraq. The next day, Tuesday, General Pilkington had flown on a mission identical to the April 14 flight, into the No Fly Zone on a Black Hawk.

There are countless pages describing mechanical functions and tests on all the aircraft involved. One section lists individual statements of death for each person killed. However, each statement says the same thing: "Death by blunt force injury." The report contains copies of innumerable documents, some as inconsequential as a statement of payment to a Kurdish farmer of $50 for a damaged onion field, and innumerable pieces of information: operating procedures, oil gauge readings, radio codes, AWACS technology, the rank structure at Incirlik, the F-15s called "Eagles," the Black Hawks called "Eagle Flight." It is difficult to wade through the superfluous material and even harder to keep the important facts straight.

After four continuous days of studying the report, I need a reprieve to get some kind of perspective on this enormous amount of information I've tried to unravel and comprehend. I've finished examining all of it, but I know some of the testimony will require more than one reading. Military and civilian leaders, with a deeper knowledge than I, will decide who will be charged and with what based on the evidence in these twenty-one volumes.

I believe there is enough serious negligence for charges to be made against several people—certainly the two pilots, some of the AWACS crew, and commanding officers at Incirlik Air Force Base. Although Danny is incensed about the behavior and actions of the AWACS crew, he often defends the actions of the two F-15 pilots. At times we argue about this.

He tells me I'm not an expert on military flying, to which I reply, "Your loyalty to the Air Force and pilots is clouding your judgment." This does cause some dissension, but since it still takes so much effort to get through each day of our lives, we don't have the emotional strength to make this a heated issue. At this point we just agree to disagree.

The newspapers continue to report the fallout from the investigation. I read that the commander of Operation Provide Comfort, Brig. Gen. Jeffrey Pilkington, has been relieved of his command. The military appears to be haggling over whether he was fired or relieved. He will return to Germany as commander of the 86th Airlift Wing at Ramstein AFB. Another report says the mission commander of the AWACS and possibly four AWACS crewmembers—and the two pilots—are facing disciplinary action.

We have begun making contact with the other families who lost a loved one in this shoot down, the beginning of a network of spouses and parents with addresses spanning the United States and Europe. Many of them tell us they are upset about the investigation's findings and concerned about the government keeping its promises. Some just want to talk, and it is comforting and helpful to have discussions without having to explain yourself. Often these other families raise the question of filing a lawsuit against the U.S. government. The press has already reported that the families of the Kurdish nationals killed in the shoot down have retained a Washington-based law firm.

Danny, being a former commander, always tells them it is almost impossible to win a lawsuit against the U.S. government over the death of an active duty member of the armed forces, regardless of the circumstances. There are rigid precedents; and some attempts to establish new precedents have gone all the way to the Supreme Court, only to be denied.

But Danny and I question the wisdom of giving others advice about this subject. We call the Legal Office at Randolph Air Force Base and ask if we can meet with someone who can give us an expert opinion. They put us in touch with a colonel who is an expert on military claims. He agrees to meet with us immediately, because he is retiring from the Air Force next week. He tells us, "My professional opinion is a lawsuit would be a complete waste of time, money, and energy. No one ever has won a claim of this kind." Then I ask him about the Kurdish families who have retained a law firm. He replies, "During Vietnam we did pay claims to civilians who were killed. The amount was under thirty dollars. The

American government will never pay anything to the foreign nationals killed on those Black Hawks. It would be a very dangerous and expensive precedent to set." I ask the colonel if compensation for the Americans is a possibility. "No. Even though the events of this mishap are tragic and are attributed to negligence, you will never receive compensation." These are the answers Danny and I had expected to hear because financial compensation for Laura's death had never been a consideration for us. We appreciate his candor and expert opinion. He confirms what we have been telling the other Black Hawk family members. I'm glad to have the issue clarified and settled because there is another unresolved concern.

A few weeks ago Danny had made a trip out to Randolph Air Force Base to purchase the medals Laura had earned before she was killed. He had requested the written criteria for the Purple Heart because he continued to believe those killed on the helicopters deserved this recognition. Danny is surprised to learn congressional language was added to the criteria for the medal in 1993, to include military members killed or wounded by friendly fire in a designated combat zone. Although we had read enough to surmise that the northern No Fly Zone was a combat area, we had not seen an official designation. Danny decided, at that time, that the prudent path would be to wait until after we read the 110 report.

The report does confirm the northern No Fly Zone as a designated "Combat Zone," and personnel assigned to the area receive combat pay. Danny is sure the decision not to award the Purple Heart was hastily made the week after the shoot down because in recent times it has become standard procedure for the armed forces to award all medals and decorations before the burial of the military member.

Now, he writes a letter to Secretary of Defense Perry and requests that Pentagon officials reconsider their original decision:

> I am convinced this award is justified for my daughter and others. In June, with my ten-year-old son by my side, I looked across the American Military Cemetery in Luxembourg, dedicated to 5,076 Americans. How many of those wounded by fratricide received the Purple Heart? How many men, wounded by our own ground fire in the dense jungles of Vietnam, or wounded by shrapnel from our own protective air cover, received Purple Hearts? I'm sure it was perceived as hostile by those who have gone before, just as it was by the personnel on the Army

helicopters, when the lead Black Hawk desperately took evasive action on 14 April 1994.

Danny then adds,

This clarification also impacts the eligibility of my daughter's name being placed on the USAF Academy Graduate Memorial Wall.

Both Danny and I feel certain that the decision not to award the Purple Heart was an oversight and that as soon as Secretary of Defense Perry receives this letter, the Department of Defense will rectify the situation.

Last week I had called the help-line number at the Pentagon to request additional time to compile my list of questions concerning the 110 report. I was told the Army lieutenant colonel who was the contact for the families would remain in this capacity for a now unspecified length of time and to forward my questions, in writing, to him. Because I'm confident the military will deal justly with those responsible for the shoot down, my concerns are more personal.

Reading the testimony of the different commanders at Incirlik, I was surprised none of them, except for Colonel O'Brien and General Pilkington, knew anything about the Black Hawk mission planned for April 14. If that was the case, how did Laura receive permission to go on the mission? Someone else knew and got her on the flight. Where did she spend the night of April 13, and where are the orders that allowed her on this mission into a designated combat zone? In the black canvas bag retrieved from Laura's apartment, I'd located an envelope she used to make notes listing people she talked to the week she was killed concerning her upcoming trip into Iraq. I write my questions, ending with:

I am enclosing copies of five documents that relate to my daughter's status in Turkey. Her original orders indicate her temporary duty status in Turkey expired on March 28, 1994. She had her orders amended to April 10, 1994, so she could go on leave and travel to Egypt. Also enclosed are two temporary gate passes to admit her to Incirlik AFB as she was legally no longer assigned there and had turned in her official gate pass. Conspicuously missing are the documents that account for her continued presence at Incirlik and military orders which give her permission to travel to northern Iraq on April thirteenth and to fly into a combat zone with Eagle Flight, on April fourteenth.

The point I am making is: Laura had to have permission and documentation to get on the April fourteenth mission. This flight was unusual because it was going outside the Security Zone. In the 110 Report, it states these flights were extremely difficult to get on. How does a lowly second lieutenant with expired orders travel to a combat zone and take part in a politically sensitive mission?

This letter is sent by registered mail on July 25. When this month began I had naively thought the release and reading of the long-anticipated official report would bring closure. I could have never predicted this twenty-one-volume monster would become a catalyst for a future "chain of events" that would continue to reshape and change the lives of the Piper family.

18 San Antonio, Texas
August 1, 1994
Monday

This summer the Air Force racks up one more devastating air tragedy. On June 12 at Fairchild AFB, in Washington state, Lt. Col. Bud Holland, practicing for an upcoming air show, stalled a huge B-52 Stratofortress and crashed it into the ground, killing himself and four other crewmembers. One of the officers killed was Lt. Col. Mark McGeehan, commander of the B-52 squadron. He had previously reported Holland's unsafe and reckless flying practices to the group commander, who took no action. As a result, McGeehan refused to let any of the pilots under his command fly on missions with Holland. That's why Lieutenant Colonel McGeehan was on the B-52 with him that day. As the B-52 flew into the ground and exploded into a huge fireball, McGeehan's sons witnessed the explosion from the backyard of their base-housing unit. No one had to tell them Dad wasn't coming home for dinner tonight.

Four major Class One incidents (where damage amounts to one million dollars or more) since March 14, with over 60 killed and 100 injured. Not just sixty killed—sixty horrible deaths: burning, breaking-apart airplanes falling from the sky, the ground scattered with charred, dismembered bodies. Sixty people, their last breath taken under terrorizing conditions. Families who have lost a loved one agonize over those last moments. How many times have I heard, "I bet she never knew what hit her. I'm sure her death was instantaneous." I'm not at all convinced Laura's was, but I'll never know. The Casualty Affairs officers, the chaplains, the Air Force, and Pentagon officials never discuss this part of the shoot down. They just keep track of the statistics. Recently I'd read the Air Force's accident record has improved over the past ten years. A small consolation to sixty families.

On August 1 General McPeak and Secretary Widnall send "A Message to the Troops." It says,

The recent Pope and Fairchild accidents and the Black Hawk Shoot Down in Iraq remind us of how lethal and unforgiving our business can be. They also remind us there is no substitute for good leadership, relevant and tough training and attention to detail. In particular the tragic Black Hawk Helicopter Shoot Down, which took twenty-six lives, is a clear indicator that we must do a thorough review of all our training and operational procedures.

The message goes on to rehash the old themes of doing more with less, being leaner and tougher, and learning to be more efficient and effective. The message concludes with, "Yes it is true we have suffered recent set-backs. But, we will learn from these experiences, build on our strengths and continue to move forward."

I begin the month of August preparing to go back to work. I'd never gotten around to making a decision about taking a leave of absence, so by doing nothing the decision was made for me. They are expecting me and I'll be there. I'm not unhappy about returning for another year of teaching, and probably it will be the best thing for me. It is something I love doing, it keeps me focused, and the days fly by. Right now I need all of those things, because, again, I find myself waiting for the next event. Charges will be made against those suspected of negligence in the shoot down sometime near the end of this month. Every military expert familiar with the 110 report seems certain charges will be brought against the two pilots and several of the AWACS crewmembers. No one believes or expects that any of the senior leadership involved will be disciplined. This confirms my conviction of who should be charged, and this is exactly what I expect to happen.

In my personal quest for information, disclosure, and truth, I may have done something I could later regret. I may have pushed the "need to know" envelope too far this time, but the deed is done and I'm faced with the consequences. During the summer I often found myself in denial over Laura's death. Intellectually, with complete certainty, I knew she was dead. However, I would find myself thinking, "She may not be dead." When the military had returned bodies from Southeast Asia, sometimes the families would have the casket opened, and the remains would be someone else's or just a few rocks and undetermined bones. Maybe Laura is being held prisoner in some little village in Iraq? As time passed these daydreams became more embellished. I began to imagine a reunion after she is released. I'd think about running to meet her and hugging her tightly, as I had done after her first summer at the Academy during a parents' weekend. I believe this unconscious daydreaming is an involuntary cognitive survival response, which gives my brain brief periods of relief from the mental anguish and stress of the past months. Or I could be just going crazy. Whatever the reason, I know it's not a healthy activity.

I had come to believe the solution to all of this was to request a copy of the autopsy report. Perhaps it is something that must be read to reach finality. I'm scared; a part of me would like to skip this step. In July, hastily, without consulting Danny or anyone else and before I could change my mind, I had written a letter requesting a copy of the autopsy, driven to the post office, and mailed it. "There," I thought, "that's done." Well, it wasn't really. As July ended I knew it would be here soon. Every day I would anticipate the arrival of the mail with dread. Trembling hands would inspect every letter, and there would be such relief when I learned it wasn't in that day's delivery.

The Saturday before I am to return to work it arrives. I know immediately what the white envelope contains. The return address printed in the corner reads, "Department of the Army, Armed Forces Institute of Pathology" and underneath, "Official Business."

I toss aside the other pieces of mail, take the white envelope, walk into the bedroom, and lock the door. Ripping open the envelope, I feel sick to my stomach, but I have to know if Laura had time to call out, "Mom" before the AMRAAM missile blew her apart. If the results are convincing—that she didn't suffer, that the end of her life was instantaneous, that she didn't feel pain—then the anguish caused by reading this will be worthwhile.

I can feel my heart pounding in my chest as I read the bullets under "Multiple Blunt Force Injuries":

A. Head: partial decapitation with loss of brain.
B. Thorax and Abdomen: multiple lacerations and contusions of lung and heart, rib fractures, fracture of spine, severe lacerations of liver and spleen, partial evisceration.
C. Multiple extremity fractures with loss of the left upper extremity, extensive whole body postmortem burning.

On the next page is the following description:

> The body is that of a severely traumatized and severely burned Caucasian female which is missing most of the head except for the presence of the base of the skull. Some of the face below the lips and pieces of skin containing brown hair posteriorly. In addition, the left upper extremity is absent, apparently having been separated at the level of the shoulder. There are third and fourth degree burns over the body with some intact skin on the right thigh, leg and foot. In addition the external body shows a huge defect with partial evisceration. . . . The injury continues down the left leg where there is evidence of a fractured tibia and fibula, the foot being only loosely attached to the rest of the body.

The section on the next page is titled "Identification": "The body is identified by dental and fingerprint comparisons of the lower jaw and a detached fragment of finger with antemortem records as Laura A. Piper. Fingerprint comparisons and anthropologic examination allows re-association of the separately submitted left arm; dental comparison allows re-association of separately submitted maxilla."

Each of the medical sections continues on in greater detail about each organ and body part, but I've read enough to have a pretty clear picture of what happens to someone broadsided by a modern-day fire-and-forget missile. My body is shaking and I'm crying, but the graphic descriptions and detail are not any worse than what I'd conjured up in my mind. In a way it is mentally cleansing to know the truth.

I convince myself that any of Laura's injuries could have been enough for her death to be almost instantaneous. I'll never know if she or anyone on that trail helicopter knew they were going to be hit by a missile. There is conflicting information in the official investigation. Testimony from a Black Hawk pilot says the helicopters were not equipped with the electronic system that warns the pilot when they've been locked on by a missile. I do know the crew and passengers on the lead helicopter knew, with certainty, their lives were in danger. They'd witnessed the shoot down of the trail helicopter, and the pilot had taken immediate evasive action to try to avoid a similar fate.

Perhaps, now, I can begin to put aside this part of Laura's death.

During long talks that often go on late into the night with other Black Hawk family members—and that's what we have begun to call those of us who lost a loved one in this shoot down—most have confided that they too had requested the autopsy report. Some had even asked for the autopsy photos and received them. Words are enough for me. I don't need pictures.

There is one more short paragraph that adds pieces to Laura's story:

CLOTHING AND PERSONAL EFFECTS: The body is accompanied by, but not wearing, two partly burned flight jackets, each with a unit patch of 6th Bn Avn on the right breast, one with no rank insignia or name plate, bearing a right shoulder unit patch from the 82nd Airborne Division, the other with a single fabric bar on the right shoulder and a partial leather name plate on the left breast with aviator wings and the legend "WO1 Eric . . . " remainder burned off. There are two trouser blousing straps and two coins, including one nickel and one dime.

Laura and I shared a common characteristic of being very susceptible to cold. I can imagine her already wearing one borrowed flight jacket in the Black Hawk. As they gain altitude she becomes cold, and the pilot of that trail helicopter, Warrant Officer Erik Mounsey, loans her his. I don't know what happened to the two coins; I know other Black Hawk families received personal articles recovered from the bodies, but I was never sent the two coins or any of the above-mentioned effects. I know it doesn't seem like an important matter, but it is. Those two coins would have been a tactile link to Laura's last living moments.

It's the very last, very short paragraph that gives me the most grief: "OPINION: 2LT Laura A. Piper died of multiple blunt force injuries. The manner of her death is an accident."

An accident is being struck by lightning or drowning in an undertow. Being killed by a missile over the safest area of northern Iraq on a clear day with only four aircraft in the area is not an accident. It is negligence.

I've read and reread the testimony of the pilots, always hoping there will be a new revelation jumping out from the page, explaining how this could have happened. The wing pilot, Lt. Col. Randy May, who had shot down the lead Black Hawk, has testified, "I want the board to know my intentions on April fourteenth were honorable." He also says, "Knowing my actions caused needless loss of life, but also much pain and suffering for others will always haunt me." After discussing his mind-set and other details about the shoot down, he concludes with: "We misidentified the helicopters, we engaged them and we destroyed them. It was a tragic and a fatal mistake which will never leave my thoughts, which will rob me of peace for time eternal. I can only pray the dead and the living find it in their hearts and souls to forgive me." At first I was impressed with the statement, but now, upon my second and third readings, I'm not. May has a degree in journalism, and being skilled at expressing your thoughts and deeds in words doesn't necessarily mean you're sincere. He speaks of himself as being "always haunt[ed]," robbed "of peace for time eternal." This is August, and neither pilot has ever publicly or privately expressed remorse to the families of those killed.

In contrast, the testimony of "Witness #26," the killer of Laura and others on the trail helicopter, is flat, cold, and emotionless. He seems sure of every action he took and feels justified in doing so. If he made an error, it was due to someone else's mistake: an Army flight plan not filed correctly, information not passed down to him, an Iraqi trap—he just seems to have an answer for everything. His testimony leaves me with more questions than before because it offers no justification for his hasty actions and multiple errors.

Before reading Laura's autopsy report until right this minute, it was never that important to me to pin a name on Witness #26. But now I'm not just angry, I am enraged, and I want to know who he is. Where else but in the U.S. Air Force can you be responsible for the torturous death and dismemberment of twenty-six people and not have your identity released? This anonymity was granted by General Oaks in a document titled "AFR 110-14 Aircraft Accident Investigation—ACTION MEMORANDUM": "The identity of the military members directly involved in the incident is to be protected to the maximum extent permitted by law." Rationally I know this is probably standard procedure, but I don't think it is irrational to want to know the identity of the person responsible for your daughter's death.

I vow I'll find out Witness #26's identity if it takes me the rest of my life. But it doesn't take that long, and it was easier than expected. It's there in his testimony. "I graduated from high school in New Fairfield, Connecticut, went straight to the Air Force Academy, graduated in 1986 with a Bachelor of Science, and continued from there to pilot training. I have no additional higher education." He continues, giving assignment dates and places and outlining his familiarity with Black Hawk helicopters:

> I've been on a Black Hawk on numerous occasions. Never have I seen the wings on it. The first time I've ever seen that is when I came here and saw the Special Operations Birds across the street on the other side of the runway here. To me a Black Hawk looks considerably different than a Hind when it does not have those sponsons and that was my impression of a Black Hawk I had. The Black Hawk did not even cross into my mind when I made that visual identification, perhaps, in fact, the only helicopter that crossed into my mind was the Hind.

Dan Murray obviously knows #26's name, but I won't ask him to violate the gag order imposed on him and on everyone else questioned in the investigation. So the search begins in our home because it could qualify as an annex to the Air Force Museum, with Danny's twenty-six-year career and three Air Force Academy graduates in our family. Military photographs hang on the wall, airplane models and military-related books line the bookcases. We have amassed a large collection of Air Force Academy yearbooks and issues of the Academy Registrars of Graduates, past and current. I start with the most recent issue of the Registrar of Graduates. I flip to the section that lists the class of 1986. The 961 names are listed alphabetically, and underneath each name is the current assignment, past assignments, and address, either current or home of record address. I know many active duty officers use their parents' address because moves are so frequent. Patiently, meticulously, I check each name, looking for a match with the information #26 gave in the accident report. On the last page, after checking 914 names, *bingo!* We have a match: Captain Eric Alan Wickson.

Laura Piper's high school graduation picture, Robinson High School class of 1987, Fairfax, Virginia.

Laura, June 1987, reporting for basic summer training at the Air Force Academy, Colorado Springs, Colorado.

Laura with her brother Sean, center, and brother Dan, right, at an Air Force Academy football game during her senior year.

Lt. Laura Piper's Air Force Academy graduation picture, spring 1992.

At Laura's father's Air Force retirement ceremony in 1993. From left, her brother Dan in his cadet's uniform; her father Col. Danny Piper; her brother Sean; her mother, Joan; Laura. This was the last time the Piper family was photographed together.

Laura snapped this photograph of a Black Hawk helicopter in Iraq the day before she was killed.

Military personnel inspecting the wreckage of the trail Black Hawk at Crash Site 1 in the No Fly Zone.

U.S. Air Force Photograph

A close-up of the Black Hawk fuselage wreckage at Crash Site 2.

Frontal view of a Soviet built Hind helicopter (left) with desert camouflage paint. This is one type of helicopter the Iraqis use. Frontal view of an American Black Hawk helicopter (right) with dark camouflage paint and sponsons. Although this Black Hawk is similar to the U.S. Army helicopters that operate over the No Fly Zone, it does not have the large American flags painted on its sides.

Side view of a Black Hawk (foreground) and a Hind (background). The Hind's distinctive double canopy is noticeable from this angle.

Rear overhead view of a Hind (left) and a Black Hawk (right).

Laura's father, mother, and youngest brother during her funeral at the Air Force Academy, 1994.

Laura's grave marker with the Purple Heart insignia.

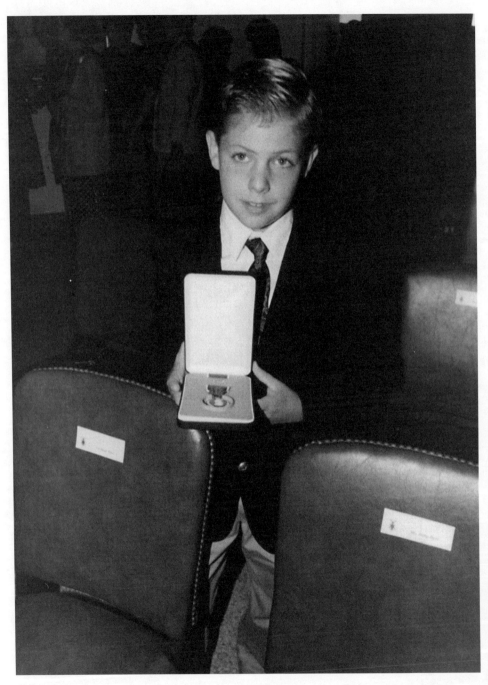

Sean holding Laura's Purple Heart medal, April 14, 1995, on the first anniversary of her death.

19. Zakhu, Northern Iraq
August 13, 1994
Saturday

The dry land near Zakhu continues to scorch in the summer sun. Nearby, scattered along slow-moving streams, are makeshift encampments dotted with tents housing Kurdish refugees. Every day more groups of displaced families, the elderly, and ad hoc groups containing orphans and widows, left from the Gulf War, arrive on foot carrying their few possessions. These impromptu settlements are a constant reminder of the horrors of the past few months. Since President George Bush established Operation Provide Comfort in 1991, the Turkish government has taken every opportunity to destroy Kurdish villages along the Turkey-Iraq border. This summer it had taken this effort to a new level of intensity. Amnesty International reports more than 800 Kurdish villages have been decimated during Turkish bombing attacks. Now more than 300,000 Turkish troops and militiamen patrol this area of southeast Turkey, and they have forced the approximately 10,000 Kurds who reside in the border villages to flee. Some groups have left for Greece and Armenia, but most have traveled into the mountainous area of northern Iraq, into the far reaches of the No Fly Zone, hoping Turkish planes won't make them a target on their next "Special Mission."

The forty U.S. Army troops stationed at "The Safe House" in Zakhu are puzzled: "Aren't we here on a joint mission to protect the Kurds from Saddam Hussein? Why do we allow the Turks to bomb and strafe Kurdish villages?" Not far from this small Army compound sits a building once built for schoolteachers. In front of the low, square building, over 200 Kurds, dressed in white burial shrouds, are conducting a hunger strike in protest of the Turkish abuse. A large banner reads: STOP THE POLITICAL AND ECONOMIC SUPPORT FOR THE TURKISH REGIME! But each day, well before dawn, the roar of the Turkish jets can be heard overhead as they streak out to conduct more Special Missions. All of this is not lost on the

143

U.S. Army troops who were almost firsthand witnesses to the death of fifteen Americans killed in the Black Hawk shoot down. Those killed had been eulogized by the American government as being on "a noble mission, defending the Kurds against the evils of Saddam Hussein." Now the American troops have begun to call this "Operation Discomfort." "We're putting American lives on the line every day, and the Turks are calling all the shots over here. We close our eyes and we're supposed to pretend we don't know they're bombing the hell out of the Kurds."

But it's more than these Special Missions that causes concern among the American military stationed in Turkey. At Incirlik AFB, where Turkey is a part of the U.S., British, and French coalition protecting the Kurds, it's no secret Turkey's main priority is containing the Kurdish rebels. Many high-ranking American officers, after serving a tour in OPC, have noted the entire operation is structured around the Turks. They have input into the rules of engagement and training, and they must approve every mission that flies. They are privy to American intelligence information, and some believe this information is used to target the Kurds on these Special Missions.

Turkey remains adamant that these leftist guerrillas are responsible for the deaths of hundreds, including innocent civilians. The country refuses to consider any diplomatic negotiations, believing this is best settled militarily. There are 20 million Kurds in Turkey, Iraq, and Syria, and this is intimidating to the Turks. The population of Turkey includes 15 million Kurds, and the Turkish government wants to thwart any attempt at Kurdish self-expression, fearing it might lead to an autonomous area for the Kurds, which would ultimately affect the borders of eastern Turkey. Turkey is a member of the North Atlantic Treaty Organization; therefore, these human rights violations should be of great concern. Brazenly, the Turkish government wants desperately to become part of the European Union. However, the European countries have rejected Turkey because of its twenty-year occupation of Cyprus and the enormity of its confirmed human rights violations.

How and why does this treatment of the Kurds happen under the eyes of the greatest military power on the planet? U.S. government officials openly admit that the strategic importance of Incirlik AFB to the Mideast is more important, when you're looking at the big picture, than human rights abuses. Turkey is crucial; it is key to gathering information and establishing an American presence in an area that accesses Iraq, Iran, Syria, and the former Soviet Union. And the United States will do just about anything to allow for its continued presence in Turkey, and the Turkish government knows that. Follow the money! Just about every year the United States chucks in about $100 million in military loans to Turkey; the total currently amounts to $453 million. Add another $1 million for training and a whopping $2.3 billion in arms sales. No ordinary citizen will ever be privy to the untold additional millions or billions that come out of discretionary funds from various government agencies, including the Department of Defense, to allow for the continued U.S. presence in Turkey.

The Turkish government requires the United States to renew its agreement for Operation Provide Comfort every six months. In June 1994 the Turkish Parliament renewed for the sixth time, but it had not been as easy as in the past because Turkey had become increasingly angry about the Black Hawk shoot down last April. Of particular concern was the American government's financial treatment of the three Turkish officers killed on the helicopters.

Secretary of Defense Perry was acutely aware that if the United States would like to renew this agreement again in December, he'd better come up with a way to find adequate financial compensation for families of the Turkish officers killed. Perry had thus commissioned a "Compensation Review" with the Department of Defense's legal team. Its purpose was to review compensation issues arising from the deaths caused by the shoot down, which in plain language meant, "Find a way to pay off the Turkish families."

The Department of Defense attorneys worked for weeks, diligently researching the options Perry might pursue to provide additional financial compensation for the families of the dead Turkish soldiers. They completed this official, but close-held report on July 28 and forwarded it to Perry. The ten-page report provided three options for payment and discussed the pros and cons of each. It made no recommendation but concluded, "Under existing claim statutes, there is no clear basis for the United States to compensate the next-of-kin of the British, French and Turkish military personnel. There are options for providing compensation, if desired. To provide compensation under these circumstances would represent a departure from past practice and could be cited as a precedent in the future."

145

The result is Perry breaks with legal tradition and sets a new precedent. At his discretion the United States will make an ex gratia payment of $100,000 to the families of each of the foreigners, because it is legally impossible to award additional compensation to only the Turkish families.

The Office for General Counsel had reported this decision might affect U.S. military morale, but the morale of the American victims' families was not even a great enough concern to be included in the Compensation Review report. However, the Department of Defense had done the appropriate legal research to know there is nothing these American families can do about this injustice, and if any of them should question Perry's decision, a host of lawyers is standing by, armed with a legal defense.

The press release is scheduled for Friday, August 26. This is a strategy the Department of Defense has been successful with before: you release the information on Friday, the government closes down for the weekend, and by Monday the issue is back-page news. The department's Public Affairs Office does not predict this news release even to be the lead news story on Saturday. The American public continues to be obsessed with O.J. Simpson.

20 San Antonio, Texas
August 26, 1994
Friday

The month of August has been too intense. I need to distance myself from the report and everything else connected to the shoot down. I can't afford to become singularly obsessed with all of this because I have a family that needs healing and a ten-year-old child to raise. But the entire issue only grows larger and more complicated. It has become the perfect time to begin the school year.

My classroom becomes a sanctuary from the outside world. Whatever personal concerns I begin the day with are lost minutes after the morning bell rings. The new school year starts with promise, new goals, and twenty-two students who need my constant attention and approval.

Sean and I easily slip back into our school routine. He is a fifth grader and a member of the morning safety patrol. I still continue to drive him to school; we just have to leave earlier. Sometimes the most enjoyable part of the day is the few minutes we spend together each morning. We're both learning life is more complicated, in many ways, since Laura's death, especially this year. We're being watched and we both feel it. Actually "scrutinized" is a more apt description. Any kid can blow a test once in a while, but if it happens to Sean, he'll be observed for depression. Other teachers can oversleep and have a bad hair day. If I come to work disheveled, others would say, "Poor Joan. She just looks terrible since Laura was killed."

This morning I tell Sean, "We'll just have to work harder to be above average so we'll be perceived as normal and blend in." I take my own advice to heart. Every day, for the remainder of the school year, I get up a few minutes earlier than before and pay extra attention to my clothes, makeup, and hair. To look your best sends the right message to others: "I'm doing well, I'm in charge of my life, and everything is under control."

In the two weeks since school has begun, I've almost come to believe this myself. It's a good feeling to be back in the routine, and although this year probably won't be fabulous, it should be O.K. "We're going to get through this; in fact, we're already off to a good start."

And that's what I say to Sean as I drop him off on Friday, August 26. It's a productive day. I stay a little later at school preparing my lesson plans for next week and then leisurely drive home. Sean runs breathlessly out to meet me. "Mom, I don't know what's going on. Our answering machine is maxed out with messages, and reporters have been calling since I got home." It could only be one thing. Legal charges have been handed down earlier than predicted. The telephone rings the moment I walk through the door. A reporter asks if I would like to give a statement in response to Secretary of Defense Perry's announcement this afternoon. Although I should be furious, I'm just embarrassed that I'm not in the information loop. I ask him to read the press release, and what it says absolutely astounds me.

MEMORANDUM FOR CORRESPONDENTS

Secretary of Defense William J. Perry announced today that the Department of Defense will make *ex gratia* payments to each of the families of the 11 foreign nationals killed in the April 14, 1994 accidental Shoot Down of two U.S. Army Black Hawk helicopters. Secretary Perry decided to make the payments in recognition of the unique circumstances related to the aircraft accident, which resulted in the deaths of 26 members of the Combined Task Force. Such payments are extremely rare. The *ex gratia* payments are not obligated by a U.S. statute or international law, but as a humanitarian gesture made solely at the discretion of the Secretary of Defense. Payments of $100,000 will go to the families of the British, Turkish and French military members killed in the accident. Additionally families of the five Kurdish workers employed by the U.S. government will also receive a death benefit from the Department of Labor. However, since that payment will be less than $100,000 the Department of Defense will augment the death benefit to equal the $100,000 being given to the survivors from the foreign military officers' families.

None of us, outside the enclave of the Pentagon, can understand how Secretary Perry reached this decision. Experts in case law governing military accidents are equally shocked. This type of payment has never been made before. Why this time, why now?

But it's Friday and the Pentagon has closed for the weekend. In the past hour I've slipped back more than a few levels from that acceptance stage of grief. I can see the hurt and anger in Danny's face. We both feel betrayed by our own government. Although we should be using Saturday and Sunday to recuperate from the week and heal our family's emotional wound, it will be another lost weekend.

The headline in Saturday's paper reads, U.S. TO PAY FAMILIES OF COPTER-DOWNING VICTIMS. Some might conclude we've been included in the financial disbursement; others are just confused. We spend the next two days on the telephone talking to our immediate families and the Black Hawk family members, expressing our common rage and frustration.

Monday, calls to the Pentagon confirm the American families are not included because our loved ones had death benefits and insurance. Well, so did the French and British officers!

Most of all, our family is stunned because Laura's death resulted in a $6,000 death benefit and no insurance. By law Laura should have been provided an additional opportunity to reconsider and sign off on insurance before traveling into a combat zone, but since the Air Force didn't bother to issue her orders for the trip, we're certain they didn't ask, "Hey, Laura, do you think you'd like to take out that insurance before you go to Iraq this week?"

The Americans are not the only ones baffled by this unusual compensation issue. Referring to a Gulf War incident in which British soldiers were killed by U.S. Air Force pilots, the commander who led the British troops in the Persian Gulf says, "I fail to understand why the United States has paid compensation over another 'friendly fire' accident in an Iraqi No Fly Zone this year but not to the victims of the earlier wartime accident."

The media will hash over this issue in the coming days. The Black Hawk families will inundate the Pentagon and their congresspeople with letters. It will seem the issue is about money, but it isn't. When the U.S. government hands over a check for an additional $100,000 to families of foreign nationals sitting next to an American service member killed on the same plane in the same incident, it says, "The lives of the foreigners are more valuable than American lives." It is ironic that the last bill for Laura's funeral was paid this week. Our share of the total for the modest burial in a military cemetery amounted to $9,000.

When I'm too upset to sleep I still sit alone outside on the deck in the dark. As I sort out the past month and especially the past few days, many thoughts go through my mind. But mostly I think, "I'm trying my best not to be a victim, but it seems as if the Department of Defense is intent on making me into one."

There's no moon tonight, but it's clear, and even with the ground clutter, the stars give off light. It reminds me of the night of April 14. I can picture the Special Operations Forces, in Iraq, wearing night-vision goggles trying to piece together Laura's dismembered body, stuff it in a body bag, and evacuate it before dawn. I think it was probably her left arm they had to go back and search for the following day.

21

Washington, D.C.
September 8, 1994
Thursday

This morning the Office of Assistant Secretary of Defense, Public Affairs, quietly releases a statement for "Immediate Release" of "Action Taken in the Black Hawk Shoot Down." There is no press conference led by the secretary of defense flanked on both sides by colonels and generals. There are no charts and maps. There are no television cameras recording the artifacts of the efforts the Department of Defense has made to reach its conclusions. There's just one typed page with the familiar dark blue band on the top imprinted with the Department of Defense seal.

The timing couldn't be better. Five long months have passed since April 14, and other events have overtaken the public's and the press's immediate interest. But during this time since the shoot down occurred, there has been much speculation about the potential charges. Will anyone be charged? Who will be charged? What will they be charged with? This is a very controversial and high-interest item because the military and the public are divided about the issue of charging individuals for their actions in a combat situation.

As in the past, Pentagon leaks have preceded this news release by at least one week. News articles have already run in the major newspapers listing what reporters believe are the accurate charges that will be released today. No one—not the press, not the military experts, not the families of the Black Hawk victims—expects to be surprised by this press release. In fact, this occasion is just a quiet, rather ordinary Washington affair.

151

22

San Antonio, Texas
September 8, 1994
Thursday

The announcement, two weeks ago, of Secretary of Defense Perry's decision to award the foreign families compensation was just the beginning of several events that have triggered an emotional setback for myself and my family.

Last weekend we had accepted delivery of Laura's shipment from Germany. The heart-wrenching finality of Laura's death had become more evident with each box and crate opened. Hastily, before losing my courage, I had taken most of her clothes to a military thrift shop, put aside many household items for Dan, who will be setting up an apartment in California next month, and stored all her personal effects in the attic. For now, there are enough loose ends in my life. It seemed important not to let all Laura's possessions remain stacked in the garage, where we would be reminded on a daily basis of the chaos and sadness in our lives. I know there will come a time when I will be able to reopen those boxes and cherish each book, photo album, and memento of her life, but not now. My wounds have not healed and there is no peace in my life.

Tuesday night, at 9:30, we had received an unexpected telephone call. "Ma'am, I've got a car on my truck that belongs to you. I'd like to make that delivery tonight. I know I'm supposed to do this in the morning, but I've got six kids and I've got to keep moving, got to keep making a living." It almost seems apropos that Laura's car would be delivered in this unexpected, haphazard manner. "Oh, one more thing," the driver continues. "I don't have a drive-off truck. You'll have to meet me over by the railroad track, where they have an unloading platform." So, at 10:30, we sat in total darkness in our parked car, at the designated point of delivery, waiting for the truck carrying Laura's car home to us. Across the highway I could see the lights of the airport. No one needed to remind me it was the same hour, the same day of the week almost five months ago that Laura last returned home, her coffin loaded into the belly of a plane that had landed in the dark just across the street.

Now it is Thursday, and I'm acutely aware this tumultuous week will reach a crescendo today because charges against those thought to be guilty in the shoot down are scheduled to be released. I know this, not because the Pentagon has prenotified our family, but because the news media has forewarned me. This time I'm not expecting any big surprises, because there has been speculation in the news all week. Reporters in the know and military experts believe with certainty that the two pilots and several on the AWACS plane will be charged.

I leave school immediately after the dismissal bell rings because I want to be home before Sean and spare him the confusion of faxes lying on the floor and the telephone constantly ringing. But I'm just not quick enough. Sean's bus had dropped him off first, instead of last. He runs out to meet me. "Mom, this is happening all over again!" Walking into the house, I think, "Today is a big step—the first step down the road of accountability for Laura's death."

This may not be the story of the day in Los Angeles, but it is here, in San Antonio, home to two Air Force families that had kids on those Black Hawks. The first call I pick up is from a reporter from the local television station. I ask him to read the official press release because although I think I know what it says, I'm not sure about anything anymore. He begins reading off the names and charges.

ACTION TAKEN IN BLACK HAWK SHOOT DOWN

The Department of the Air Force announced today that the appropriate Air Force commanders have made disciplinary decisions in regard to six aircrew members involved in the April 14, 1994 shoot down of two U.S. Army Black Hawk helicopters by two U.S. Air Force F-15 aircraft over northern Iraq.

1. Twenty-six charges of negligent homicide and two charges of dereliction of duty have been preferred against Lieutenant Colonel Randy W. May.

Charges of dereliction of duty have been preferred against five members of the AWACS crew. They are:

153

1. Major Douglas Martin, the airborne mission director "Duke" on the AWACS plane, three counts.
2. Major Lawrence Tracy, Mission Crew Commander, four counts.
3. Captain Jim Wang, Senior Director of the Mission Crew, five counts.
4. First Lieutenant Joseph M. Halcli, the Enroute Controller, four counts.
5. Second Lieutenant Ricky L. Wilson, the Tactical Area of Responsibility Controller, four counts.

The charges against these individuals will now be investigated pursuant to Article 32 of the Uniform Code of Military Justice. An Article 32 hearing is the military equivalent of a grand jury. The primary purpose is to inquire into the truth of the matters set forth in the charges and to decide whether the matter should be tried by court-martial or disposed of otherwise. Administrative action may still be taken against other individuals.

I keep waiting for him to say the name "Captain Eric Wickson," but it's never mentioned. How can this be? The person who was most negligent, the person whose egregious mistakes were the first link in the chain of events isn't even charged!

I think back to the last sentence in the press release: "Administrative action may still be taken against other individuals." Maybe the charges against Wickson are more severe and will be released under a separate cover? Every time I reread his testimony I become more convinced that the rules of engagement were not adhered to and continue to question why Wickson acted so hastily and aggressively. Too many questions that need answers! Certainly Wickson's actions were not so far above reproach that it could be assumed he is innocent. After all, when charges are preferred against an individual, it just means there is enough evidence to suggest the possibility of guilt. Why not allow Wickson's testimony and deeds on April 14 to be examined?

The next day, Friday, we don't call the Pentagon. We decide on a wait-and-see approach. As we talk to the other Black Hawk families over the weekend, we urge caution. "Give the Air Force an opportunity to make this right." We're still the loyal, true-blue Air Force family, although lately there have been cracks in the foundation of this relationship. We don't discuss this openly, but even Danny has begun questioning this loyalty. He has not even received an answer from his appeal to the Department of Defense for awarding the Purple Heart to the victims of the shoot down.

The Pentagon remains silent. Frustrated, unable to restrain myself any longer, I call. Officially, I'm told that there still is the chance further charges will be released. Unofficially, the officer says, "I don't know what to tell you. Many people are shaking their heads about this one. You're not the only one who is baffled."

Late in the evening on Monday I receive a telephone call from an American reporter in Europe who writes for a newspaper distributed to overseas military bases. Any news of the shoot down is an important story in Germany, home to the pilots, their fighter squadron, and the Black Hawk detachment. The reporter tells me he is doing a cover story about the shoot down and Lieutenant Colonel May. He asks for my reaction to the recent charges, and later we talk off the record. He says, "I've been a reporter over here for quite a while and I've got a long list of sources, but no one will tell me the name of the lead pilot. As far as I've been able to find out, he's never made a public statement. The Air Force is really protecting this guy." At first I hesitate to give him Wickson's name, but why should I protect his identity? It is time for Wickson's name to be part of the public domain. I give him the name and explain the circumstances of how I obtained it. A few days later the reporter calls back. "I was able to get someone to confirm Wickson as the lead pilot, and I've air expressed a copy of the newspaper with the article in it to you."

A few days later, when I arrive home from school, a large white envelope is tucked under the doormat. The first words I read are the headline: AGONY OF IRAQ DOWNING ALSO FELT BY FELLOW FLIERS. Continuing down the page, the expected quote from one of May's pilot buddies jumps out: "It's one of those things where you sit back and say, there for the grace of God go I." Each pilot interviewed feels compassion for May, although they do say they've never read the 110 report, nor are they familiar with the details or chain of events that caused the deaths of twenty-six people. A commander is quoted as saying, "This incident has had a sobering effect among pilots. It's easy for pilots who sit in powerful multimillion dollar flying machines to sometimes lapse into a false sense of infallibility." Another pilot and friend of May's says, "I also knew Lt.

155

Laura Piper, it makes such a tragedy that much tougher to accept." An attorney is also quoted: "The military had no choice but to press ahead with charges because of the pressures brought to bear by the families of the victims and the other countries that suffered losses." I believe this attorney is overstating the influence of the Black Hawk family members. I certainly don't have the impression the Pentagon is concerned about what we think.

The article gives a synopsis of the events leading to the shoot down and ends with a quote from the 110 investigation report: "As Lieutenant Colonel May had passed over the wreckage site after he fired the Side-winder missile he remarked, 'Nobody's there. Nobody could survive that.' " Yes, that is almost true, but I know it's not the whole truth. The report had prefaced that quote with the words "expletive deleted." The Air Force had deemed May's actual words too shocking, too inappropriate to be included, but they weren't curse words. The first words May spoke as he passed the burning disaster below were, "Stick a fork in them, they're done!"

Also on the front page is a picture of May standing in front of a furled American flag, speaking into a microphone. Underneath is a five-paragraph statement written by him and released by his attorney. He uses this public forum to offer condolences to the families and loved ones of those who died. Now I know this situation does not arise often enough for a Miss Manners ruling, but it seems to me the proper place to address these condolences is in a personal letter to each family, not on the front page of a newspaper read only by the American military community in Europe. I suppose he thinks one of the victim's families will read it and send a copy to the other family members, as I later do. Perhaps someone needs to inform him of the causes of death for each of the twenty-six people killed on April 14. The victims on those helicopters didn't just die; they were burned, dismembered, and mutilated.

He continues, "I accept responsibility for the role I played in this tragic accident. My decision to fire was the last action in a long chain of events involving a number of people and agencies. The decision to fire was based on human error and in a perfect world it would have never happened. . . . I was not derelict in the performance of my duties. I am innocent of the charges which have been brought against me."

Then he thanks the military and civilian community for the outpouring of their support. I can accurately surmise May has been inundated with support from the active duty and retired fighter pilot community. Without reading the 110 report, without accurate knowledge of what happened that day, they believe in his innocence. Furthermore, they, like May himself, believe the pilots are the real victims in this unfortunate incident that began with "such good intentions."

But I can't fault anyone for not reading the 110 investigation because, in reality, who has time to read a twenty-one-volume report? I'd come to think, and military reporters have confirmed to me, that this is often a Pentagon strategy: "Release an inordinate amount of information that is overwhelming to the average reader. Put everything you can think of in there, it doesn't matter, just stack up the pages with obscure and barely related documents." I know less than 25 percent of the entire report contains information that is of real importance. Nonetheless, I'm grateful for anything that helps me piece together the chain of events on April 14.

As September draws to a close Danny is relentless in his passion to get Laura and her colleagues the Purple Heart. He continues to enlist the support of the other Black Hawk family members in writing letters to the Department of Defense and their individual members of Congress. There's strength in numbers.

Just this week I received the telephone number of Eileen Thompson, the widow of Army Col. Jerry Thompson, the outgoing commander of MCC Forward in Zakhu, Iraq, and a passenger on the lead Black Hawk helicopter. That flight was to have been Jerry's final mission. He had completed his tour and was scheduled to return home on Wednesday, April 20. He is remembered as a person who was a devout Christian, a dedicated family man, and a commander who took extraordinary care of his men. Jerry did return home on April 20, but in a silver, flag-draped coffin.

When Eileen answers the telephone she knows exactly who I am from the articles written about Laura and Jerry that had appeared in the *Washington Post* last April. As we talk I can tell she is having great difficulty coping with this tragedy. "I've got boxes of sympathy cards and letters to acknowledge. I don't believe I'll ever want to read that 110 investigation. In fact, it's still sitting unopened in the living room. Last week Jerry's personal shipment arrived from Iraq and it's in the garage. . . ." I can identify with every heartbreaking obstacle. With reluctance, because the timing isn't right, I bring up Danny's crusade for the Purple Heart. Eileen says, "Jerry has a drawer full of medals; one more isn't going to bring him back." Her comments mirror my sentiments. I just can't see the importance of the Purple Heart. It will involve a long fight requiring more energy than I'm capable of giving. I share my feelings with Eileen and end the conversation with, "Someday you'll have questions and will want to know what's in that 110 investigation. When you get to that point call me because I've read every page."

23

San Antonio, Texas
October 1, 1994
Saturday

This month we defect and join the other side. After months of trying to recover from each new Department of Defense directive, we have no choice. At first the Pentagon had fired warning shots over our heads, but lately it's been aiming at our hearts. This is not a lightly taken decision. At one point we added up the time that just our immediate family has spent in the Air Force, and it amounted to over forty-two years. We'd waved the white flag and asked them to reconsider some of their decisions. Until now we had remained the voice of reason and tried to justify to the other Black Hawk family members each Pentagon decision. This voice of reason will now be replaced by a voice of activism. Henceforth, the Black Hawk family members will be a united front. For the first time, this week, we speak out in an interview with a Washington-based reporter.

WASHINGTON. In a major turnaround, the parents of 1st Lt. Laura Piper say they are fearful that those responsible for the death of their daughter and 25 others will not be held accountable for their actions. The Pipers were the people who initially chastised news reports for trying to place blame for the accident. This week the Pipers spoke out for the first time of their "growing concern" that the Pentagon's actions in the wake of the April 14 accident will amount to nothing more than a whitewash. "I'm worried that uncaring generals will be persuaded by unknowing colonels," said retired Colonel Danny Piper, a 26-year Air Force veteran with over 4,500 hours of flying time. Initially, the Pipers were opposed to disciplinary action. "We wanted to believe this was just an accident," Joan Piper said. But after poring over the thousands of pages of testimony and reports searching for clues as to why their daughter had been killed, the Pipers came to the conclusion that not only were those charged in the accident suspect, but several others as well. The Pipers became increasingly convinced that their daughter died not because of some freak accident in which high-caliber professionals made human mistakes but because of people failing to do their jobs properly. In the next few weeks, the military justice system will address those concerns.

In yet another effort to retain what is left of my mental equilibrium, I vow to restore tranquillity to my life, and the key word for October will be "normal." I am aware the AWACS Article 32 hearing will be held at Tinker AFB in Oklahoma City, beginning on October 11, but because of my commitment to my family, school, and my class, I'm not planning to attend. We're making every attempt to be the average family that eats dinner together and goes to their son's football games on the weekends.

One evening I'm surprised to get a call from Eileen Thompson. She begins with polite casual conversation but almost immediately gets to the point. "I'm ready to know what's in the 110 investigation." Up until now she'd been relying on the press releases and information passed to her by Army friends. Finally at one point she'd said, "There seem to be some missing pieces to this puzzle." I paint a broad picture of some of the things I know and make some suggestions about which parts of the report would be most helpful in linking together the chain of events that led to Jerry's death.

Eileen is angry at the Air Force over some of its more recent decisions. This doesn't surprise me. All of the Black Hawk family members feel that most of the responsibility for the shoot down, the denial of the Purple Heart, the compensation to the foreigners, and the recent inequitable legal charges falls solely on the back of the Air Force. I'm tired of defending the Air Force. It's time the families become aware of the bigger picture. "Eileen, I've been closely following these events since the beginning, and I'm unaware of the Army publicly criticizing any of the Air Force's rulings. At the top level of leadership the military is together on this, including some of the Army's top brass who have held your hand and mourned with you this year. To preserve the integrity of the armed forces, they're prepared to sacrifice the few for the many. The few, in this case, happen to be Jerry and Laura." I don't know how Eileen initially reacted to my words and I understand how difficult it is to question family loyalty to the Army, but eventually she actively joins the Black Hawk family members.

Columbus Day brings a much needed three-day weekend. I spend the days quietly catching up on the chaos that still constantly threatens to overtake our lives. Monday morning this tranquillity is interrupted by a call from an Oklahoma television reporter. "My station is doing a nightly series on the Article 32 hearing. We've uncovered many interesting facts about some of the AWACS crewmembers that have been charged. For instance, one of Captain Wang's former instructors has told us that he had Wang medically checked out for narcolepsy. It seems Wang, who was supposed to be controlling fighter aircraft, had fallen asleep during a check ride, not once, but twice. We'd be very interested in getting your perspective on this hearing. Would you consider doing an interview?"

Through all the past events the press has become an ally. They always have the inside information first and their accuracy has been remarkable. Because I have no intention of attending the hearing, it might be helpful to have the watchful eyes of a reporter in Oklahoma City who can keep me informed of any unusual events. We consent to the interview, the crew flies in that afternoon, and we tape from our house. As they prepare to leave, the reporter says, "If you don't mind I'll give you a call every night before I go on the air and keep you informed."

On the night of October 11, he makes good on his promise. "Two of the AWACS crews have waived their rights to a hearing. Maj. Doug Martin 'Duke' accepted blame for his part in the accident and requested his case be handled administratively or referred speedily to a court-martial. First Lt. Joseph Halcli, the Enroute Weapons Controller, withdrew after his request to divide the joint hearing was refused."

I don't find this surprising, because last week Major Martin had sent a written statement to the *Air Force Times*. The wire service had picked it up, and it had made the daily papers. He'd said, "Somebody has to accept responsibility for this tragic accident. If my Air Force and my country deem that I must bear that burden, then I accept their decision. This accident was caused from the top down. There were breakdowns in communication, equipment limitations and missed windows of opportunity to foresee and prevent this tragic loss of life. Because of radar and electronics limitations, the AWACS crew and myself did not know the Black Hawks were still flying. In the absence of higher headquarters' guidance, we presumed the Black Hawks were conducting standard operations in the Security Zone and had landed."

This serious statement contrasts considerably with Major Martin's rather flip testimony in the 110 report. Some of his answers were memorable:

> 71Q: Did you observe that [radar track of the helicopters] at the actual time of occurrence?
>
> 71A: Not that I recall, Sir. Once again I don't—this—pay that much attention—I do not strictly concentrate. I'm more concerned with other matters than—
>
> 75Q: When you discuss the radar and IFF contacts disappearing, what is your knowledge of the physical appearance of those types of contacts on your radar screen?
>
> 75A: Sir, my area of expertise doesn't lie there. I'm like a pig looking at a watch. I have no idea what those little blips mean.

The next part of the reporter's conversation is the most upsetting. Four of the Air Force officers who held top leadership positions at Operation Provide Comfort have declined to testify at the hearing. Brig. Gen. Jeffrey Pilkington, commander of OPC; Brig. Gen. Curtis Emery, commander of OPC's Combined Air Forces; Col. Douglas Richardson, director of OPC's Operations; and Col. Rusty O'Brien, commander of OPC's Operations, Plans, and Policy, have decided to use their right to remain silent. I'm disappointed in the Air Force and, most of all, in the integrity of these leaders.

I'm glad I didn't clear my calendar and leave my family to attend these hearings. These latest developments lead me to think this is just a formality. Even if the crewmembers are presumed to be sufficiently guilty to be recommended for a court-martial, the convening general of the court can recommend only a reprimand or an admonishment. Reporters always ask, "How do you think these crewmembers should be punished?" I don't think the military or society at large is best served by a prison sentence for any of those charged. But I do want accountability, not just a slap on the wrist. An immediate general discharge from the military and loss of accrued benefits would be sufficient and equitable.

When the reporter calls again Friday night, I'm unprepared for the latest update. "Joan, I've been privy to the schedule of witnesses to be called next week. Captain Wickson is going to testify on Wednesday. And he's going to do it under a grant of immunity!"

This time the Pentagon has fired a bullet that has pierced my heart. Any hopes that Wickson would later be charged are dashed. You don't have to be a military legal expert to know something strange is happening. Sometimes even I wonder if this isn't all part of a devious scheme designed to destroy the victims' families piece by piece. Of course, the Pentagon is closed until Monday morning, and I can't confirm any of this. But I am certain of one thing: if Wickson is going to be in Oklahoma on Wednesday, so will I! Over the interminable weekend I call the other Black Hawk families and give them the latest news. The key word of the month, "normal," is no longer part of my vocabulary. Perhaps it is time for me to face the reality of this living nightmare: normality is neither a reasonable nor a foreseeable goal.

Monday morning the Pentagon confirms that, indeed, Wickson has been given testimonial immunity, but that does not preclude him from later prosecution. The deal is this: Maj. Gen. Eugene Santarelli had already granted Wickson immunity to testify at Lieutenant Colonel May's Article 32 hearing scheduled for November 7. Thus, he also was granted immunity to testify in the general AWACS hearing, already under way. The reason? Wickson needs to be able to give an accurate account of the events leading to the shoot down. However, military observers speculate the general had other reasons to grant Wickson immunity. Santarelli, a fighter pilot and crony of Air Force Chief of Staff McPeak, may have been acting on orders to prevent the pilots from taking any of the blame for the shoot down. The word "whitewash" again begins to haunt me.

A "whitewash" also is a very disappointing action to me because last week I'd read an encouraging commentary by Gen. John Loh, the commander of the Air Combat Command. He'd addressed the characteristics of a good commander, especially during these recent difficult times, and had ended the piece thusly:

> *But a crime is different than a mistake.* The distinction lies in the culpability of careless or negligent acts or the degree of premeditation and willful disregard for directives, regulations and sound judgment. Commanders must realize the difference between mistakes and crimes, and, in

the case of the latter, must display the moral courage to protect the loyal many at the expense of the disloyal few.

His words led me to think Loh does not believe Wickson and May made an honest error in judgment. However, my larger concern is the likely possibility that the Pentagon has orchestrated a yet undisclosed second act to Wickson's immunity.

As for Wickson being scheduled to testify on Wednesday, well, the Pentagon isn't quite sure. After numerous calls from other Black Hawk family members, they concede. "Yes, Captain Wickson is scheduled to testify on Wednesday. Although this will be an open hearing, the public will not be allowed in the hearing room because classified material may be discussed. We have set up a viewing room downstairs with a closed-circuit television to broadcast the unclassified portion of the hearing. You can attend, but it may be emotionally uncomfortable as some of the AWACS crewmembers who have been charged and their families will also be in the same room." The Pentagon just doesn't get it. Emotional discomfort is not a consideration at this point.

I quickly schedule a personal day of leave from school and make an airline reservation. Connie and Cleon Bass will be traveling with me, and Kaye Mounsey, the widow of the pilot who had loaned Laura his flight jacket, plans to fly in from California.

We're in the midst of a Texas-size rainstorm as Danny drives me to the airport Tuesday evening. Waiting for our flight, the Basses and I watch the runways illuminated with lightning and listen to the thunder crash above the roar of the jet engines. Is this an omen of things to come? I'm a nervous flier, even under the best of conditions, and the turbulence on the flight to Oklahoma subdues us all. In the dark plane, watching the rain beat against the windows, I reflect on my motives. My only objective has been clear from the very beginning: I need to see the person responsible for Laura's death, and this may be my only opportunity. It's not important to Danny. In fact, he doesn't even want to be there.

Tomorrow is going to be O.K. I'm glad I'm not going to be in the same room as Wickson. I don't want to meet him, talk to him, or even look him in the eye. Watching him testify over the closed-circuit television set is going to be a good thing. I can watch him, listen to his testimony, and, best of all, I'll be invisible to him.

24. Oklahoma City
October 18, 1994
Tuesday

Our plane touches down in Oklahoma City at exactly 9:00 P.M. One of our goals is to be as unobtrusive as possible. We've waived the offer of an Air Force escort from the airport; however, for convenience we did accept lodging at the Tinker AFB visiting officers' quarters. It's after 10:00 when we check in, and the clerk gives us a message from Kaye Mounsey: "I'm in room 410. When you arrive, come by."

Over the past few months we've talked to Kaye often. Through our conversations I feel I've come to know Erik. He'd grown up in a Los Angeles suburb close to the international airport, which inspired his boyhood dream to someday be a pilot. After college he'd joined the Air Force and gone through flight training. When he and Kaye were married and knelt at the altar, the left sole of his shoe had read "Top" and the right sole "Gun." Toward the end of pilot training he'd discovered that flying fighters wasn't for him. He cross-commissioned into the Army and began his love affair with Black Hawk helicopters. Kaye says he often brought flight manuals on vacations because it was so important to him to keep current with the systems and the missions. I've also spoken to Erik's parents, Sarah and Ray Mounsey. They are quite a family and have even pulled closer together since Erik's death. All of them will try to ensure that Erik and Kaye's two-year-old daughter will grow up with vivid memories of her father.

We talk late into the night. Each of us verbally recollects our own personal journey that has brought us together in this small hotel room in Oklahoma. Finally good sense prevails; we have an early wake-up call in the morning. The hearing is scheduled to begin at 9:00 A.M. sharp. We want to arrive early because we don't want to make a grand entrance. Our plan is to be in our seats, blending in with the surroundings, as the rest of the spectators begin arriving.

In the morning, just as we are preparing to leave, we receive a phone call. "The hearing has been delayed until ten o'clock." We drive around the base during the daylight and get our bearings. It's decided we'll find the building, take our seats, and wait. As we prepare to enter the parking lot of the large two-story, rectangular, flat building, a security policeman stops our car and tells us none of the spectators will be allowed to park until fifteen minutes before the hearing begins.

When we return others are arriving. We can tell by their stares they are well aware of who we are. Keeping to ourselves, we sit down and wait for the hearing to begin. Judging by the size of the crowd, Captain Wickson's testimony appears to be the high point of the hearing. Everyone is curious about this pilot, and few know much about him. The Air Force had never officially released his name until this week.

The television screen begins to flicker, and I'm getting butterflies in my stomach. It's very much like riding a roller coaster. First, the suspense and anticipation of slowly climbing the hill, and then, when you finally reach the top, you begin to brace yourself for the steep drop and the sharp curves. I catch myself holding on to the edge of my seat. The hearing begins.

Wickson is light complected, with a medium build and no defining physical characteristics. Certainly no one would suspect on the basis of his appearance that his actions caused the needless deaths of twenty-six people. But then I wasn't expecting someone who looked like a serial murderer. It immediately occurs to me that Wickson is actually responsible for more deaths than most mass murderers, but the Air Force has made every effort to protect Wickson, and this morning he is testifying with privileged immunity solely because his intentions were honorable.

Today I begin putting faces on the main characters who are responsible for Laura's death. Many of the AWACS crewmembers are sitting in folding chairs surrounding me, also watching Wickson on the television screen. Everyone connected with the case who knows the people who have been charged is adamant about what good people, what nice guys they are. Even Dan Murray said this.

Col. Bryan M. Caldwell, the legal counsel to the officiating hearing officer, begins the proceedings: "This is an open proceeding. We will only break when we have a need to discuss classified material. This is not a trial, but an investigation. We are gathering information to determine if there will be a trial, just like in Lieutenant Colonel May's upcoming Article 32 hearing."

Caldwell tells us, "I've had two thirty-day deployments to Incirlik, Turkey, for fighter training. I still have some idea of what it is like flying in that arena and how threatening and dangerous those mountains can be when you get up close and personal when you are flying low and fast."

He begins with the questions, easy ones first. Wickson is questioned about flow sheets, briefings, and radio modes.

Suddenly Wickson appears to have a muscle spasm. His head jerks down toward his left shoulder, which instantaneously rises up. Then five minutes later it happens again. Sometimes I can tell Wickson is trying to control this strange spasm. He tightens his jaw and tenses his neck until the cordlike muscles protrude. What is this? We're not even into the difficult portion of the testimony yet. I try to concentrate on the testimony, but these tics are distracting.

Wickson is questioned about a previous experience, shortly before the shoot down, when he picked up two unknown low, slow targets out in the No Fly Zone. On that day Wickson's was not the first aircraft in the No Fly Zone, and AWACS had told him to back off. Wickson assumed these helicopters were part of a UN flight. When he'd encountered almost the same situation on April 14, why didn't he recall that similar encounter?

These nervous tics become more pronounced as Colonel Caldwell begins his questioning about the specifics of the April 14 shoot down. "Why did you need to engage so quickly? Could you have spent more time asking AWACS to gather information? Did you even consider spending more time with AWACS?"

Wickson looks directly at Caldwell and confidently replies, "Not after I positively VID'd them as Hinds. Once I had no doubt that they were Hinds and that I'd met all the Rules of Engagement, the next step was to shoot them down."

This reply takes my breath away and has a chilling effect on the audience. It had been relatively easy to remain detached as I had read and reread his testimony in the 110 report. But today Wickson's monotone, expressionless manner of speaking gives another dimension to these familiar words. I grab hold of Connie Bass's hand. We had hoped he would disclose some new revelation, but he continues with answers that I recognize verbatim from the 110 report. It occurs to me that Wickson's entire testimony has been rehearsed.

Caldwell asks about the radio calls specifically related to May's confirmation of the helicopters' identities. Wickson's answers continue to coincide with his original testimony: Wickson ID'd the choppers as Hinds, and May conducted his own identification pass and confirmed to Wickson. Wickson then radioed AWACS, "Tiger Two has tallied two Hinds, engaged."

Wickson is questioned about May's immediate response after they'd just fired the missiles and downed the choppers. Wickson, the flight lead, had called the shots and made all the decisions. Until this point May had not questioned any of their actions; he had simply complied with all of Wickson's directives. But immediately after the shoot down May unexpectedly took the initiative and struck out on his own, something a wingman shouldn't do. Caldwell asks, "What happened after the missiles were fired?"

"I blow out south, and I make a radio call that says, 'Tiger, blow out south.' My concern here is that I want to—I have yet to look south, south of the thirty-sixth parallel. I want to sanitize the area. I don't know if those guys are up here for a trap and the hair on the back of my neck is rising. My wingman says he's coming back left for a reconnaissance pass. That's not what I wanted to do, but at the time it sounded like maybe we should just do one. We went over—did a northwest to southeast pass over the crash site and didn't see anything. Again I tell him to blow out south. He doesn't do it. He says he's coming back around for another visual recce pass. This didn't make me happy. I wanted to blow out south, but he has already committed to coming back around for a reconnaissance pass and I wanted to keep neutral support so I come back with him. This time we are going to run up the valley in the opposite direction. I make a directive on the radio that says, 'Tiger Two, after this reconnaissance pass, blow out south.' "

Breaking for lunch, we talk about Wickson's tic. Connie says maybe he is just nervous. I reply, "If he gets that nervous testifying with immunity, what's he like in the air, flying a fighter, under combat conditions?" This nervous condition haunts me. Teachers are trained to identify young children who might have limiting medical conditions requiring further professional evaluation. If I had a child in my class who displayed the exact physical response that Wickson demonstrated this morning, especially under stress, I would consider Tourette's syndrome as a likely possibility. Coincidentally, I had just read a book about Tourette's. Although most people associate this affliction with the involuntary blurting out of obscenities, that's the worst-case scenario. The milder cases entail symptoms that might be as innocuous as excessive blinking.

We return to the hearing and listen to more questions about radio calls, and as Wickson answers the uncontrollable nervous tics continue with the same regularity as this morning. All day his voice has remained flat and emotionless, almost as if he were reciting a grocery list, not the actions leading to twenty-six deaths. In numerous instances he'd been asked to speak up or move closer to the microphone. But finally there is a question that lights up his eyes and raises his voice above a monotone: "Would it be fair to say that you'd rather be flying up at twenty-seven thousand feet than one thousand feet down the mountain?"

"No, I'd rather—"

"You'd rather fly up high?"

"No, I'd rather fly low. It's more fun!"

For someone testifying under immunity, Wickson has offered no new information, no new insights. One of the other attorneys questions Wickson: "As a result of this incident, have you been disciplined in any way?"

"No. I have been grounded, so I guess 'yes' would be a better answer. But no, I have received no administrative or disciplinary action."

"I guess this wasn't your idea to get immunity?"

Without hesitation Wickson replies, "I didn't volunteer for immunity. I received a letter on my desk ordering me to testify at this hearing and an Article 32 hearing for Colonel May. With that letter came a Grant of Immunity so that I would not be able to plead the Fifth."

This last answer shocks me. I had just assumed that Wickson's attorney had requested immunity. Very interesting that the most culpable individual was instantly immunized by the Air Force. Generally the person with the lesser responsibility of guilt is immunized to nail the person more responsible. I wonder why the Air Force chose this strategy. Publicly, the Pentagon had rationalized this decision to immunize Wickson by saying, "We need an accurate accounting of what happened that day, and we didn't want Captain Wickson to take the Fifth Amendment." Certainly Lieutenant Colonel May could have also given an accurate accounting, so why did they choose Wickson? Now Wickson has testified, and his story has remained consistent with his testimony in the 110 report. During this hearing none of the attorneys ask Wickson if he would have testified without immunity. Maybe that's another one of those details I'll never know.

For the remainder of the afternoon Wickson answers miscellaneous questions from attorneys who are trying to fill in gaps in their knowledge, to further help their client's case. During Wickson's replies the strange jerking tics become distracting to the point that those of us watching and listening to his testimony have difficulty attending to his answers. But there are a few questions and answers that stand out.

Wickson is asked if he had seen Black Hawks equipped with sponsons before. He replies, "Yes, the Special Forces Black Hawks which are very close to where the F-15s were parked at Incirlik Air Force Base. But they are slightly different because they're equipped with a seven foot refueling boom on the front of the nose." Toward the end of the day an attorney questions Wickson about the visual identification: "And you weren't close enough obviously that you could see a flag or marking of nationality on the helicopters?" Pausing for just a moment, Wickson replies, "I've learned that since the accident. At the time of the accident I thought I was." This last answer seems strange and it also doesn't ring true, because in the 110 report Wickson had testified he didn't see any flags or markings.

Late in the afternoon the questions taper off, and finally Wickson is excused. He made his case that the AWACS crew had failed to inform him of friendly aircraft in the area and the Army helicopters were squawking the wrong radio code. So how could he be at fault?

It's been a long day, and certainly worth the trip to Oklahoma. Immediately after the hearing we leave Tinker Air Force Base and drive to the airport for our trip back to San Antonio tonight. Tomorrow it's back to my regular life.

The AWACS Article 32 hearing continues for two more weeks. During the remaining days the television reporter does call with some of the news. He tells me that his photographer tried to get a picture of Wickson the day he testified but was unsuccessful. No one saw him enter the building or leave later that afternoon. I don't believe that was just an unlucky break.

The reports coming out of Oklahoma look discouraging for the AWACS crewmembers charged. The electronic tape that recorded their mission on the morning of April 14 clearly shows the helicopters on several of the crewmembers' radar screens. It therefore has been concluded that the crew had enough information to avert the disaster. Attorneys blame the Air Force for failing to train the AWACS crew properly. To this accusation Colonel Caldwell replied, "The training program, in my view, is not relevant."

The accused AWACS officers testify that helicopters are not part of their responsibility and that they follow their flights as a courtesy. But the AWACS operations manual says, "Helicopters are a high interest track and should be hard copied every five minutes in Turkey and every two minutes in Iraq. These coordinates should be recorded in a special log book, because often radar contact with helicopters is lost and the radar symbology can be suspended." Did these AWACS crewmembers read their own operations manual?

The mission crew commander, Major Tracy, charged with failing to adequately supervise the crew, had refused to give testimony for the 110 report. For the Article 32 hearing, however, he does testify, saying his crew believed that helicopters were not included in their orders. He was monitoring the safety of the AWACS plane, and he doesn't remember everything that was going on at the time of the incident. One of Tracy's commanding officers had counseled him earlier in the year because he'd never completed an advanced degree, nor had he attended any of the expected professional schools for someone of his rank. The commander had said, "It's incumbent upon me to point out the recent statistics for the promotion board—if you are an up-and-coming guy." But perhaps Tracy was not an up-and-coming guy, just an example of what the military calls "active duty retired."

Captain Wang, the weapons director, had failed a couple of check rides and, with his record, probably never would have been put in a position of responsibility. But the Air Force had just instituted an early-out program and lost many qualified weapons directors, thus Wang was moved up to a position of greater responsibility. It was revealed he had been seeing a mental health professional because of, among other things, marital problems. The counselor had made a written recommendation to Wang's superiors that he be closely watched.

After countless witnesses had given hundreds of hours of testimony comprising two long weeks of tedious legal proceedings, the hearing concludes. Colonel Caldwell must now make recommendations on all five cases to the commander of the 8th Air Force, who will decide whether to court-martial the officers, discipline them administratively, or dismiss the charges. The decisions are expected within the next two months.

Regardless of Caldwell's recommendations, the ramifications for all of the AWACS crews deployed around the globe and here at Tinker, where they are trained, are considerable. After the shoot down their credibility had instantly plummeted, and every crewmember had to be recertified. One crewmember said, "In Operation Provide Comfort, AWACS' crews had to prove themselves once again. We really had to work to show that we can do our job. For a while, AWACS couldn't make a call without being second-guessed."

Thus the shoot down had forced the entire AWACS wing at Tinker to take another look at everything, including all the training and certification programs. Now, every Air Force officer who trains to become a controller will use the AWACS testimony and information from the 110 report as a "bible" on how not to control aircraft or conduct a mission.

Back in San Antonio, I've had time to think about my day in Oklahoma. It was a helpful experience to finally get a look at Wickson. But that day brought more questions than answers, specifically concerning Wickson's medical condition. The press had seen it, but no one will talk about it. Has the Americans with Disabilities Act had this far-reaching an effect? I know it's not considered appropriate to mention someone's nervous condition, but the circumstances in this case are unique. Wickson flies multimillion-dollar fighters loaded with live ammunition, and twenty-six people met their deaths in a horrible way.

25.

San Antonio, Texas
October 22, 1994
Saturday

The first cool front arrives over the weekend, reinvigorating San Antonio and south Texas. It's the time of year for football games, homecoming dances, and Halloween. This year we're sitting on the bench, just sideline observers to these frivolities of leisure time. It requires all our energy just to accomplish the necessities of each day. Since coming back from Oklahoma, I again try to get our lives back into a normal pattern. Why does it have to be such a concerted effort? A part of me says, "Give it up. It's time to let it all go." But I know this short span of time to seek out answers will soon be over, and then it will be too late. If I let it go, will I have regrets for the rest of my life? Will a part of me always be asking questions that I was too tired to find the answers to now? Will Sean's and Dan's children, my grandchildren, someday ask me what happened only to have me tell them I don't know? In my darkest hour what keeps me going is Laura. She was a fighter, a believer in the truth, a hard-charging, do-the-right-thing person. I owe it to her memory to find the answers and seek the truth. Isn't that what families do?

This week Danny finally received an answer from the Pentagon concerning his July letter asking for reconsideration of granting the Purple Heart to the shoot down victims. The answer was short, succinct, and to the point: "No, the Department of Defense will not authorize the award of the Purple Heart. The determining factor used to make a decision as to whether a service member is eligible for the receipt of the Purple Heart in a 'friendly fire' situation is whether the individual involved was 'actively engaged' with the 'enemy' during the time he or she was injured or killed. These circumstances did not exist in connection with the incident in which your daughter was killed."

The Pentagon is unaware that Danny won't take no for an answer. He'd politely requested the powers that be to take another look at their initial decision, but they refused to give it a second review. They are standing firm with the decision they had made in haste just a few days after the shoot down. This only makes Danny more determined because, first of all, the Pentagon is wrong. As mentioned earlier, in 1993 a congressional resolution added new language to the long-established criteria for the Purple Heart that allowed eligibility for individuals engaged in armed conflict in peacekeeping situations. In peacekeeping missions there is no official "enemy." Secondly, he has to fight for what he believes is right for Laura and all the victims.

Spearheaded by Danny, the Black Hawk family members continue the letter-writing campaign to their individual representatives. The other critical avenue to success is the press. The lawmakers in Washington, D.C., who oversee the Department of Defense are strongly influenced by public opinion and publicity. Because we are very private people, this is the hardest step. Some mornings, when a news piece has just been published in the daily paper, I fantasize about living anonymously in a distant country. For some reason, New Zealand always comes to mind. Public grieving is abhorrent to me, and I've never been good at asking for anything. Each time we do an interview I seem to lose a piece of myself. Afterward I'm emotionally drained.

However, we persevere, and this afternoon we spend several hours doing an interview with a major news service. We get some satisfaction from the fact that they're still interested in the story, because their interest gives Laura's death importance and our concerns and questions credibility. It's good for us to know that others not personally connected to this shoot down also are questioning some of the more recent events. Sometimes we think it's just us—blame is a big part of grieving. Are we blowing this out of proportion? Should we accept the Department of Defense's decisions? Should we just lie down and die?

After the interview I just want to go to bed and start life over tomorrow. These thoughts are interrupted by a ringing telephone. "My name is Georgia Bergmann. My son, Tony, was killed in the Black Hawk shoot down. My daughters and I are traveling through San Antonio, and we'd like to visit with you tonight." Somehow all the Black Hawk family members had overlooked Georgia. Tony's last name was Ellner, and the first name listed under his next of kin in all the documentation was his noncustodial father. This month Georgia had taken her daughters on a trip to Florida, touching bases along the way with Black Hawk families whose hometowns coincided with their vacation route. In fact, this had become almost the real intent of her journey. Even though six months have passed since our children were killed, there still exists such a need to continue talking about it—to make it real. Our immediate families are tired of listening, and some never wanted us to discuss it in the first place. This support group of Black Hawk families has become a life ring in the sea of survival.

We welcome Georgia into our home. Sitting in our den, amid the paperwork, photos, and remnants from this afternoon's interview, Georgia tells us about her life and her son, Specialist Mark Anthony Ellner. Tony's father made his early childhood difficult. Desperation and a strong will to save her children forced Georgia to flee with them to a battered women's shelter and file for divorce. Without financial support from her ex-husband, she became a single parent and the sole breadwinner for her family, and she'd done it well. Tony was a kid who could learn from adversity and rise above it. Remembered as well mannered and obedient, he mowed lawns and painted the houses of his elderly neighbors while growing up. He grew into a normal, polite teenager who ran cross-country, loved photography and the arts, and earned a perfect 4.0 grade point average all through high school. After high school he'd enlisted in the Army because it was his best chance to get to college and make something of himself. A crewmember on the lead helicopter, and therefore a witness to the violent explosion that ripped apart the trail helicopter in midair, he was the youngest of the Black Hawk victims. No longer a boy and not yet a man, Tony was one week shy of completing his first year in the Army.

It doesn't take any convincing for Georgia to join the Black Hawk family group. She'd spent the summer reading the 110 report. If Tony was not in a situation of being actively engaged with an enemy, what do you call his last moments of terror, feeling the heat and violent vibrations from the trail helicopter's explosion? The crew and passengers in that lead helicopter knew they were going to be killed, they just didn't know the killers were wearing flight suits bearing U.S. insignias. Georgia left our house armed with copies of documents and samples of letters requesting the Purple Heart. This was the last stop on her trip; tomorrow she heads for home and joins the battle with the Department of Defense for the Purple Heart.

The dining room that once held sympathy cards, news articles, and documents of Laura's death that I'd scrupulously boxed up and put away over the summer is beginning to fill up with paperwork again. Stacked on the floor and on the table are the twenty-one volumes of the 110 report, copies of correspondence Danny has sent to Washington, miscellaneous press reports, and official documents. In the past month unknown people have sent us documents and reports pertaining to some aspect of the shoot down. We have come to appreciate any source of information that sheds more light on the shoot down and the even more perplexing follow-up. Sometimes even the Pentagon sends us new information.

Each day, on my way home from work, I start preparing myself for what I might find when I arrive. Sometimes I drive by the house first, surveying the front steps to see if there are any UPS packages or envelopes before I park in the garage. Always, I try to get home as early as possible before Sean does to clear the answering machine and intercept packages and mail. Last week we'd had a near disaster.

Sean had arrived home first and retrieved a large brown envelope leaning against the front door. He could feel through the paper that there was a videotape inside. As I walked in the back door, he was just getting ready to pop the tape in the VCR. With no notice, the Pentagon had mailed us a copy of the video taken by the Kurdish farmer from the roof of his house. The accompanying letter explained that the second part of the farmer's tape, which showed graphic footage and immediate details of the crash site, had not been included. We sat together, hyperventilating in unison, and Sean pressed the play button. As the tape began we saw a beautiful, lush, green valley with craggy mountains in the background. Very low, beneath the ridgeline of the mountains, are two Black Hawk helicopters peacefully flying in lead-trail formation. The camera pans to a fighter plane with an easily discernible double tail, which Sean identified as an F-15. Then the tape ends.

Sean rewound it, and we watched it a second time, trying to find any additional details. Again, the helicopters, the F-15 . . . and then, looking very closely, we spotted a small silver missile being released from the F-15 and traveling through the air just before the screen turned blank. This footage seems benign compared to the television and movie violence we're all exposed to on a regular basis. The average person might view this tape and say, "What's the big deal?" But for us, from the safety of our living room, six months after the events depicted, it was a chilling experience to view the backdrop of Laura's last living moments in a remote area, half a world away. After the events of the past months, Sean and I were too desensitized to overreact. We've learned to survive, and to do this you have to continue putting one foot in front of the other and carry on with the business of life.

The Article 32 hearing for Lt. Col. Randy May is scheduled to begin on November 7 at Sembach Air Force Base in Germany. This week there have been rumblings in the press with headlines such as WHEN IS A MISTAKE A CRIME? Many defend May with quotes like "This is the cost of doing war" or "If this pilot is found guilty, what message does this send to other pilots who put their life on the line every day protecting America?" Even I admit there is another side to this story—May and Wickson's side. From reading their testimony in the 110 report, I know they are confident of their every action and that their intentions were noble and honorable.

Although their testimony does seem credible, Danny is not so sure of this anymore. He has come to believe May and Wickson knew before they exited the No Fly Zone that they'd shot down friendlies. He bases this on evidence in the 110 report. Immediately after the shoot down the pilots were queried by AWACS to confirm they had shot down Hind helicopters, not Black Hawks, and calls on the emergency radio frequency immediately began flooding the air in an attempt to rouse the Black Hawks. Danny also believes they used their auxiliary radio, on the flight back to Incirlik, to get their facts straight before they landed.

Some days I question all our perceptions. Perhaps the Air Force is right—perhaps the pilots did do everything right and just made a simple human error. But there are too many unanswered questions. In the 110 report not once does an investigator ask a senior flying commander at Operation Provide Comfort if the pilots adhered to the rules of engagement. Most of all, I have a need to hear General Pilkington, the ultimate commander of OPC, justify the actions of his pilots.

It has been reported in the news that May's attorneys have interviewed hundreds of witnesses. I am confident one of them will be General Pilkington and, most likely, others from the Operation Provide Comfort command structure who can verify whether or not the ROE and other standing orders that prevented a tragedy of this magnitude for the previous three years were followed. It is believed May is the first person to ever be tried in a friendly fire incident. Twenty-six counts of negligent homicide, one for each person killed—these are serious charges requiring important witnesses and careful questioning. The stakes are high. If May should be recommended for a court-martial and be convicted, he could face twenty-six years in jail. But in my heart even I know that would be overkill, and virtually no one expects that to happen.

I've made a decision. Next month, at the hearing in Germany, if these commanders do testify that Captain Wickson and Lieutenant Colonel May did indeed do everything right but made a justifiable human mistake at the conclusion of the long chain of events, then I will give it all up and I will let it go.

26

Sembach Air Force Base, Germany
November 7, 1994
Monday, 9:00 A.M.

In a small, detached building located on Sembach Air Force Base, in central Germany, Lt. Col. Randy May's pretrial Article 32 hearing is about to begin. In contrast to the open hearing of the five AWACS crewmembers, held in Oklahoma City almost three weeks ago, this is a closed hearing. There are no television cameras broadcasting the testimony and proceedings to private viewing rooms for the family and press. In fact, most of the personnel stationed at Sembach are not even aware May's hearing is beginning this morning. The Air Force is taking no chances with any intrusions. To prevent any unauthorized photos, the windows of the building have been covered with brown paper. The reason for all of this secrecy? Major General Santarelli, commander of the 17th Air Force at Sembach, has ordered these precautions on the grounds that classified information will be discussed. During the AWACS hearing classified information was also discussed on a regular basis. When a question evoked a classified response or a classified document was reviewed, the hearing officer ordered the closed-circuit television cameras turned off and cleared the hearing room of anyone who did not have a need to know.

May's two attorneys are circuit defense counselors, the Air Force's most senior defense lawyers. Both have been with May since the very beginning, when they were dispatched to Incirlik AFB to represent him immediately after the shoot down. Although May expects to be exonerated, recently he has interviewed a top civilian attorney who has an excellent reputation defending military clients. In the event he is recommended for a court-martial, he will hire the civilian attorney to lead the two military attorneys in his defense.

The hearing is called to order at 10:00 A.M. Present in the room are Col. Edward M. Starr, the official investigation officer; the two government attorneys; May; and his two attorneys. The first order of business is the reading of the charges against the accused:

Charge I, Specification 1: the accused is charged with negligent dereliction of duty for not making a positive identification of the helicopters.

Charge I, Specification 2: the accused is charged with negligent dereliction of duty for allowing the engagement to continue despite his own lack of a positive identification of the helicopters.

Charge II: the accused is charged with 26 counts of negligent homicide.

1. That 26 people are dead.
2. That their death resulted from the accused's failure to act, and to clearly convey to his F-15 flight lead that he could not confirm the identity of two suspected Iraqi Hind helicopters, after having been directed by the F-15 flight lead to confirm their identity, and by allowing an engagement with the helicopters to occur when he could not confirm the helicopters were Iraqi Hinds.
3. That the killing was unlawful.
4. That the accused's failure to act which caused the death amounted to simple negligence.
5. That under the circumstances, the accused's conduct was prejudicial to good order and discipline in the armed forces or was of a nature to bring discredit upon the armed forces.

The list of charges is serious, impressive, and long. As the officer concludes by reading each of the twenty-six names of the victims, he often has to stop to catch his breath.

The most important thing in this trial, the one overriding issue foremost in the minds of all the attorneys and Lieutenant Colonel May, is that the one charge of negligent homicide hinges on the two counts of dereliction of duty. If May's attorneys can prove he is innocent of those, he cannot be found guilty of negligent homicide. The defense will have to prove that (1) May did positively identify and confirm the two helicopters as Hinds and that (2) by making a positive identification of the helicopters as Hinds and confirming this information to the flight lead, he thus had no reason to stop the engagement of the helicopters.

Next, the defense and the prosecution discuss their agenda. May will read a prepared statement, and although over 100 witnesses were interviewed, only one witness will be called to testify at this hearing—Capt. Eric Wickson—and he will testify with immunity.

The government begins its case: "It is not necessary to detail the evidence before the visual identification pass." The attorneys make it very clear the entire case against May depends on what transpired during the one- to two-minute interval from the time immediately after Wickson called, "Tiger One has tallied two Hinds, confirm" until the time of missile impact.

This will be the third time Wickson has given testimony of the events that happened on April 14. He is asked: "When you asked Colonel May to confirm your visual identification, what were you expecting him to do?"

Wickson replies, "Hey, does what you see jive with what I just saw?"

"And as I understand from talking to you, you don't remember the exact language that was used, but was there any doubt in your mind that he confirmed what you saw, which was two Hind helicopters?"

"No, I don't remember the words, but I remember thinking to myself that he saw the same thing I did."

Two more times during the morning Wickson is questioned at length about the sequence of the radio calls. Both times he remains steadfast with almost identical answers. "My best recollection is after I conducted my visual identification pass, I asked May to confirm. He replied, 'Stand by,' and then conducted his own identification pass. He confirmed the identity of the helicopters to me with a radio call. I then made the call to AWACS, 'Tiger Two [May] has tallied two Hinds, engaged.'"

"Are you certain in your mind that the correct sequence is that the accused confirmed the identities of the helicopter to you before you called AWACS with the 'engaged' call?"

"Yes, sir. My recollection is that he confirmed [the identity of the helicopters] and then I made the 'engaged' call to AWACS."

"That it happened in that sequence?"

Wickson nods and says, "Yes, sir."

The government representative now presents as evidence May's testimony from the 110 investigation discussing what he saw when he made

181

the VID of the helicopters. Last April, May had testified that although his experience provided him no reason to believe they were not Hinds, he only identified two helicopters, not whether they were hostile or friendly. According to May, "I did not identify them as hostile—I did not identify them as friendly. I expected to see Hinds based on the call my flight leader had made. I didn't see anything that disputed that. I've played that sequence over in my mind. I don't believe I ever came off and called, 'Tally Hind.' I called, 'Tally two' at that point, and the identification was based on what my flight leader called."

This answer had been confusing to even the 110 investigators. So one more time they had questioned him about the significance of the "Tally two helicopters" call. May had attempted to clarify his last response by answering, "I saw a lot that indicated they were Hostiles, but I didn't see enough that I wanted to, no kidding, put the chips down and say, 'No kidding, those are Hinds.' He [Wickson] had already made that designation. He had already called AWACS and said, 'We're engaged with two Hinds.' "

Clearly Wickson's and May's testimonies conflict concerning this radio call. In the chain of events of a fighter intercept and engagement, this radio call is more than crucial. It means life or death for the crew of the targeted aircraft. At this point in the hearing two very different scenarios are developing. The first is this: Wickson is strong in his belief that May did confirm two Hinds. He also reiterates, to the best of his recollection, that after he asked May to confirm the identification of the helicopters, May replied, "Tally two." Wickson then radioed AWACS, "Tiger Two has tallied two Hinds, engaged." And the second: May, twice in that initial April testimony, says that he did not confirm two Hinds but only that he confirmed two helicopters. May believes Wickson called AWACS with the "engaged" call before he (May) called, "Tally two."

The defense brings May to the stand. He reads his prepared statement: "I maintain that everything I saw when I passed the trail helicopter convinced me it was an enemy Hind. . . ." Succinctly and methodically, he explains why:

1. My statement today is stronger than my original testimony last April and it is based on my careful recollection of events. . . .
2. I maintain that the flight leader [Wickson] called AWACS, stating,

"Tiger has tallied two Hinds at low altitude, engaged" before I made my "Tally two" radio call back to him.

3. I state that Wickson's use of the term "engaged" signified the identification portion of the intercept was now over. Wickson's "engaged" call was an override to his previous "confirm" directive.

4. I did confirm the identification by saying, "Tally two." This call was made not in response to the "confirm" directive, but in response to the subsequent "engaged" call to AWACS. I meant I had identified both target aircraft in sight.

May concludes with, "An honest human error on my part was the last link in a long chain of human and institutional errors which resulted in the tragic loss of life. I contend that while a great tragedy has occurred, there has been no negligence, no dereliction of duty, no criminal culpability. I am innocent of the specifications brought against me."

The hearing ends at 4:00 in the afternoon. May had read his statement, and Wickson, the one witness called, had testified with immunity and answered 432 questions. Two days later Investigating Officer Starr recalls Wickson and asks an additional sixty-one questions about the visual identification pass. Wickson's answers are identical to all his previous replies.

Whatever the outcome of this hearing, the testimony of May and Wickson and their famous radio calls will become infamous. At pilot training bases across the United States and at fighter lead-in programs, where pilots are trained to fly fighter aircraft, these radio calls will be used as the poorest example of radio communications possibly ever given by pilots during a combat intercept.

Three days after the conclusion of May's hearing, Starr completes his report and recommendations concerning the defendant's guilt or innocence. The report states:

> Both pilots have, I believe, done their best to remember the events, given the stress of the incident, the literal moment in time we're dealing with, and the fading memory with the passage of time. . . . There are several different scenarios that could have happened between the visual identification and the release of the missiles. Colonel May's guilt or innocence depends on which facts are to be believed.
>
> If you believe the scenario in which Wickson made the radio call

"AWACS, Tiger Two has tallied two Hinds, engaged," the accused was quite likely negligent and referral for court martial would be warranted.

After examining all the available evidence, I am not persuaded these are the facts. My initial difficulty with this scenario is that it is highly unlikely a pilot with the maturity, experience, and obvious skill possessed by the accused would:

1. Fail to carry out his flight leader's command by making an ambiguous response.
2. Sit idly by while the flight leader relied and acted upon an erroneous interpretation of his ambiguous response. . . .

Reasonable people may differ as to what they think about the sequence of the pivotal statements in this case. Both possibilities, that I've spent time discussing, are reasonable interpretations. For me, whether these charges warrant trial by general court martial comes down to which sequence of events one believes. Reasonable grounds do exist to believe that the accused committed the offenses alleged. I do not believe that the accused answered the flight leader with an ambiguous response, but I can't say it would be unreasonable under the evidence to believe this. . . . I recommend that these charges be dismissed.

This recommendation and a summary of the Article 32 hearing will now be sent to Major General Santarelli. He will decide to either take Colonel Starr's recommendation or refer May for a court-martial.

The events of May's Article 32 hearing were more than unusual. With only one witness called, there were no other statements to corroborate May's or Wickson's testimony. Nor was there testimony from any of the Operation Provide Comfort commanders, especially General Pilkington, who could have explained the operating procedures and rules of engagement. And it would have been relatively easy to secure him as a witness because Pilkington was still stationed down the autobahn at Ramstein AFB.

Also, Colonel Starr based most of his assumptions of innocence on May's good character, "maturity," and "skill," overlooking the fact that despite these impeccable credentials, he'd still shot down an American helicopter. Perhaps it was just too incomprehensible for him to think that a United States Air Force fighter pilot could commit so negligent an act.

Additionally, under the Uniform Code of Military Justice (UCMJ), there is no such thing as "simple" or "gross negligence"; there is just "negligence." Any evidence of negligence is enough to warrant a court-martial, and Starr even says in his report, "Reasonable grounds do exist to believe that the accused committed the offenses alleged."

More importantly, Major General Santarelli won't know there was a conflict in the testimony of the two pilots regarding the sequence of radio calls, because Starr's report only alludes to it. Furthermore, the report makes no mention of May's reversal of testimony concerning the identification of the helicopters and of his incentive to change his testimony between April and November. If May's testimony in this Article 32 hearing is believed, "that I'd positively identified the helicopters as Hinds," the dereliction of duty charges will be dismissed and, hence, the twenty-six counts of negligent homicide. If Major General Santarelli takes Starr's recommendation to dismiss all charges against May, it assures that neither pilot will ever be charged or held accountable for their actions or misactions in this matter.

In San Antonio Danny and I wait for Major General Santarelli's decision. We know the testimony and radio calls are complicated and require close scrutiny, but to an experienced fighter pilot like Santarelli, it will be an easy take. It's not close to an even bet that he is going to go with Starr's recommendations because Santarelli is just another general who can't help rooting for the pilots. However, when we have the presence of mind for logical thought, we know the larger reason for a finding of innocence is that this judgment will end the 17th Air Force's legal responsibility in the case. Common sense tells us they would like to close the book on their chapter of the Black Hawk shoot down.

Privately, we still harbor some small hope that at least one of the pilots will be held accountable.

27

San Antonio, Texas
December 1, 1994
Thursday

Connie and Cleon Bass had spent Thanksgiving Day with us, and as we sat down to dinner and said grace, we had difficulty finding much to be thankful for. It would be an understatement to say, "1994 has not been a good year for us." Also, we were all acutely aware this holiday was another one of those "firsts"—our first Thanksgiving without Anthony and Laura. This in itself would have made the day solemn enough, but the Department of Defense had scheduled a press release the preceding week.

On November 17 the Air Force had announced that the investigating officer who had overseen the AWACS Article 32 hearing recommended that only two AWACS officers be disciplined. Specifically, Capt. Jim Wang, the senior director, could face a general court-martial, and 1st Lt. Joseph Halcli, the enroute weapons controller, has been recommended for nonjudicial administrative punishment. They were found directly responsible for the accident by failing to inform the fighters and the AWACS crew of the helicopters' location. Wang received the more severe punishment because he was Halcli's immediate supervisor. The judge recommended that dereliction of duty charges be dropped against the other three officers, although they still could be punished by nonjudicial means. Lt. Gen. Stephen Croker, commander of the 8th Air Force, will make the final ruling, but he is under no obligation to use the judge's recommendation.

As we lingered over our Thanksgiving turkey, we found it difficult to restrain our frustration. Seven months after the shoot down the smoke had cleared, and this is what we saw: the lead pilot, Captain Wickson, has been granted immunity. The second pilot, Lieutenant Colonel May, will most likely have all charges against him dismissed. Of the five AWACS crewmembers, three will have charges dismissed, one faces administrative

186

discipline, and one lone captain may be court-martialed. Twenty-six people have been killed, and one captain on the AWACS plane is responsible?

Under these circumstances how could any of us give up the fight? How could we just let the death of our loved one go? We've been down this path before, and we have absolutely no hope that the two generals who will make the final decision will rule on the side of stricter accountability. Judging from the past events, we're betting on an even more lenient ruling.

During the next few weeks we receive, anonymously in the mail, copies of the two Article 32 hearing reports. We'll never know who provided us with these documents, but they give us much needed insight into this soap opera of accountability. The report from May's hearing is the most disturbing. One witness called, a two-minute sliver of time judged, and the hearing officer bases his decision on May's past fighter pilot record. Other Black Hawk family members request copies of these reports from the Pentagon, but they are deemed unreleasable until all the legal proceedings are concluded. Most of us have purchased fax machines for the purpose of immediately sharing information and contacting our lawmakers in Washington, D.C. The fax machines hum.

I begin a mental countdown to Christmas because this year I'm dreading the holidays. The best plan for me would be to leave town and ignore them completely, but Christmas is still important to a ten-year-old child. In one of my best efforts so far "to do the normal thing," I begin the holiday preparations. Many of our immediate family members have decided to join us. They don't explicitly say it, but mainly they're coming to help make the holidays, this first Christmas without Laura, brighter and to give us their support. I appreciate their thoughtfulness, but the thought of putting up cheery holiday decorations, crowded shopping malls, and preparing the holiday food is totally overwhelming, and because I work until the week before Christmas, normal exhaustion forces me to get a late start. I make a personal vow to put all these Black Hawk issues away during Christmas week. Talking to the other Black Hawk family members, I find that they too have independently decided on the same strategy. However difficult it is for all of us, we will make the most of the holidays. Laura's death has reinforced how much we need to be thankful for each day and for those around us.

Monday morning, December 19, is my first day of vacation. My mother and mother-in-law arrived over the weekend, and we're doing "just" O.K.

Yesterday we decorated the Christmas tree, and this morning we plan to get an early start shopping. The mood is pleasant and cheerful as they drink coffee and watch the morning news while I prepare breakfast. Then, without warning, the newscast flashes film footage of the Black Hawk crash site. While these two elderly matriarchs watch the helicopter that carried their granddaughter to her death smolder, the announcer says:

> The Air Force disclosed today that Captain Jim Wang, the supervisor of air controllers aboard the airborne warning and control system aircraft, on duty during the friendly fire shoot down of the two Black Hawk helicopters, will face a court-martial at Tinker AFB, Oklahoma. He is charged with three counts of dereliction of duty. Charges against the four other AWACS crewmembers were dismissed. If convicted, Wang could be sentenced to three months confinement and dismissal from the Air Force.

The next day, Tuesday, it's almost a repeat of the day before. Again the film footage of the crash site, and this time the announcer says:

> The Air Force announced today that Major General Eugene Santarelli, 17th Air Force, has dismissed charges of negligent homicide and dereliction of duty against Lieutenant Colonel Randy May. This action ends Santarelli's consideration of criminal disciplinary actions against U.S. Air Forces in Europe personnel who were associated with the incident, including the lead pilot and commanders of Operation Provide Comfort. However, the decision does not include administrative action against anyone involved in the incident. Captain Eric A. Wickson, flight lead, was never charged because evidence revealed Wickson made a reasonable mistake.

I would like to say that we were expecting this news and that we'd shielded ourselves from these two latest bullets fired from the Pentagon. But they hurt nevertheless. I thought back to October, when Danny had said, "I'm worried that uncaring generals will be persuaded by unknowing colonels." This accountability issue involves far more than uncaring generals and unknowing colonels. I do not believe that Generals Santarelli and Croker made these decisions independent of the higher chain of command. I believe the Air Force built a defense around the pilots by manipulating the official 110 report, in which it never questioned any of the Operation Provide Comfort commanders about the pilots adhering to the rules of engagement or the necessity of determining the nationality of the helicopters before letting go with high-powered missiles. If the pilots failed to follow the rules, or, as the report says, if they "over-simplified" the rules of engagement, would that be a reasonable error?

This just doesn't seem right. I don't know why I should care, but I am embarrassed that the Air Force has put itself in the position of having to defend the fact that one captain is responsible for twenty-six deaths. Last July the chairman of the Joint Chiefs, General Shalikashvili, had said of the 110 investigative report, "There were a shocking number of instances where people failed to do their job properly." Secretary of Defense Perry had leaned into the microphone, looked directly into the camera, and said, "Our third promise to the families of the victims was to address accountability . . . This investigative report is the starting point."

The Department of Defense did not give the families of the victims prior notice of the news release, as it is required to do by law. This final statement by the department deeply offends me. No one ever can make me believe that Captain Wickson made a reasonable mistake. A reasonable mistake doesn't result in twenty-six lives lost. It's almost as if the Department of Defense has sent each of the Black Hawk families a personal message:

Merry Christmas
from the Pentagon
We won!
P.S. Try to enjoy the remainder of your holidays

And we do try to enjoy the holidays, but this last blow almost makes it a fruitless effort. For the remainder of the week our family doesn't discuss Laura or the shoot down. It's almost as if we had a 700-pound gorilla sleeping in our living room. We can see him, smell him, and hear him beating his chest and growling. No one mentions him and we all pretend he isn't there. When we're not looking he runs through the house creating chaos and havoc. Every day we scurry about cleaning up the mess and repairing the destruction. We all hope the day never comes when we're too tired to continue this routine and the gorilla takes over our house and eventually our lives.

28. San Antonio, Texas
January 1, 1995
Sunday

Yesterday, the last day of the worst year of my life, I took down the Christmas decorations and packed away all the remnants of 1994. I want this year to start off fresh, clean, and organized. These mindless tasks had allowed my mind to wander places I don't usually give it permission to go. I'm firm in my resolve not to enmesh myself in pity, repeating the affirmation, "Change is a part of life, and I'll build on my experiences of this past year and try to make them a strength." If I make this my goal, there is no need for New Year's resolutions; and, realistically, I don't have high expectations for the coming twelve months. I really don't know what to expect at all.

One thing is certain: the Black Hawk families have not been successful in any of their pursuits, and many are discouraged. But adversity strengthens Danny's determination, and he begins the New Year with a greater resolve to accomplish what are now the top three items on our agenda:

1. Accountability
2. The Purple Heart
3. Equal compensation for the American families

Accountability tops the list because it is abhorrent to Danny, as a former commander, that those who were responsible and have had charges dropped will be able to continue their Air Force careers, flying fighters and directing aircraft.

The Pentagon has begun answering the requests from our members of Congress for reconsideration of the Purple Heart. In its correspondence to our individual congresspeople, the answer is always, "No, the military members on the Black Hawks were not actively engaged with the enemy." Over and over, it continues to give the same explanation, ignoring the more recent 1993 congressional language. The Pentagon concludes its letters with, "We regret the Pipers' loss," and it uses language that implies that our grief-stricken condition preempts clear and rational thought. The Department of Defense, with subtle apologies for the Black Hawk families' taking the unnecessary time of their lawmakers, attempts to victimize us further. I'm still not convinced the Purple Heart is important enough for this expense of energy and contemptible treatment by the U.S. government.

The first week in January Secretary Widnall attempts to make military history and does succeed in making front-page headlines. Last month, after the Air Force dismissed all the charges against everyone except Captain Wang, Widnall had scheduled a meeting with Secretary of Defense Perry. She urged him to join her in stopping Wang's court-martial. Why? Many high-ranking military officials were disgruntled by a sole captain being singled out as accountable for the Black Hawk shoot down. This request by Widnall is unprecedented, and the odd thing is she doesn't need Perry's permission to stop the court-martial. She could call it to a halt on her own, but she asks Perry to share the responsibility of this no-win situation. On the one hand, exonerating Wang would be seen as an indictment of the military justice system, and after the strange results of Lieutenant Colonel May's Article 32 hearing, it wouldn't be a wise decision to open that can of worms. On the other, if Widnall lets this court-martial stand, Wang will be perceived as a scapegoat, and the press knows that behind every scapegoat is another government or military cover-up. Dilemmas, dilemmas! Perry refuses to join Widnall in exonerating Wang. This leaves Widnall with no choice. She decides not to intervene because if she does, she will be the first service secretary in recent military history to stop a court-martial.

On Monday, January 9, the Air Force issues a press release specifying the date for Captain Wang's court-martial. The trial is scheduled to begin on March 13 in Oklahoma City at Tinker Air Force Base. The last sentence reads, "All sessions of the court martial will be open to the public except when classified information is discussed." I have mixed feelings about attending. I'd like to go, but could I sit through the trial proceedings and listen to the people responsible for Laura's death testify that the shoot down was everyone else's fault but theirs? Laura's birthday is March 18, and it will be another one of those "firsts." She would have been twenty-six years old this year, and not only is her future gone, but so is part of mine. No, it just wouldn't be a good idea to be in Oklahoma City on Laura's birthday. The biggest determining factor is that I can't miss work or leave Sean for two weeks. Once again the circumstances of life make the decision for me.

Captain Wang excels in his role as the scapegoat, doing numerous television and print interviews. This publicity keeps the Black Hawk shoot down in the news, especially when Wang blames the commanders of Operation Provide Comfort, insisting he acted properly based on his training and the available information. Some of his defenders, mostly crewmembers on the AWACS plane with him, say, "You've got one captain being held accountable, and he didn't shoot anything."

There is still enough public curiosity about the shoot down for the television news magazine programs to have an interest in Wang. The story has many of the elements of a sensational saga: a scapegoat, a possible cover-up, state-of-the-art weapons, two violent explosions, and grisly deaths. The major stumbling block is the fact that the events and cast of the shoot down are just too complicated. They just don't lend themselves well to sound-bite journalism. The investigative work would be too labor intensive, and then the journalists would have to simplify the events so the average television viewer could understand the whole story.

However, a *Primetime Live* producer and journalist Sam Donaldson do begin to take an interest in these events. Wang's court-martial, which has been receiving national attention, makes the shoot down newsworthy enough to pursue. The Black Hawk families have some reservations, but it's decided it might be in our best interest to participate. The publicity from a major television news segment might generate more attention than the letter-writing campaign. For the next two weeks all of us cooperate with the producer, contributing information, personal stories, and documents.

Reporters routinely request information under the Freedom of Information Act, but sometimes it can take months or years for the military to release documents. The producer calls the Pentagon and asks for a copy of the twenty-one-volume 110 report. Later that day he says to me, "I knew something was amiss when the Air Force said they'd mail a copy of the report out today. Joan, this is a common Department of Defense media strategy honed to perfection during the Gulf War. After a military news event the Pentagon would go on the offensive and release reams of information. This would make them appear very cooperative and forthcoming, but in reality, they'd always hold back the critical, important facts." It's startling to hear a professional journalist repeat what I'd come to believe.

As the producer begins building and writing the television segment, he asks if anyone has a photograph of Captain Wickson. The answer is no, because Wickson has been protected from the media and all publicity. It has always seemed almost too odd that the main character in this chain of events is virtually anonymous. The producer finally resorts to locating a copy of Wickson's 1986 Air Force Academy yearbook for the purpose of using Wickson's graduation picture. Because I've shared with him my observations of Wickson's physical manifestations at the Article 32 hearing in Oklahoma and my suspicion about Tourette's syndrome, he calls me immediately after procuring the yearbook. "Joan, you won't believe Wickson's Academy nickname! 'Blinky' is printed under his picture." I find this more than a coincidence, it's incredible!

The night before we tape, the Black Hawk family members get together for dinner and later meet at our house for dessert. For many, it is the first time they have met face-to-face. Most of us, including Georgia Bergmann, Kaye Mounsey, Eileen Thompson, and Connie and Cleon Bass, have spoken on the telephone during the past nine months, but some have not been in touch with anyone. We gather around the fireplace in our den, and Danny leads the conversation as we listen to each person's journey from April 14 to this point in time. Before tonight we were a group that fate had cast together, loosely united to accomplish the objectives necessary to bring closure for ourselves. After tonight Danny inspires all the family members to feel a renewed sense of commitment and energy to accomplish these goals for the loved ones we lost.

All of us have members of our immediate family who have asked us repeatedly to put away these Black Hawk issues, to just let them go. Danny tells them not to give up because this will ultimately affect the entire group's effort. It is one of life's most awful experiences to lose a son, daughter, or spouse, but in this incident our treatment by the country for which our loved ones gave their lives has added another dimension of grief and difficulty. Having one another gives us the encouragement to continue.

Earlier in the week Sam Donaldson and the production crew of *Primetime Live* had taped interviews with members of the AWACS crew. The producer had tried to persuade Captain Wickson and Lieutenant Colonel

May to be interviewed. The producer said, "I don't care what the military says, the story about how this happened centers around the pilots." Wickson and May declined to participate. A wise decision on their part, considering nine months ago, immediately after the shoot down, they never dreamed they would get off so easily.

Danny and I have always been under the impression some of these news shows use shoddy methods to achieve spectacular, inaccurate results that boost their ratings in the highly competitive business of television news. This could be the truth, and it is the main reason we had not consented to do a major interview like this one before. You have to give up control, and there are no guarantees on the finished product. But after taping today we were impressed with Donaldson's in-depth knowledge of the details concerning this entire incident, not just the shoot down, but also the Pentagon's subsequent actions. Many of his questions and concerns are our questions and concerns. Sometimes you get so close to an issue, you can't be objective. How many times have all the families asked themselves, "Is it just me, or do others see the same things I do?"

I was worried Donaldson might put us on the spot, perhaps even interrogate us about our audacity to question decisions made by the Pentagon. My concerns were ill founded. When we finished the three-hour taping session, he stayed to talk with the families and to pose for photographs with each of us. One of his assistants reminded him it was time to leave if he was going to catch his flight to Washington. He replied, "Get me on a later flight. This is important. I want to stay and finish visiting with the families." It may have been a small thing, but to the Black Hawk families, even a small act of kindness will be remembered.

The thirty-minute segment runs the first week in March, and we watch it alone at home. It is accurate, concise, and well done. They use photographs, charts, computer-generated graphics, and videotape to illustrate the complicated chain of events on April 14 and since April 14. Yet I'm just not sure the viewers have been left with the right message.

The next morning is another one of those days when I wish I were living in New Zealand, but I go to work instead. I know all my colleagues have seen the program, and I'm not comfortable talking about it. But sooner or later you have to confront the gorilla, or it will gain control of your life. Finally, at lunch, the segment becomes the topic of discussion. A teacher, whose father is a retired Air Force officer, says, "My father and

I watched you on *Primetime Live* last night, and he says the shoot down is part of the risk that people in the military take. Laura knew the risks, and so what's the big deal?"

I believe she is saying what many believe to be true. After twenty-six years as an Air Force wife of a pilot, I understand acceptable risks better than most people. If Laura had been hit on that helicopter by an Iraqi missile, that's an acceptable risk. If the F-15 pilots and AWACS crew had conducted the mission properly and made a human mistake, that's another one of those acceptable risks. However, pilots acting with undue haste in a careless and reckless manner, without performing an adequate visual identification of two benign helicopters, is not an acceptable risk. It's negligent homicide.

29.

San Antonio, Texas
April 1, 1995
Saturday

It's coming. We're counting down the days, and no one wants to talk about it. No, it's not a long-awaited celebration or a holiday tagged on to a three-day weekend. It's the first anniversary of the Black Hawk shoot down. The end of a very long, terrible year. And I can't say I see any light at the end of this dismal tunnel.

The Black Hawk families have discussed for some time how each will spend April 14, 1995. Most will visit cemeteries and place flowers on the graves of their loved ones. Even for a long weekend, the distance to Colorado is too great. Like most other events during the past year, we'll just take it as it comes and again let the circumstances of life dictate our decision.

Almost one year and still no progress on any of the objectives the families had agreed to work so hard for in January. Although we have nothing to show for our efforts, we have decided to add a fourth goal to our previous list. We want a congressional hearing and an investigation to determine why just one person has been held accountable. This time we want the real truth, not the Air Force's version of the truth. The families have begun to forward requests to Congress, even though we know an independent investigation can't be accomplished until after Wang's court-martial, which has been delayed until May.

Most of the people charged and later exonerated are getting on with their Air Force careers and their lives. Wickson and May met a Flying Board last January to determine if they should be returned to flying status. Not surprisingly, the Air Force decided yes, they should. I'm told May is planning to retire, and no one seems able to tell me where Wickson is. I wonder if he's back in the cockpit of an F-15, being hailed as some kind of antihero by the fighter pilot community.

Tuesday, April 4, when I get home from work, Cleon Bass calls: "Joan,

196

the Department of Defense has backed down and is awarding the Purple Heart. They didn't make this decision on their own; Congress had to put pressure on them, and they gave in. We finally have succeeded in this battle."

Last July this quest for the Purple Heart had begun as Danny's solitary effort, so I want him to know about the victory immediately. I try to call him, but he calls me before I have a chance to dial. The Air Force had contacted him at work, and for the first time in longer than I can even remember, he sounds upbeat: "Joan, they want to know when and where we want to hold the ceremony, and they'd like to do it next week." The best possible day would be next Friday, which is coincidentally not only Good Friday, but also April 14, the exact anniversary of the shoot down and Laura's death. It would be a fitting tribute to mark this dark occasion.

I learn later in the day, from the television news, that Congress had ordered the Army and the Air Force to reconsider the Purple Heart decision in its 1995 Defense Spending Bill. The Pentagon reversed its stand after determining that U.S. troops will increasingly encounter dangerous situations without actually confronting hostile enemy forces. An Air Force spokesperson on the news says, "After a careful review this strict interpretation of the Purple Heart regulation was considered inconsistent with the emerging service doctrine concerning U.S. involvement in peacetime operations and operations other than war. Another factor that justified their decision was the hostile environment in which the helicopters were shot down."

Although Danny had pointed out countless times to the Pentagon that this "hostile environment" was a presidentially declared combat zone and that the necessary governmental language already existed to award the medal, it had refused to concede. I'm happy for him, but the victory would have been sweeter if his Air Force had independently made this decision much earlier. Looking at the larger picture, questioning the Pentagon's decision on the Purple Heart was a positive effort. Not only will the Black Hawk victims get the decoration, but in the future American troops involved in peacekeeping efforts around the globe will be recognized for combat military decorations. It acknowledges that war and combat exist under peacetime conditions.

On Friday, April 14, Danny, Sean, and I again drive through the gates of Randolph Air Force Base. The ceremony today will be held in the Clark

Rotunda on the first floor of the Randolph landmark, the Taj Mahal. In a short, dignified ceremony, surrounded by our friends, the military representative presenting the award reminds us the Purple Heart is America's oldest military decoration, having been established by General George Washington in 1782. A short speech follows that remarks on Laura's sacrifice for our country and the sacrifice we have made by losing her. He hands the medal to me and I pass it to Sean.

Danny walks to the podium and thanks those who have stood beside us this past year. He shares some of his most vivid memories of Laura, remembering our travels through Europe. "Once on a trip to Paris, we had happened upon a small café that was a favorite gathering place for the French philosopher Voltaire. Sitting at the rustic tables and eating lunch, we had read some of Voltaire's quotes to our children. One of those quotes seems to fit the occasion today: 'To the living we owe respect and to the dead we owe truth.' I still owe my daughter the truth and I intend to find it."

Everyone is taken aback by Danny's statement, especially the active duty commanders who have attended the ceremony. But when Danny spoke his tone was sincere and gentle, and these remarks couldn't help but tug at the hearts of some. Later, after the ceremony had ended and our friends and the press had left, a few of those commanders came up to Danny: "If I were in your situation, I would be doing the same thing." Most of them have children who are Laura's age, and they understand Danny's commitment.

In the rush of the Monday morning following the three-day Easter weekend, Sean asks if he can bring the Purple Heart to school. I'm surprised. He doesn't talk about the shoot down or Laura very often. "Mom, it's too sad to think about, so I just put it out of my mind." And I understand that, wishing this coping mechanism worked for me. This fifth-grade year has been difficult for him, even with an understanding teacher. Often schoolmates question him about Laura's death. What kind of helicopter was she on? Why was she in Iraq? What type of missile blew up the helicopter? I'd asked Sean what he does when this happens. He replied, "I leave and go to the bathroom or get a drink of water, because I don't want to answer them." This request to bring the Purple Heart to school and call attention to himself and the shoot down seems like a step forward, so I put it in a bag and hand it to him.

Later that afternoon his teacher calls: "It was probably my most touching moment in all the years I've been teaching. Sean got up in front of the class, showed the Purple Heart to everyone, and told his classmates about its origin and the history. He told them last Friday it had been presented to his sister, who had been killed in Iraq one year ago. When he was finished one of the students asked, 'What does this medal mean?' Sean hesitated for a few moments and then replied, 'It means my sister is a hero.' "

This past year many people had asked, "Why the Purple Heart? Laura is dead, what difference does it make?" I had even agreed with them. Now I know why it was worth every moment of effort Danny and the other families had expended. It is for the children like Sean who'll grow up without having that special person who loved them so unconditionally. Now they can remember that father, sister, or brother with more profound memories, because they are heroes.

30

San Antonio, Texas
May 1995

ate this afternoon, shortly before I begin my soccer-mom carpool
routine, the telephone rings, and a male voice introduces himself
as Dr. Alan Diehl, a former civilian Air Force safety official: "For
some time I've been wanting to contact your family, and today I realized
I can't put it off any longer. I have several interviews and press releases
scheduled for this month, and I wanted to talk to you personally before
you read them in *Time* magazine or the newspaper."

He has caught my attention. I whisper to Sean, "Put on your soccer
shoes and get your water bottle; I'm going to be on the telephone until
it's time to leave." Diehl tells me he is a research psychologist who has
previously worked as a senior safety official for the Air Force investigating
military aircraft accidents. "After the release of the investigations for the
Pope AFB midair collision and the Black Hawk shoot down that killed
your daughter, I decided to break my silence. Last fall I compiled my
concerns in a report to the secretary of defense, the Air Force, and several
members of Congress. I've heard nothing, so that gives me no choice but
to go public with my information. It was a difficult decision because I
come from an Air Force family and my brother is an F-16 pilot.

"I've come to realize the investigation of military accidents has spun
out of control. There are a number of reasons, but I'll come to the point.
These crash investigations are routinely sabotaged by officers seeking to
please superiors, hide culpability, and avoid embarrassment."

While Diehl is talking, Sean is pacing the floor and pointing to the
clock. If he is late for practice, the penalty is running several times around
the soccer field. Today I'm having another one of those overlaps between
my normal life and my other life. I explain my soccer situation and tell
Diehl that I'm sure Danny would also be very interested in listening to
what he has to say. "Could we call you back tonight?"

"Sure. I know from reading about you that you're in touch with the other Black Hawk families; perhaps you could relay this information to them? . . . Oh, one last thing. After I sent that report to Washington, I was labeled a whistle-blower and was involuntarily assigned to a nonsafety position. It wasn't unexpected and I knew the risk. When I think of families like yours who have been hurt by misinformation, it's easier to accept the consequences of doing the right thing. Every accident in which people are hurt or killed is a lesson for which we pay in blood."

Danny calls Diehl back later that evening. It is crucial to have a professional substantiate what we already have come to believe, and we think this information will be helpful in trying to get a congressional investigation started. Most of all, for Danny, it's more concrete evidence that there is another side to the Air Force he served in for twenty-six years. It's unfathomable to lose a child, but for him, there is the additional loss of belief in a system he'd risked his life for.

Several days later the Pentagon fires a missile aimed directly at my family. Another phone call around 10:30 P.M., and a deep voice with a Southern inflection says, "Is this Mrs. Piper? I've been keeping up with the Black Hawk shoot down since the beginning, and I'm real sorry about your daughter. I work out here at Randolph Air Force Base, and I'd like to keep my job so I don't want to reveal my name. Thought you'd be interested in knowing Captain Eric Wickson is stationed out here for the next few months. He is going through pilot instructor school and then has a follow-on assignment to Columbus AFB in Mississippi. When he gets there he is going to be a flying instructor. I just didn't want you running into him unexpectedly if you were out here shopping or at the medical clinic. Good night, ma'am."

I'm convinced this person is telling the truth, but before I overreact Danny makes a telephone call the next morning and confirms this information. Later I call the Basses and tell them. Ending the conversation, I remark to Cleon, "How could the Pentagon put the pilot who killed Anthony and Laura in our backyard? This is cruel and unusual punishment. Is this a payback for the Purple Heart or a character test to see if one of us kills him?"

On Saturday Danny and Sean take the dogs and go out to the Randolph AFB skeet range, something they do a few times a month. This morning they're distracted because they're thinking about Wickson. Of course, they can identify him only from the description I've given them and the outdated Academy yearbook photograph. As they leave through the back gate,

Danny drives on the perimeter road adjacent to the golf course and jogging trails. He and Sean, involuntarily, check out the faces of each runner, and both believe they spotted Wickson jogging. Maybe they did, maybe they didn't; but nonetheless, going out to Randolph for a morning of shooting or golf is no longer an innocent escape.

While they're gone it occurs to me how easy it would be for me to kill Wickson. I can't even believe I'm thinking along these lines. I've never even spanked my children. But the thought persists. Danny has been stationed at Randolph four times, so I know the building where Wickson shows up for training every day, I know where the visiting officers' quarters are, and, most of all, I know exactly what he looks like. Also, I have a car with a Randolph gate pass on the bumper and a variety of guns at my disposal. I'm not sure how to use a gun, but I figure it couldn't be brain surgery, judging from the idiots I've seen on the news who have been involved in a shooting. O.K., so I could put the gun in the trunk, drive through Randolph's front gate, wave to the security guard, drive to the flying squadron, then sit and wait. After I shoot him I won't make a getaway; I'll stay and own up to it. I'll probably end up in prison, where I can teach, read books, and work out at the gym—it almost seems less stressful than the life I'm living at this point.

Then I think about Sean and how it wouldn't be fair to him. It's been hard enough losing Laura, we have a far from normal life, and then his mother goes to prison. I can just hear him telling his friends, "I won't be able to play in the soccer game on Saturday. We have to go to the prison in Huntsville and visit my mom." I better try to turn off these destructive thoughts.

I focus on finishing out the remaining few weeks of school. Work has been a good thing. Teaching has given my life normalcy, and this year it will be especially hard to see my students go. A good feeling comes with doing your job well and touching twenty-two lives in a positive way.

It's May 14, Mother's Day, and I'm peacefully reading the Sunday newspaper in bed, trying to keep my emotions under control. This holiday is almost a day of mourning for those who have lost a child. Today I'm going to use Sean's strategy: I'm not going to think about anything that makes me sad or angry. As I open the local news section of the paper, a familiar name jumps out from the page: "Pilkington." The article says the general will be assigned as the vice commander of the Air Intelligence

Agency at Kelly Air Force Base, right here in San Antonio. Could this be another encrypted holiday greeting from the Pentagon?

Happy Mother's Day
Thought you might be comforted by having
General Pilkington and Captain Wickson
living in your beautiful city.
Best regards,
Your Friends at the Pentagon

I'm becoming bitter, and I think it's not so much because Wickson and Pilkington will be living in the same city with us; it's because this is clear evidence they are not only getting on with their lives, they are achieving and moving on to better things. Perhaps Wickson doesn't believe that flying a trainer is a job promotion, but he still has his wings and is still flying despite being responsible for the deaths of twenty-six people. And this upsets me the most, because I still believe he has a nervous condition that should prevent him from flying. I'm angry the Air Force doesn't realize he is a danger in the air and is unfit to be a flying instructor.

I doubt the feelings of the Bass and Piper families were even considered by the individuals who handle personnel assignments for the Air Force. But it does make us wonder. I have Wickson on the north side of town and Pilkington on the south side of the city, and it is my strongest wish that I never see either one of them.

When I'm not too distracted by nearly having Pilkington and Wickson as neighbors, I try to keep up with the details of Captain Wang's upcoming court-martial. He has hired a civilian lawyer to head his military defense team, and a Chinese American civil rights group is helping fund his defense. Wang has appeared in almost every major newspaper lately, including the *New York Times*. He apparently still doesn't understand why he is being court-martialed and jokes that he has begun to understand the old adage "Military justice is to justice as military music is to music." He continues to claim that the AWACS controllers were receiving no signal from the Black Hawk helicopters. "Six people, six sets of eyes looking at the scope—and we saw nothing, no indication that those were friendly helicopters." The major piece of the prosecution's evidence is the magnetic tape that recorded what was on the radar screens between the time the fighters entered Iraq and the time the missiles were fired. It clearly shows that the helicopters were on the screens of the controllers, but Wang contends the tape is inaccurate.

Wang says, "The Air Force refused to press charges against the pilots and many facts about the case remain classified, including the Rules of Engagement. So my court martial may be the only chance the public will have to find out what happened in the skies over Iraq on the morning of April 14, 1994."

The words "only chance to find out what happened" echo in my mind during the coming days. The trial portion of the court-martial will begin the first week in June. School will be over; there is no reason I can't attend. Danny and I discuss this. I tell him, "I have this need to be there, and I think one of us should attend. First, because it sends the message that the families of the victims are interested, and more importantly, it will be the only opportunity to see and listen to the people who were responsible for Laura's death. I still have such a need to know every detail. It is not a choice for me. I have to attend." Danny can't take off two weeks from work, and he agrees one of us should go. Arrangements are made for Sean to visit his grandmother. Hastily I make airline reservations and call Tinker AFB to request base lodging. I'm finishing school on Friday, and on Saturday I'm leaving for Oklahoma.

31

Tinker Air Force Base, Oklahoma City, Oklahoma
June 3, 1995
Saturday

When I arrived in Oklahoma City late last night, it was evident this city had radically changed since my last visit here in October 1994. Barely two months have passed since the Alfred P. Murrah Federal Building was bombed, and this week the city is completing the cleanup of the tons of rubble. But that's the easy part. So many horrific deaths—and I know how bumpy the long road to recovery will be for everyone who lost a loved one. Some will never get over it, and downtown Oklahoma City will forever be a reminder and a shrine of sadness.

I plan to stay for most of Captain Wang's court-martial, but I will leave before the jury is sequestered to decide Wang's guilt or innocence. I believe Wang should be held accountable, but that is not my greatest concern. I don't want to be in a courtroom filled with emotion when the verdict is announced. If he is found innocent, I'll be an outsider unable to share any of the defense's jubilation. If he is found guilty, I will be able to share his sense of unfairness about being the only person accountable for twenty-six deaths. The verdict is not my reason for shouldering the expense and inconvenience of taking two weeks out of my life to be here in Oklahoma City. It is the only chance I'll have, ever, to personally see almost every individual who shares this responsibility with Wang. And perhaps after this is all over, I will have achieved some measure of inner peace.

The Basses decided to attend the first week of the trial, and my son Dan has received permissive temporary duty orders to attend as well. His decision surprised me. "Mom, if you're going, I want to be there and share this with you. This is something I need to do." I believe this will be a good experience for him. A second lieutenant doesn't have the time to read a twenty-one-volume report that explains in detail how his sister was killed. I'm thinking the testimony at this trial will fill in the blanks for him. Sometimes, because he is apart from us, I forget his own difficulties with Laura's death. Although very opposite in personalities, they were always close, rarely arguing as children. As they grew older this relationship deepened, when they were both at the Air Force Academy, just two classes apart. When Dan was going through his "doolie" first year, Laura would sneak him a candy bar or a pizza. In Laura's personal effects we found every note and letter Dan had written to her. This trial will also be a once-in-a-lifetime opportunity for him to not only hear the details of the shoot down, but to see the people who were responsible. And that has real importance because this episode of our lives will be a permanent part of our family history, and when I'm gone I'd like someone else to be able to tell this now long and complicated story.

Wang's pretrial hearing began two weeks ago. During that time his attorneys had filed a motion to have his case dismissed. They claimed top-level commanders, including Defense Secretary William Perry, had made public comments about the shoot down that encouraged targeting Wang as a scapegoat. The motion was denied. His attorneys also pointed out to the judge the legal inconsistencies in the way Wang was charged compared to the two F-15 pilots. The judge refused to address the issue.

It was during this pretrial period that I had decided to attend the court-martial. This time I wanted to be in the courtroom, not downstairs staring at a television for two weeks. Therefore, I had filed my own motion, requesting that families be allowed in the courtroom. After much discussion the judge granted us permission to sit in the back, with the condition that when classified material was discussed the court would go into a closed session and we would have to leave the room.

Early Monday morning the Basses, Dan, and I arrive at the same building we had been to last October. The courtroom is upstairs, and as we are directed to the stairway we are just not sure what to expect or how we'll be treated. We intend to stay in the background. Our worries are unfounded—the atmosphere is friendly and cordial. One of the attorneys passes us a list of witnesses scheduled for this week and a possible list for next week. The first name on the list, to be called today, is Capt. Eric Wickson. The attorney tells us they had asked the judge to also provide Lieutenant Colonel May as a witness, but this request was denied because the judge said one pilot's testimony would be enough. General Pilkington is scheduled to testify the middle of next week.

Almost immediately after we are escorted to our seats, the trial is called to order, and Wickson appears through a side door, sits down, and is sworn in. This time I'm sitting where he can make eye contact, and without a doubt he knows who we are. He is a changed person from last October. Clearly this is a guy who is getting on with his life. He has lost some weight, looks fit, and is wearing a new style Air Force blue uniform. After all, he was never charged with anything, now knows he never will be, and he's back in the cockpit. Granted, the cockpit this time is a trainer, but in his situation he should feel damn lucky.

His testimony begins, and it is essentially the same old story, told now for the fourth time. The only difference is that today he speaks with complete self-assurance. Given the chain of events that occurred before he called AWACS with "engaged," he asserts, he was entitled to hit the pickle button and off-load an AMRAAM. He is confident, sometimes even arrogant, and his nervous condition that was so evident in October is barely noticeable today. Yes, he does blink often and sometimes he tightens his jaw, which prevents this strange tic from progressing further. The time passes quickly, and the judge calls for an early lunch before the cross-examination.

Dan and I are hungry—we hadn't eaten breakfast—and as we have only an hour, we need a place close by. I take him to the Napoleon Deli, where I'd eaten last October. Just outside the front gate of Tinker, it is a favorite hangout for the AWACS personnel. Today the small restaurant is a sea of green flight suits, but I don't pay much attention, because this is the first time Dan and I have had an opportunity to talk. Dan spots Major Tracy, the mission crew commander on the AWACS with Wang. We both have seen Tracy several times on television giving interviews with Wang. I really have to take a close look, because today he appears different. He is wearing sandals and surfer shorts, his shirt is hanging out, and it is apparent he hasn't shaved in several days. Leaning back in his chair with a pair of Ray Ban sunglasses perched on his head, he is holding court amid the military members who have gathered around him. It's evident Tracy is a celebrity in the AWACS community, just another guy who has also gotten on with his life.

The remainder of the afternoon is uneventful, until 2:30. The attorneys are finished with questioning Wickson, and because of his flight training schedule, he will be unable to come back and testify at Wang's sentencing hearing, if Wang is found guilty. For that reason, the defense requests the court be adjourned to take a video deposition from Wickson. The judge agrees and the courtroom empties. We've been sitting for several hours, and it's decided we'll walk downstairs and get a soft drink. After we leave the courtroom and exit through the common area on our way to the stairs, I can feel something is just not right. Out of the corner of my eye, I see someone in a blue uniform approaching me. Oh, shit, it's Wickson! I don't want to see or talk to him. But he continues to walk toward me.

The room becomes silent, everyone freezes in their positions, and all eyes are on me. They have a valid concern that I might become hysterical, as this "mother meets daughter's killer drama" plays out before them. The Basses conveniently hurry down the stairs, but I can't move, I'm too far into this. With Dan standing beside me, Wickson approaches and says, "I know who you are, and I heard you want to talk to me."

"I don't know who told you that, because I've never wanted to speak with you."

Looking me in the eye, he says, "I wish I could change what happened."

Everything is moving in half time as I reply, not sure what is going to come out of my mouth: "Look, this is very uncomfortable for me. I don't know what to say, except that I hold you personally accountable and responsible for Laura's death. It appears things are going well for you and you're getting on with your life." He shrugs his shoulders and someone calls his name; the video camera is ready to tape.

The next morning when we arrive Major Tracy is in the common area, still dressed in his California surfing clothes, unshaven. He's drinking coffee and socializing with some of the AWACS people. He ignores us and we do the same to him. From his interviews we know he believes the AWACS crewmembers are the real victims of the shoot down. Later it becomes evident he's here to give moral support to Captain Diedre Bell, the air surveillance officer on the AWACS with him and Wang, who has been called to testify this morning. Captain Bell has known Major Tracy since her first Air Force assignment. She was a second lieutenant and brand-new to the Air Force when they were stationed together in Korea. Previously she had testified, "I think he's super." Bell was already in Incirlik when this AWACS crew arrived. She had agreed to extend her stay and join the crew once she found out Major Tracy was the mission crew commander. Her actions on April 14 are not under suspicion. She was seated in the back of the aircraft and was the officer who sent the attention arrow to Wang before the shoot down. That arrow had blinked "trouble" for one minute on Wang's screen, and immediately after that he had given permission to Lieutenant Halcli to drop the helicopter symbology. Captain Bell's testimony is very important. It can make or break the credibility of the front crew, especially Wang and Tracy.

As she takes her seat and begins answering questions, I recognize her; she was seated at Tracy's table eating lunch and joking with him yesterday. Today she has undergone a personality metamorphosis. Now she is reserved, almost shy, and her voice is barely audible. Nervously, she repeats her testimony, almost verbatim, from the 110 report, adding no new information.

The remainder of the week is spent listening to supporting testimony from expert witnesses about the technical capabilities of the AWACS. Although this is all pertinent to Wang's case, it is often boring and tedious, but we don't miss a word. Toward the end of the week we are shown the video taken from the camera that was filming one of the radar screens. This is the same video that had been partially erased after the shoot down. After the courtroom lights dim we see a radar screen with the time of 10:23 noted on the bottom. On the screen are four blips—two for the fighters and two for the helicopters. This tape is emotionally more difficult to watch than the Kurdish video of the F-15s shooting down the helicopters. As the clock at the bottom of the screen ticks closer to the moment of Laura's death, I silently scream, "Somebody do something!"

It's frustrating because all of the primary crewmembers had the four blips on their screens and the ability to make simple, basic switch actions to identify the blips. More importantly, if the AWACS crewmembers had any reason to question the pilots' hasty actions or decisions, they had the authority to tell the pilots to back off. The tape ends at 10:28 because the staff weapons director, Capt. Mark Cathy, had mistakenly erased all the events recorded thereafter when trying to view the shoot down he had slept through. But by 10:28 the damage was done. The F-15s were close enough to the Black Hawks for their radar symbology to converge.

One of the differences between a military court-martial and a civilian trial is the military jury members may submit questions to the witnesses. And all of these ten jury members are sharp. Seven are command pilots, and of these, five are Air Force Academy graduates, one was promoted early three times and is a B-2 squadron commander, and another is a Rhodes scholar. They all have the necessary background to ask the right questions, and throughout the week they exercise that right as each witness testifies. Their questions clarify the complex testimonies and are often the same ones I would ask.

On Monday and Tuesday of the second week, three Black Hawk pilots, all with experience flying in Operation Provide Comfort, testify. These helicopter pilots are professional in their demeanor and credible in their testimony. They all say it's always been standard procedure for helicopters to remain on the enroute radio frequency once they enter Iraq. In fact, several times the Black Hawk pilots had questioned this procedure, and AWACS had told them, "Don't worry, stay on the enroute frequency. We know where you are." It was discovered after the shoot down that the Black Hawk squadron had not been provided with the updated Air Tasking Order that specifies "all aircraft should switch to the classified AOR code after they enter the gate into Iraq."

The helicopter pilots testify about the frustration of working with the commanders at Incirlik and how they perceive the Black Hawks to be the stepchildren of the OPC mission. Six months before the shoot down, in October 1993, they had complained that the fighter aircraft were not complying with the directive to stay above 10,000 feet and that they were using their radar to lock on to the Black Hawks an unacceptable number of times. Therefore, there was an urgent need for the Black Hawks to be talking on the same frequency as the fixed-wing aircraft.

But nothing was implemented, nothing was changed until after the April shoot down. Then these situations were immediately corrected, and additional safety procedures were instituted.

After lunch on Tuesday Lt. Ricky Wilson, the AOR controller on the AWACS, is sworn in with immunity. He was responsible for controlling all the aircraft inside Iraq in the No Fly Zone, but he was looking south in the wrong direction when the Black Hawks were shot down. At 10:23, when Wickson had radioed the location of his radar contact, "Tiger One is hits, bull's-eye 030 for 50," Wilson had replied, "Clean there," meaning he didn't see anything. At this point Lieutenant Wilson says he made two calls to Wang. The next time Wickson had called, saying, "Tiger's contact, bull's-eye 030 for 50, low, slow," at 10:25, Wilson had replied, "Hits there." This meant he saw unknown helicopter radar symbology on his scope.

The attorney asks Wilson, "Did you feel you needed help during the mission?" He replies, "No."

I believe he is telling the truth and, to boot, is a good person but a poor excuse for an Air Force officer. His responses to the attorney's questions are slow, and even now he isn't quite sure of his job responsibility on that April 14 mission. I pray to God he never has the opportunity to control aircraft again. As I think these words a senior AWACS officer sitting behind me leans over and says with disgust, "This is a crew that never should have been together." Later in the day one of the attorneys tells me, "If you think Wilson was a poor witness, you should have heard Lieutenant Halcli [the enroute controller who had testified on the Friday before I arrived]. All he could remember was he went to the commissary when he arrived in Turkey."

The next witness called is Captain Cathy, the staff weapons director who was asleep in the back of the AWACS aircraft during the shoot down and erased a critical portion of the videotape immediately after the shoot down. Earlier this week Captain Fuller, the AWACS tanker controller, had testified that during his crew's incoming briefing, when they'd first arrived at Incirlik, Cathy had said about helicopters flying in the No Fly Zone, "They're there but don't pay any attention to them." Now the defense asks him, "What was your purpose on the mission?" He immediately replies, "It was an over-the-shoulder ride. I was their 'answer man,' just to answer any questions they might have." Cathy says he had seen helicopters out in the AOR before, past Zakhu, but he really didn't feel it was necessary to brief crews about the Delta Point system to determine a helicopter's destination. He proudly makes a point of not knowing what the Black Hawks do: "It was some kind of a squirrelly mission." One of the jury members then asks Cathy if he logged instructor time while he was sleeping.

Captain Cathy's prior experience might have made a difference on April 14 if he'd been awake and on task. During the midafternoon break an embarrassed AWACS officer who had sat behind us and listened to Cathy's testimony asks me, "I bet you think AWACS is just a cesspool of stagnant people?" I am unable to give him a truthful answer.

By Wednesday morning Dan and I are weary of sitting in a courtroom, but we are anticipating this afternoon. The first witness after lunch will be General Pilkington. I somehow know that if any new revelations are to be disclosed during this trial, they will come from him. However, quite often during the past year my expectations have been wrong, so I realize there are other possibilities. Is Pilkington going to side with the Air Force and testify that the pilots did everything right and just made a reasonable mistake? Why has he waited so long to testify? Is it because he's been waiting to be granted immunity? I need some answers to these questions that have kept me guessing for so long.

Brig. Gen. Jeffrey Scott Pilkington enters the courtroom and is seated. He is a trim, distinguished, fiftyish officer who looks the part of an Air Force general. This is the first time since the shoot down that he has publicly testified—as the commander of Operation Provide Comfort, this seems unusual. People have been charged, charges have been dismissed, and now at the tail end of the legal proceedings, Pilkington is called as a witness. But as with everything else connected to this tragic chain of events, there is a story behind this event.

Expectedly, last April, he had had no input into the investigation of the shoot down. Later, when the 110 report had been released and he had read all the testimonies, he was taken aback by the lack of knowledge the investigators had of the operations that governed Operation Provide Comfort. In his opinion, the investigators took a very narrow focus and asked questions of the AWACS personnel and pilots that only the most senior commanders would have been able to answer. This resulted in making the people who had been questioned appear ignorant. Then, when the same investigators had interrogated him, almost one month after the shoot down, they had not even bothered to ask him—the person who had the right answers—the same questions. Additionally, Pilkington, based on his knowledge of the rules of engagement and procedures, had expected a number of the AWACS crewmembers, Captain Wickson, Lieutenant Colonel May, and possibly some of his staff members and even himself to be brought to trial. In the fall, after he had left Incirlik, he had been informed, to his surprise, that those in the OPC chain of command were being assigned legal counsel to help guide them through the legal proceedings that would follow. When he had chosen not to testify at the AWACS Article 32 hearing last October, he was not hiding behind the Fifth Amendment. Rather, his Air Force attorney had advised him there would be ample opportunity to give open testimony in the expected upcoming court-martials, which never came to be.

Now today he has traveled from Germany to sit in this seat and answer questions that no one has had the authority to answer before. He will be forthright and truthful, because he, like almost everyone else who has testified previously, has a grant of immunity. He begins by stating that he is currently the commander of the 86th Airlift Wing and the commander of the Kaiserslautern Military Community but that in July he will report for a new assignment as vice commander of the Air Intelligence Agency at Kelly Air Force Base in San Antonio, Texas.

The defense begins by questioning Pilkington about the ROE. For the past year expert after expert has debated whether these rules were flawed or too aggressive. Pilkington surprises everyone by stating, "The Rules of Engagement were adequate and it was not within my responsibility to recommend changes, because they had been issued to me from the Joint Chiefs of Staff. I'll add that on numerous occasions in the presence of the Secretary of Defense, various congressmen and dignitaries from the United States Government and other governments, the Rules of Engagement for Operation Provide Comfort were regularly touted as the perfect Rules of Engagement for the type of operation we were conducting. The comparison universally drawn was that the Rules of Engagement for OPC were as good as we'd ever had and were as good as we could hope to get."

The remainder of the first hour is spent discussing radio frequencies. Pilkington is aware that the AWACS used the enroute radio frequency in Iraq for the Black Hawks. It had been briefed as a safety measure because the helicopters weren't equipped with Have Quick radios.

The next line of questioning concerns the Delta Point system used by the AWACS to pinpoint the location of the Black Hawks. Pilkington believes this system is standard on all AWACS missions. In reality, the defense was unable to locate even one AWACS crewmember at Tinker who could testify that he or she had ever used it.

Pilkington is asked about the threat posed by a Hind helicopter. "There would have been no threat to Coalition air operations by an enemy Hind helicopter, only to the Kurdish population." He is questioned about the mission of these particular F-15s. "The mission of the F-15s, the first flight in on the fourteenth of April, was the same as the mission of the first flight in the No Fly Zone every single day for the last eleven hundred days prior: to make sure it was safe for the AWACS to enter the restricted operating zone. That was the only purpose of their mission."

The defense asks why none of the commanders at OPC flew F-15s. "I had a great problem with the fact that we didn't have an F-15 flier on the permanent staff. I had requested one from my superiors repeatedly because of the delicate political situation. There was no tolerance for mistakes or unprofessional flying at OPC. I had regularly sent people home for the least violation in terms of the rules. It turned out the majority of the people that I was sending home were F-15 pilots."

Next on the agenda is the matter of altitude restrictions for fighters. Pilkington says, "I regularly, routinely imposed altitude limitations in northern Iraq. On the fourteenth of April, the restrictions were a minimum of ten thousand feet for fixed wing aircraft. This information was in each squadron's Aircrew Read File. Any exceptions had to have my approval." One of the defense attorneys consequently asks, "Did Colonel May or Captain Wickson obtain your personal approval to fly below ten thousand feet on the fourteenth of April 1994?" Pilkington curtly replies, "Negative."

The defense follows this last answer by asking if the pilots broke the rules of engagement, but the judge objects because it is irrelevant to the hearing. If the defense can prove the pilots broke the rules, then how can jury members find an AWACS crewmember guilty?

Thus the defense lays more groundwork for that conclusion with the next question: "When the F-15s attacked and shot down the helicopters, did they expose the AWACS to other air threats?" Pilkington replies, "Yes, when the F-15s went down to investigate the helicopters, made numerous passes, engaged the helicopters, and then made more passes to visually reconnaissance the area, AWACS was potentially exposed for that period of time."

One of the jury members asks the general, "Would you expect the Flight Lead to coordinate with AWACS if they weren't immediately threatened by the helicopters?" Pilkington replies with the second most important answer he will give today: "You know, there's two things that can happen when you hit that pickle button and one of them is pretty good, but the other one is so bad that you have to be cautious. No one that has the authority to use deadly force and uses that deadly force without being personally threatened is, in my mind, not living up to their responsibilities." In an answer to a follow-up question, he says, "I don't understand and I will probably never understand Wickson's mindset."

His last sentence gives me chills, because that's what I have tried to understand all year. It has just never added up how Wickson picked up two unidentified radar hits and seven minutes later shot down two helicopters that, even if they had been Hinds, were flying low, slow, and straight—not even close to an immediate threat to the F-15s or to the AWACS. If the general doesn't understand this situation either, this raises considerable questions, and the biggest one is this: What was Wickson thinking, what was going through his mind? I keep going back to his apparent nervous condition. Did the anxiety aggravate a nervous reaction that precluded rational thought and logical actions?

Finally, at the end of Pilkington's testimony, with less than fifteen questions remaining, he gives his most important answer today. Wang's civilian attorney asks: "General Pilkington, I'm seeking only a yes or no answer. Based on your understanding of the pilots' visual identification, is it your opinion that the Rules of Engagement were in fact violated by the pilots?" Pilkington answers, "Yes."

Everyone in the courtroom gasps. When Pilkington answered "Yes," all my efforts to be here for two weeks became validated. The jury probably won't find Wang guilty, but this is a small price to pay for finally hearing the truth.

The session is adjourned for the day. Before I make my usual calls to Danny and some of the other Black Hawk family members, Dan and I list the mistakes the pilots made on April 14, which Pilkington testified to earlier today. None qualifies as a reasonable error.

1. Identified a Hind helicopter as a threat to the AWACS, when both helicopters were flying south through the mountains of Iraq in the opposite direction of the AWACS that was approaching orbit in southern Turkey.
2. Exposed the AWACS to additional air threats while they'd identified and engaged the helicopters.
3. Violated the altitude restriction of 10,000 feet without permission.
4. Didn't coordinate with AWACS before engaging.
5. Violated the rules of engagement.
6. Failed to perform a proper visual identification of the helicopters.
7. Misidentified the helicopters.

As the court-martial proceeds, the remaining witnesses are anticlimactic. Major Tracy is called as a witness on Thursday, now looking almost professional in his military attire. He states that he is on terminal leave, meaning he hasn't worked one day since the shoot down. "I put in my retirement papers two months before the Shoot Down. They offered my career field a fifteen-year retirement and I jumped at it." He recounts vague details of the events on April 14. His concluding statement says is all: "Neither myself or my crew, including Captain Wang, did anything wrong on the day of the fourteenth. We could have maybe done more right, but we didn't do anything wrong."

The prosecution's interrogation allows Tracy's true character to shine. "Major Tracy, you're testifying under a Grant of Immunity given to you just last week. You refused to talk to the Government before you had that Grant of Immunity, just like you refused to testify before the 110 Accident Investigation Board, correct?" Tracy answers, "Yes." The prosecutor continues: "But during that time you have told your story on several national broadcasts that include *Primetime Live,* the *Today Show* and *Good Morning America.* You held press conferences and were quoted in several newspapers. In fact, you've become somewhat of a celebrity. Isn't that true?" Major Tracy tries to justify his conduct. "Not to tell my story. To tell how Captain Wang is being held up as a scapegoat."

Tracy, even with immunity, is nothing more than a further embarrassment to the Air Force. Wang may be the scapegoat, but Tracy continues to portray himself and the rest of the crew as professional victims. It's partly his actions and behaviors during the past year that have labeled this particular AWACS mission a "Ship of Fools." The rumor is that Major Tracy will pursue a teaching career after his imminent early retirement. If that is true, God save the children.

Captain Wang is sworn in late Thursday, and the defense begins its questioning. He is soft-spoken and hesitant, and his answers to simple questions are long and detailed. Often, in his eagerness to display his AWACS expertise, he extends the answer longer than the defense would like. He says Lieutenant Wilson is an above-average controller, and since all of us in the courtroom had been firsthand witnesses to Wilson's testimony, we begin to question Wang's judgment.

After a lengthy recounting of his training, the remainder of Wang's testimony centers on the radar returns on his screen prior to the shoot down. Wang gave permission to drop the helicopter symbology from the screen at 10:21. When the F-15 pilots called unknown radar contacts, he says, "The Black Hawk helicopters were not even a thought in my mind." At 10:23 the AWACS screens begin to show IFF signals from the helicopters. Although the returns were intermittent, they indicated a positive friendly response from the electronic equipment aboard the Black Hawks. Wang maintains they were not green dots that would indicate friendly aircraft, just brown dots that signify unknown aircraft. This is not consistent with the magnetic tape that shows green friendly dots on his screen that day. But green dots or brown dots, the important point is that Wang concedes he personally did not take even one single switch action, which is basic knowledge to all controllers, to determine the identity of the radar returns. For seven minutes no one aboard the AWACS made an effort to identify this friendly response, even though the F-15s had called out an unidentified contact in the same area. Not one crewmember, including Wang, can adequately explain this troubling scenario.

On Friday Wang finishes testifying. Over the course of the past two weeks, I have watched him intensely. He is not a bad or evil person. I have seen him with his son, and by all appearances he is a caring and loving father. He is quiet, reserved, and I'm sure fairly intelligent, but he was promoted to a position beyond his capabilities, and it appears he has company in that respect. In fact, all of the AWACS crewmembers have testified they were a good crew, but after listening to their testimony for two weeks, I know this crew was incompetent, and an unbiased legal expert would undoubtedly conclude many were grossly negligent. It is not my wish that they should go to jail. I just want them to be held accountable and never fly another AWACS mission—ever.

Tomorrow morning will begin with the closing arguments, but I've listened to everything I need to hear and probably more than I wanted to. It is time for me to leave. As Dan drives me to the airport, we talk. Both of us have gotten what we came for. Dan has heard the story and seen the main characters, and more importantly, we have finally heard the truth. Even that doesn't make Laura's death any easier to put to rest, because I now have definitive proof the circumstances weren't acceptable. However, I do feel the return of an energy or a life force that has been missing from my life. For the first time during this interminable year, I have optimism about the future and expectations that I will be able to deal with more than just the immediate and the necessary.

I've even enjoyed some of this time spent in Oklahoma, especially sharing this experience with Dan. In many ways we have always been very much alike, and these past two weeks have been a reaffirmation of our strong relationship. We've always enjoyed each other's company; it is a blessing for a parent to see that continue when your child becomes an adult. This last year I've learned to take my blessings wherever I can find them.

I give Dan a long hug at the airport—it has always been emotionally trying to part with my children and more so now. We are grateful for this experience, but definitely we both are eager to leave and get back to our other lives.

32

San Antonio, Texas
June 20, 1995
Tuesday, 10:30 A.M.

Back in San Antonio, summer, like many other events this past year, has begun without me. But now I feel a sense of renewal, an urge to do things I've put off because I've barely accomplished only what I've had to. This energy surprises me. I want to paint the house, clean out drawers, and redirect my life. Maybe, just maybe, I've reached a new level on this journey to acceptance. I'm not sure about this new, improved version of myself that has recently begun emerging, but I am positive I want this new life to count for something.

Then again, perhaps I can attribute these feelings to being gone for two weeks, because it felt so good to come home, to be with my family after being constrained in a courtroom. The experience was not only something I had to do, in many ways it was an adventure, and even more than that, it was two weeks of complete immersion into the chain of events of April 14. Most likely, that is the key to what has come over me. Grief experts say you have to retell a horrific event over and over until you desensitize yourself to it. Only then can you begin recovery. I admit to myself this is true, because I don't want to think or talk about this anymore. I just want to be left with my memories of Laura, minus the events and circumstances that have brought me to this place in time.

Over the weekend I did put all of this out of my mind, almost forgetting that the final conclusion has yet to be determined. Sean returned from visiting Danny's family, and my mother arrived Sunday for her summer visit.

Dan called Monday night with the latest news from Tinker AFB. Tuesday morning the judge will give instructions to the jury, and they are to be sequestered until they reach a verdict. No one expects them to take long, because under military law, where the maximum punishment is less than ten years, only two-thirds of the jury members must concur.

Tuesday morning, even though I keep saying the jury's finding is not important, I still feel a sense of anticipation because events of this past year have conditioned me to expect the unexpected. I get up early and go to the gym, so I can be home when Dan calls. I'm home by 9:00, and I spend the next ninety minutes trying not to watch the minute hand slowly move on the big clock in the kitchen.

At 10:30, the telephone rings, and I know this is it! But it's not Dan. It is a reporter from our local news station. He tells me the verdict just came over the wire services. The finding is "not guilty."

This verdict is not a surprise, but my anger does surprise me—and it's not aimed at Wang. Fourteen months have passed since the shoot down, and I know this "not guilty" verdict is really the last event in the long, tangled chain. Beneath the anger is the indescribable frustration of knowing this really is the conclusion. Not one person is to be held accountable for Laura's death. Ultimately the Pentagon has won and we have lost. Sure, we can say we have put up a good fight for information, compensation, and accountability, but was it worth the price? I'm not sure, because each time we lost, it was almost like losing Laura all over again.

Dan finally gets a call through to us at 5:00 in the evening. From a pay telephone at the airport, he says, "Mom, after the verdict was announced, it was crazy. I couldn't find a free telephone, and then when I got back to my room, to pack my things, your line was busy. This is what happened: the jury did a nullification. They didn't find him innocent; they acquitted him of the charges. It was explained to me that a nullification occurs when a jury—based on its own sense of justice or fairness—refuses to follow the law and convict in a particular case even though the facts seem to allow no other verdict but guilt." Dan's explanation justifies the situation because testimony throughout the trial proved that the negligence was too widespread for one senior director to be held accountable. I can hear Dan take a deep breath before continuing. "Just a few minutes ago I ran into one of the jury members, here at the airport. I went up to him and asked how the jury arrived at their decision. He told me without a doubt Wang was guilty, but too many others screwed up for them to convict."

The next morning Wang's verdict is front-page news, overshadowing even the O.J. Simpson trial. But the headlines in the San Antonio Express News are disturbing: BOOK CLOSES ON FRIENDLY FIRE DEATHS and ALL CLEARED IN FRIENDLY FIRE DEATHS. Expectedly, Wang is elated and says he would like to continue his Air Force career: "My goal is to continue working aboard AWACS aircraft." He talks about how the past months have affected his life:

> There was a lot of stress, with the glare of the national media, the uncertainty of my Air Force career and the possibility of going to jail for nine months. Some members of my unit lost confidence in me, my marriage was strained and even my children felt the pressure. My eleven-year-old stepson was questioned at school by other children who had heard their parents discussing the case and didn't understand the facts. One child remarked, "I heard your dad was the one who shot down a helicopter and killed a lot of people."

Now that Wang has walked out of the courtroom a free man, he publicly questions why he was the only person held accountable. "I want to say the fight is nowhere near over for me. I want a congressional hearing or investigation into why I was the only person charged."

Although I can accept the verdict, the response by Secretary Perry, after having pledged to the families that there would be "full accountability," is hurtful and insulting. Yesterday, after learning of the Wang verdict, he said, "I accept that verdict. It is not correct to say that no one has been punished. There have been many officers held accountable. Administrative actions have been taken. No one has been sent to jail, that is true; however, many officers' careers have been very adversely affected by this."

Maj. Gen. Nolan Sklute, the Air Force's top legal officer, tells reporters at the Pentagon, "An incident like this does not necessarily mean that the conduct of all those involved rises to the level of criminal culpability. I'm satisfied with the handling of the case." He was probably overjoyed. Fourteen months later, and I'm betting not one Air Force officer, regardless of what Secretary of Defense Perry says, has faced any serious repercussions. Even if Pentagon officials had orchestrated this, it couldn't have turned out better for them. Now they can close the book on this black chapter of Air Force history.

Throughout the next week the press, members of Congress, and legal experts vehemently and publicly question this version of Air Force accountability. The military rarely releases the results of administrative actions taken against its members, but the outcry about no accountability for twenty-six deaths forces its hand. The military makes public the list and punishments. Eleven people were reprimanded:

1. Brigadier General Curtis Emery II, Commander of Operation Provide Comfort's Combined Air Forces—letter of admonishment
2. Captain Joseph Halcli, AWACS Enroute Controller—letter of reprimand
3. Major Douglas Martin, Airborne Command Element "Duke" on AWACS—letter of reprimand
4. Lieutenant Colonel Randy May, F-15 Wing Pilot—letter of reprimand
5. Colonel James O'Brien, Commander of Joint Operations, Operation Provide Comfort—letter of reprimand
6. Brigadier General Jeffrey Pilkington, Commander of Operation Provide Comfort—letter of admonishment
7. Colonel Douglas Richardson, Operations Director, Operation Provide Comfort—letter of admonishment (already removed from his file)
8. Major Lawrence Tracy, AWACS Mission Crew Commander—letter of reprimand
9. Captain Eric Wickson, F-15 Flight Lead—letter of reprimand
10. 1st Lieutenant Ricky Wilson, AWACS AOR Controller—letter of reprimand
11. Captain Jim Wang, AWACS Senior Director—court-martialed and acquitted

Major General Sklute says the letters could affect Air Force careers, but other military legal experts say it is doubtful. What do these letters mean?

Letter of Admonishment: This letter serves as a warning and is usually not entered into personnel or squadron files.

Letter of Reprimand: A letter of strong criticism written by superiors. There are two kinds: one is kept as part of one's record for two years; the other is delivered to the recipient, never a part of one's record but just a warning.

To the Black Hawk families, these letters don't represent accountability. They are as innocuous as a slap on the wrist.

We hear the frightening news that Lt. Ricky Wilson, the AWACS officer who was looking in the wrong direction at the time of the accident, is now in training to be an AWACS air surveillance officer. Colonel May could be reassigned to a staff job, but that is an almost expected job progression for someone with his experience and rank. And, of course, Wickson is flying as an instructor pilot. Of the eleven officers charged, if they are not preparing to retire, each is moving forward in his career. Contrary to what Secretary of Defense Perry says, the Black Hawk families don't see anyone adversely affected except ourselves.

Despite my rage and frustration about no accountability, I am aware that it is time to let go of this. I believe I now know the truth and as much as I will ever know about the events of the shoot down. Now our questions center on what happened afterward—actions and events that not only left no one accountable, but allowed all the officers involved to continue unscathed with their military careers. It is time to turn this over to a higher authority with the clout and power to ask the right people the right questions. Danny and I compile a list of our most immediate concerns that can be answered only by a congressional investigation:

- Was information intentionally left out of the official investigation, and were specific questions not asked to preclude the pilots and commanders from being court-martialed?
- Was Lieutenant Colonel May's hearing orchestrated for a finding of "not guilty"?
- How far up the chain of command did the responsibility for these legal decisions and actions go? We don't believe Major General Santarelli acted autonomously in dropping all charges and granting Wickson immunity. Good sense tells us he was following orders. But from whom?

And now Danny has new information, which will allow us to request a specific independent government investigation that could give us the answers to our questions. This spring he had become aware of another friendly fire cover-up that had taken place during the Persian Gulf War. Army Cpl. Douglas Lance Fielder was killed one day before the end of the war. A disabled tank had left his unit stranded in the Iraqi desert. While they waited to be rescued they were fired upon, and he was killed. The U.S. Army told his parents Iraqi forces had killed him, and Fielder was awarded the Bronze Star with a "V" for valor. His family did not learn he was a victim of fratricide until two of the survivors from his unit called them and told them the true circumstances of his death. The rounds that killed Fielder were fired from a U.S. Army Bradley fighting vehicle. The American officers who ordered the shots to be fired were awarded the Bronze Star for their heroic efforts involving conflict with an armed enemy.

Corporal Fielder's mother, Deborah Shelton Harris, pursued the truth and eventually received a government investigation. As this story made the headlines Danny spoke with Mrs. Harris, and she put him in touch with the General Accounting Office (GAO) investigator she had come to trust.

While I had been in Oklahoma Danny had called Washington and briefed the investigator on the Black Hawk shoot down. The investigator had said, "In your case, just any congressional investigation won't do. You'll need an impartial investigation, and our group can't guarantee impartiality. This is the way it works: Most likely, the House or Senate Armed Services Committee would sponsor this investigation. They could and, from my experience, would control the parameters of whom we talk to and what we look at. You need to contact Senator William Roth, chairman of the Permanent Subcommittee on Investigations. His group is your best chance for truth and impartiality because they don't report to another committee or agency, plus they have the authority to subpoena reluctant witnesses."

Now, with the days ticking down to August, when Congress adjourns, Danny seeks another opinion from a friend who is considered to be a Washington insider. He reiterates what the investigator had said. He tells Danny, "The GAO has a reputation as a 'rotten organization'; although it is strong on the bottom with earnest and skilled professionals, the leadership is weak. Whenever the GAO finds evidence of wrongdoing, they too often cover it up and write it up" (meaning they leave out the most damning evidence when they write their conclusions in the official report).

So after months of trying to obtain a GAO investigation, and with time now running out, Danny changes his focus. He begins another letter-writing blitz to Congress and specifically to Senator Roth requesting assistance in getting his group to do an independent investigation.

And we both take time to write one more letter. On April 25, 1994, just two days after Laura was buried, President Clinton spoke at the Black Hawk memorial service in Washington, D.C. He'd said, "They're all heroes and we owe it to them to honor their lives and to answer the questions of their families, to find the answers which they rightfully seek." Now Danny and I send President Clinton a letter, as a reminder, in the event he has forgotten this promise. We never receive a reply or even an acknowledgment.

33 San Antonio, Texas
July 1995

I n cold, hard, uppercase, bold print, last week's newspaper headlines
had read, BOOK CLOSES ON FRIENDLY FIRE CASES. For the Black Hawk
families, that couldn't be further from the truth. We send another
round of letters to our Washington lawmakers expressing anger over this
Air Force version of accountability and use this as one more justification
for an investigation by Senator Roth's Permanent Subcommittee on Investigations. Letters are also written to various higher-ups in the Air Force,
asking them to review their actions. But it's almost as a courtesy that
we make this request, because from past experience we know that only
Congress can make them accountable. Time is short to try to achieve any
of these objectives, for when Congress returns after the August recess, this
will be old business and quickly forgotten. We not only write letters, we
call, we fax, and, most of all, we pray.

Danny had approached several attorneys about representing the Black
Hawk family members in a class action suit. The answer was always
consistently the same: "No one wins a case like this against the U.S.
government. Your only recourse is through congressional action."

By now Danny and I have become savvy about how business is conducted in Washington. We are well aware that although Congress receives
a multitude of very serious requests for congressional investigations, few
are granted. Outrage and allegations are not sufficient; almost conclusive
evidence of malfeasance must be provided. Therefore, we make every
effort to supply our members of Congress with concrete information to
back up our claims, and this includes excerpts from official testimony and
copies of documents.

So once more we comb through the volumes of testimony and the
stacks and files of documents in our possession. This is not an easy task
because, in the past year, we have filled a tall, three-drawer filing cabinet,
several large economy-size plastic tubs, and our dining room with relevant

paperwork. Since Christmas, our last attempt to put everything away and actually use the room for eating, we've just let materials pile up and spill over to the floor. Even with best intentions and efforts at organization, the long table and buffet have become a repository for Danny's letter-writing campaigns and various disorganized papers.

As the summer heat suffocates south Texas, we begin shuffling through all this information and sorting it into manageable stacks. Late one night we come across two documents we don't remember reading, and we're not even sure how they came into our possession. So many people and unknown sources had faxed and mailed us documents, it had become more than information overload. Through the past year I had become the reader, sorter, and organizer. Although I had thought I'd given everything a cursory glance, obviously these two papers had escaped my attention.

At first they seem insignificant, but as we read them we are stunned. The two faded photocopies are affidavits signed and attested to by two F-15 pilots from the 49th Fighter Squadron in England temporarily stationed at Incirlik in May 1994. They fell under the command of Maj. Gen. James Andrus, who led the 110 investigation immediately after the shoot down. He had ordered these pilots to recreate the circumstances of Wickson's and May's visual identification of the Black Hawks.

Thus, on May 5, 1994, less than three weeks after the shoot down, an F-15 and a Black Hawk helicopter flew out to a remote area of Turkey. The F-15 pilots flew eighteen passes past the Black Hawk with all possible variations of the descriptions given by Captain Wickson and Lieutenant Colonel May in their testimony. After they landed at Incirlik AFB the Air Force captain flying in the rear seat reported the following: "I could not identify the UH-60 [Black Hawk] as friendly until passing over, and looking in front of the aircraft, about 500–1000 feet above the UH-60, and 1000 feet in front. I never saw the American flag on the helicopter. We made 18 passes on the UH-60."

The pilot in the front seat had a video camera to record the visual passes. In this affidavit he says:

> Positive identification required flying over, and in front of, the helicopter at a distance of 1000–2000 feet slant range. I did not see American flags on any of the passes. . . . The primary feature I used to confirm the aircraft was a Black Hawk was the nose shape and size/width.

Again this feature could not be seen clearly until almost abeam the aircraft and in the turn just in front of and above the helicopter. Maintaining sight of the helicopter after the initial sighting was difficult and required constant visual contact. I found it easy to believe any dark shape was the helicopter if it was in about the position where I expected to see the Black Hawk.

This affidavit is more than compelling for two critical reasons. First, this evidence was not included in the 110 report. Second, this proves that Wickson and May made an inadequate visual pass in their attempt to identify the helicopters.

Danny and I question why this recreation of the shoot down—ordered by Major General Andrus, accomplished by pilots under his command, and done at the expense of taxpayers—was never included in the 110 report. Could that be an oversight? To our minds, no. The twenty-one-volume report contains such insignificant information as the $50 disbursement for a Kurdish onion field and the history of the oil pressure on the F-15s—certainly these documents are of more importance. For the first time we have evidence to conclude that damning proof of the pilots' negligence was excluded from the 110 report.

Moreover, the pilots who flew the recreation reported that to adequately identify the helicopters they had to fly in front of them. This proves Wickson and May could not have executed a proper visual identification. Both testified they'd exercised every effort not to get out in front of the helicopters. But, just to confirm our beliefs, we look up their testimony in the 110 report and reread the portion that describes how they came to identify the helicopters as Hinds.

Wickson says, "I passed to the side of the helicopter because the one thing I worry about is getting out in front of him. I know a Hind can employ ordnance out the nose." The pilots who flew on May 5 said the identification required constant visual contact. Wickson had testified, "Flying over the top of the helicopter at a speed of 300 miles per hour, I was trying to keep my wing tips from hitting mountains and I accomplished two tasks simultaneously, making a call on the main radio and pulling out a guide that had the silhouettes of helicopters. I got only three quick interrupted glances of less than 1.25 seconds each."

Lieutenant Colonel May had originally testified he couldn't identify them as Hinds, but then he changed his mind last December, claiming, "I could identify them as Hinds," in a successful effort to avoid being charged with twenty-six counts of negligent homicide. His description of the visual identification is even more disturbing: "I deliberately stay high as I try to slow down. . . . I pass down between fifteen to two thousand feet slant range and find myself five hundred feet above the trail helicopter. My left wing is low and as I look out the left side of the aircraft down at the trail helicopter it gives me a view of the top part of the helicopter's side. . . . I maneuver to the left, kick in the afterburners and pull off to the North."

Additionally, the pilots of the recreation flight flew closer to the helicopters than Wickson and May. Under optimum conditions of not worrying about enemy traps or dealing with the anxiety and rush of adrenaline, they still could not see even one of the six, two-by-three-foot American flags on each helicopter. General Pilkington had testified: "That visual identification required the pilot not only to determine the type of aircraft, but the nationality [flag or fin flash] and then to ensure that the aircraft was not medically marked. That was clearly stated in the Rules of Engagement and I believe that was understood by all pilots in the operation."

Unlike the conclusion reached by the Air Force, there is nothing here to even suggest the pilots made a reasonable mistake. It is every pilot's responsibility to make sure he or she understands with complete clarity the rules and procedures set for each theater of operation to which they are assigned. At Operation Provide Comfort and in every other fighter squadron, there is a set of operating procedures, ATOs, and rules of engagement collectively called an "Aircrew Read File." Although all pilots are briefed on the information, it is their personal responsibility to individually read and memorize this information and then sign off after they have done so. The pilots assigned to Operation Provide Comfort were not overtasked. Wickson had even testified, "Coming down here was a relief. Once you get down here it's a totally different environment. The previous month kind of drops off your shoulder".

The most horrific mistake, to us, is that "Wickson and May ultimately failed to exercise the discipline and care entrusted in military members who have the authority to discharge deadly weapons." By the time an Air Force pilot becomes initially trained to fly an F-15, more than $6 million has been spent on his or her training. Wickson and May also were certified beyond that basic level. May had testified, "I'm qualified to do about everything," and as squadron commander he should have been. They were both more than basic "six-million-dollar men."

Air Force Lt. Col. Tony Kern, a former KC-135 and B-1B commander who is now a professor at the U.S. Air Force Academy, has authored a book titled *Darker Shades of Blue: The Rogue Pilot*. He says, "A single act defines a rogue—and 'one-act rogues' are just as dangerous at that moment in time as the most undisciplined pilot in the sky." He uses Wickson and May as prominent examples of one-act rogues. Writing about the Black Hawk shoot down, he comments:

> Mistakes happen, but there was no rush to shoot these helicopters. The F-15s could have done multiple passes, or even followed the helicopters to their destination to determine their intentions. Hindsight is always twenty-twenty, but to say that a mindset for action was not a part of this equation is to deny the obvious. A chain of errors does not excuse a highly trained pair of professional combat pilots for a gross miscalculation and failure of judgment. This was a rogue act.

Last September, when Laura's shipment of household goods had arrived from Germany, we had unpacked cartons of books. She and I had always shared a love of reading; the difference between us was Laura saved all her books, including textbooks from the Academy. As we sifted through these Danny came upon a text, *Law for Commanders*, from a class she had taken at the Academy. Even back then, he had realized this might be a handy source in the future. While I was sitting in the garage, flipping through the pages, one particular quotation caught my attention, and over the past months it had become ingrained in my conscience:

> There is a special need in the military to make the killing of another as a result of simple negligence a criminal act. This is because of the extensive use, handling, and operation in the course of official duties of such dangerous instruments as weapons, explosives, aircraft, vehicles and the like. The dangers to others from such acts is so great that society demands protection.

Danny and I had learned previously that under military law there is no distinction between simple and gross negligence for an individual charged with negligent homicide. Just to make sure, we call a military attorney. He confirms this information and confidentially says, "The 110 report went through two legal reviews, one in Europe and one in Washington. With the advice of top military lawyers the Department of Defense chose their words very carefully when they concluded the pilots made a reasonable error. So the department was admitting that, yes, an error was made, but it was reasonable, not negligent; therefore, the chances were slim to none that either pilot would be held accountable."

Several times during the past months and through the various legal proceedings, Pentagon officials and officers who were charged to carry out legal responsibilities had said repeatedly, "There is no criminal culpability in this case." But Danny and I now know that is not true.

Even the inquiry officer who, last August, determined the original charges against those involved in the shoot down had stated in simple terms, "Belief that someone is negligent means more than just a chance of conviction for an individual to be charged." He had also said, "The term 'criminal' may seem harsh to describe an officer whose crime involved misstep rather than motive—but violation of an article of the Military Justice System makes the violator a criminal regardless of intent." However, that same inquiry officer who had charged Lieutenant Colonel May still failed to charge Captain Wickson. And, to me, that has always been one of the most perplexing pieces of this puzzle because charging Wickson would have only said, "Let's ask some more questions, and then, if the evidence suggests guilt, let a military jury decide his fate."

Lieutenant Colonel May stated repeatedly, "Our intentions the morning of April fourteenth were honorable." Their honorable intentions did not cancel the failure to exert enough discipline to follow the rules and guidelines, explicitly intended to prevent an incident like this one.

As the middle of July approaches, Washington begins to respond to our requests, and for the first time the Black Hawk families are encouraged. The House of Representatives' National Security Subcommittee on Military Personnel will conduct a hearing on the Black Hawk shoot down. This hearing, scheduled for August 3, will examine the accident investigation and the judicial actions that followed.

But the most important, the most hoped for news comes on July 17. Danny and I are elated! Everyone's hard work and dedication have finally come to fruition. Today we are informed that Senator Roth has authorized an investigation into the shoot down.

This is the best thing we could ever hope for because not only is it the most prestigious investigation authorized by the U.S. government, but Roth's committee is beyond the reach of influence of the Department of Defense. Additionally, the investigators are respected professionals, and this committee can issue subpoenas. This subpoena power is a powerful tool for a military investigation, because if a military member lies under oath while giving testimony before this committee, the result is penalty under civilian law. We know the Pentagon will not be forthcoming with witnesses and information, so subpoena power is essential.

This hearing by the House of Representatives and, more importantly, the Senate investigation cause great concern at the Pentagon. On July 24 the Pentagon orders the Air Force to reexamine the disciplinary and administrative actions for those involved in the shoot down. This is deemed serious enough for the deputy defense secretary to order the Joint Chiefs of Staff to review the corrective actions taken during the past year against those charged and determine whether further action is necessary. They have one month to submit their findings.

We also become aware the new chief of staff of the Air Force, Gen. Ronald R. Fogleman, who had recently succeeded General McPeak, has begun his own review of accountability at the request of Air Force Secretary Sheila Widnall. Now, with the involvement of Congress, there is more at stake than accountability. This time it is the Air Force's integrity.

As July comes to a close it is the first time the Black Hawk families feel real hope. We have spent the past year seeking the truth and accountability because that's what families do. Maybe one has to be truly hopeless, as all of us have been, to appreciate this new feeling. And in the largest sense this is more than a hearing or an investigation. We have come to learn that some members of Congress are loyal to the Department of Defense. Despite our pleas, they have either ignored the Black Hawk families or openly expressed their displeasure with our efforts. Now we know there are some lawmakers in Washington who take time from their other duties to listen and care for those people they represent. Isn't that what governments should do?

34.

San Antonio, Texas
August 1, 1995
Tuesday

This week marks the end of my summer vacation, except there was no vacation for the Piper family. Nonetheless, it has been a summer well spent. For the first time since the shoot down, we feel a sense of accomplishment because soon we will be able to turn all this information and our questions over to Senator Roth's committee, which will begin its investigation in September.

This Thursday the House's National Security Subcommittee will hold its hearing on the shoot down. Although many Black Hawk families will attend, Danny and I will not be there. In July Danny had provided the committee with a written list of our concerns and spoken with the staff on numerous occasions as they prepared the agenda and questions to be addressed. Congressman Bob Dornan of California, who is presiding over the hearing, had called Danny and had spoken to him for over an hour trying to persuade him to attend and make a statement. After much consideration Danny declined. Perhaps Congressman Dornan and some of the Black Hawk families misconstrued Danny's motives. After all, hadn't we worked diligently this past year to get Congress's attention? During our late night telephone calls to each other, hadn't we hoped and sometimes prayed for a hearing? But that was then and this is now. It's a "Be careful what you wish for because you just might get it" scenario.

Congressman Dornan's own motives might be pure, but Danny knows any of the information gleaned from this hearing could be used by Congress and the Department of Defense to thwart the Senate investigation. Even though we have been granted this prestigious Senate investigation, nothing in Washington is a sure thing. Additionally, only one afternoon has been set aside for Dornan's hearing, not long enough to address how or why information was intentionally excluded from the 110 report, the manipulation of the military justice system, the lack of accountability, and the unfair compensation issue.

The other Black Hawk families will have to represent us, because we have a desperate need to step back and take some time for our other life. The court-martial, the "once again" victimization by the Pentagon over its version of accountability, the energy and time required to request an investigation, and the search for evidence of malfeasance have taken a toll on our family life and have sapped our personal energy. Next week, when I go back to work to prepare for the new school year, Danny and Sean will be off on their own adventure. They have planned a driving trip through the western states. They need this time together, and I need some personal space.

On Wednesday they gather maps, pack the truck, and head out for wherever their interests take them on this spontaneous trip. After we say our farewells I walk back into an empty house. After the chaos of the past year, the quiet solitude is more than I could have hoped for. There is just enough time to recuperate before I begin another year of teaching, and, unlike last year, this time I'm anxious to begin. I would like to put the events of this summer behind me, but I know from past experience that this may not be a realistic objective so I just focus on my immediate priorities.

Thursday afternoon I do think about what is transpiring at the congressional hearing in Washington. There is a truth to being there in spirit, because I know it required both a financial sacrifice and an emotional risk for the other Black Hawk families to attend. After the hearing is concluded those who did travel to Washington will continue to be reminded not only of the shoot down, but of their personal loss. Each regression into the past seems to intensify the grief. I am confident they will rise to the occasion, because we all have become experts at doing so, even on short notice.

Very late in the evening Eileen Thompson, Georgia Bergmann, and the Basses call from their hotel to tell me what happened. I'm not surprised to learn the hearing was called to order at 10:30 this morning and was not adjourned until 7:30 tonight. Congressman Dornan has a reputation in Congress as a "loose cannon" and a "grandstander," but today the families believe his actions were appropriate and genuinely heartfelt. He had said, "I will pursue this issue in the same manner as if my child had been on one of those Black Hawks." But as some of the congresspeople who serve on this committee read their statements, it became clear they misconstrued the purpose of this hearing. In their minds, this was more about friendly fire.

Steve Buyer from Indiana was the best example, the same Steve Buyer who was having breakfast with General McPeak on April 14 when the general was notified about the shoot down. As the Black Hawk families listened to his statement, they came to believe he viewed this shoot down from the perspective of the Pentagon and McPeak. He'd said to them, "The issue of Friendly Fire is a reality of the heat of battle. I want you to know that there is a great degree of uncomfortableness from me when there are those who seek the military court martial system for forms of accountability under Friendly Fire. We have to recognize that war is ugly and very dangerous. Finally I want you to recognize that I view that good men and women do make poor decisions."

Another congressman said to the families, "Maybe today we can help you control part of the sadness." The issue, for the families, is not accepting friendly fire as the cost of war or controlling our sadness. No one needs to say to us, "Let me explain this to you one more time and see if you get the big picture." It is Congress that doesn't see the big picture, because the Department of Defense has portrayed us as emotional lunatics in its letters responding to our individual congresspeople. And who wouldn't believe the Department of Defense over the perceived irrational survivors? That is why all of us tried to set aside our grief this past year and force ourselves to exercise rational, logical thought because the responsibility of providing the burden of proof could come only from us. As I talk to the family members in Washington, we remind one another we had accomplished that objective, because we were able to convince Senator Roth to conduct his own independent investigation. His committee is perhaps the only one in Washington that's not in some way connected to or in the back pocket of the Department of Defense.

The only Air Force members who appeared at the hearing today were General Pilkington and Major General Andrus. They each gave a statement and later answered questions. General Pilkington reiterated the F-15 pilots' failure to adequately identify the helicopters by not getting close enough to distinguish the national origin, required by the rules of engagement. Next, he discussed how the investigation was conducted and the events that followed. Most of what he said had been previously stated at Wang's court-martial. But the families were impressed with his candor and sincerity.

Perhaps the most telling testimony came from Major General Andrus, who is also a career fighter pilot and was considered knowledgeable and experienced enough to be tasked with investigating the worst friendly fire incident in Air Force history. He testified, "The F-15 pilots should have identified both the aircraft type and the markings. That is, the aircraft origin. And if in fact it would have been a medical aircraft, they should have determined that." Congressman Dornan had asked, "If you pass one time and you are at an angle or an altitude or a distance to where you look out and you cannot see anything, is it customary to make another pass and take another look, or is that prohibited?" The families had been surprised when Andrus candidly replied, "Sir, as a pilot, I would have made another pass. You would never fire until you know what you are shooting at."

This testimony is more than compelling because Major General Andrus never pursued whether the F-15 pilots actually adhered to the ROE during his investigation into the causes of the shoot down. This had always seemed duplicitous because both pilots, Wickson and May, had testified in front of him at the beginning of the 110 investigation last April that they saw nothing to determine the national origin of the helicopters. More importantly, Andrus failed to take note that Wickson's assumption that the helicopters were Iraqi Hinds caused him to skip a step in the visual identification process, the vital step that requires pilots to confirm national origin by a flag or fin flash. If Captain Wickson and Lieutenant Colonel May had taken that single step, Laura and twenty-five others would be alive today.

As Congressman Dornan adjourned the hearing he'd said, "As regarding the future, it is clear to me that there remains a number of issues that would benefit from a further examination by the GAO. We shall soon provide suggestions for their review."

Just before I end my conversation with the family members, we remind ourselves this isn't over. Not yet. Yes, we got the Purple Heart. Yes, we have gotten our Senate investigation. The two items left are accountability and compensation. Now there is a special need to make financial compensation a priority, and we expect this to be the most difficult objective.

After the shoot down none of the American families had even given a thought to financial compensation. But one year ago this month, when Secretary of Defense Perry had made the decision to award $100,000 to each of the families of the foreign members who were killed and exclude the Americans, it became an insult. Danny has tirelessly pursued this issue all year, but to no avail. As with every other issue we have fought for, the Department of Defense has stood firm.

When a monetary claim is requested, especially in a wrongful death, the victims always say, "It is not about money." Although, earlier, I too made this claim, I need to clarify a point here: indeed, it is always in some way about money, because in our culture financial remuneration represents more than monetary value. This financial payment to the foreigners caused an enormous amount of pain and suffering to the Black Hawk families because it devalued the lives of our loved ones. American families who are asked to sacrifice their young adults on foreign soil for a dubious cause deserve more consideration than Secretary of Defense Perry gave us when he decided upon this ex gratia payment for everyone on the Black Hawks except the Americans. Simply put, the Black Hawk families believe he placed foreign nations above the interest of the most loyal of American families.

Now one of the Black Hawk families has an immediate need for this money, so the financial aspect becomes primary. Last April, two weeks after the first anniversary date of the shoot down, Laura Colbert, wife of Army Specialist Jeffrey Colbert, a crewmember on the lead Black Hawk, watched as her youngest child, Beth, was airlifted by helicopter to Boston. Soon after, Beth was diagnosed with acute leukemia. Laura's benefits and those of her children had just changed from active duty to retiree status. The first three weeks of critical care cost $98,000. By the end of July, with no end of treatment in sight, the bills totaled over $200,000. Yes, the military will pick up some of the cost, but not enough. The financial compensation Laura receives as a widow is barely above the subsistence level.

Danny remains optimistic, and I know when he returns from his trip he will intensify his efforts. But I've come to believe that no one wins anything from the Department of Defense. It is stronger and more far-reaching than an entire government of a medium-size country, and maybe even then I'm underestimating its power. I hesitate to say it, but I'm beginning to believe it is more powerful than any of our three branches of government.

Danny and Sean call each night from a different location. It is wonderful to hear the enthusiasm in Sean's voice. "Mom, today we saw Chimney Rock, just like the pioneers on the Oregon Trail!" It's clear Sean is having a wonderful experience. After I relate the details of the hearing, Danny believes he made the right decision. And he did, because Sean will never be eleven years old again. We've always made our children a priority, but under our present circumstances it has been difficult. In the scheme of life the hearing won't amount to a blink, but missed opportunities with a child can be everything, because there are no second chances.

35.
The Pentagon
August 10, 1995
Thursday

Deep inside the recesses of the Pentagon, with the customary ruffles and flourishes, Air Force Chief of Staff Gen. Ronald Fogleman is introduced. He slowly walks to the podium for this official, highly touted briefing and press conference. The crowded briefing room is standing room only for high-ranking Air Force officers, staffers, and the press. They all are well aware of the topic for this briefing, which they have been required to attend. Although they are clear on Fogleman's objective today, they don't know what the outcome will be. It would be an understatement to conclude that all the senior commanders are wondering how this will affect them, because the Pentagon, famous for its leaks and infamous for its rumors, has been buzzing all week.

General Fogleman, whose voice in itself commands authority, speaks in his most serious tone. He relates the details of the Black Hawk shoot down and how last month he was ordered to review the administrative and personnel actions taken against those who were negligent and charged:

> The fact that the conduct of some individuals did not give rise to criminal prosecution or conviction should not end the inquiry into the appropriateness of their actions. Air Force standards require that people display the extraordinary discipline, judgment and training that their duties require and that the American people expect.

Fogleman says that his review convinced him that in several instances people failed to meet Air Force standards and that this was not reflected in their records:

> Therefore, I have written and issued supplemental performance evaluations for several officers whose actions demonstrate a failure to meet Air

Force standards. Keep in mind that the purpose of these performance reports is to provide an official record. Administrative actions which are not visible to promotion boards and go away after a period of one or two years do not properly document the individual's performance. I am also taking actions concerning assignments. I have directed that the F-15 pilots and certain AWACS crew members be disqualified from aviation service and duties for at least three years. I took these measures because the actions of these officers demonstrated a failure to meet Air Force standards. I am also concerned about the actions of senior officers who failed to appropriately record the conduct of those involved. This is unacceptable. The Black Hawk incident was serious. Lives were lost—our people did not meet Air Force standards. Now, we are holding all involved accountable.

Videotapes of this briefing will be distributed to every Air Force military installation on the globe, where it will be mandatory viewing for all officers.

Some have called this past year "the grimmest chapter in Air Force history." Now General Fogleman's "get tough" message hopes to end that chapter. Fogleman has his critics, who say military members in war zones will now become gun-shy. But Fogleman and other top military leaders contend this case was different because "flagrant" mistakes made the need for accountability paramount.

I wonder where "flagrant" falls on the mistake-accountability line. Fogleman leads me to believe flagrant mistakes are more serious than reasonable mistakes but still not serious enough to label the mistake negligent. I think the Air Force leadership is making this up as they go along because they don't want to admit that sometimes mistakes are crimes.

36

San Antonio, Texas
September 1995

From our nightly telephone conversations, initiated from remote motels scattered across the western states, Danny had learned of General Fogleman's actions. The Pentagon had sent us the official transcript of the briefing and a copy of the videotape. After I had read the pertinent sections from the transcript to him, we had discussed the Air Force's newest revised version of accountability. We found it either embarrassing or interesting, depending on one's point of view, that last month Secretary of Defense Perry and the Air Force's top legal officer, Major General Sklute, had publicly been so accepting of the old version. Now with a Senate investigation looming on the horizon, the Air Force, we believe, decides to cover its tracks.

One year ago, when charges had been filed, we might have been satisfied with this improved version. After the 110 report had been released, even though it was not an accurate accounting of the shoot down, it had been very clear to us that Air Force standards had not been met. The pilots should have been grounded and the AWACS crew relieved of their positions controlling aircraft for the remainder of their careers. The Black Hawk families were never out for blood or incarceration, we just wanted what was fair and equitable, and more than that we wanted to ensure those responsible never had the opportunity to make another deadly error. Although it is too long overdue, this decision does bring the Black Hawk families some measure of peace.

Danny and Sean returned from their road trip last month bursting with stories about every national park, monument, and tourist attraction from South Dakota to New Mexico. Ten days of intensive driving and sight-seeing. For me, the pace would have been grueling. For Danny, compared to the past year, it was relaxing.

They had pulled into the driveway on a Sunday afternoon, and Sean had started school the next morning. This is probably the ideal antidote

241

for middle school anxiety. Without missing a beat, we all fell back into the rhythm of the school year. New clothes, pristine notebooks, and eager faces represent a symbolic New Year for teachers. I want this September to be the beginning of a better year. Last year was spent pursuing our objectives and seeking the truth. This "New Year" will be a time to let go of the anger and hurt and start rebuilding our lives.

This week we receive a letter informing us that the GAO's Office of Special Investigations has been authorized by the House of Representatives' National Security Subcommittee on Military Personnel to conduct an investigation of the Black Hawk shoot down. This is primarily a result of Congressman Dornan's hearing held last month. The House subcommittee is asking the GAO to determine if (1) the 110 Accident Investigation Board had met its objectives, (2) the subsequent military justice investigations had followed established guidelines, and (3) the Department of Defense and/or Air Force had improperly or unlawfully influenced these investigations.

Now we will have two investigations, one by the House of Representatives and another by the Senate. We should be pleased, but Danny and I know the only investigation that stands a chance of uncovering the truth will be the Senate investigation. Although we have achieved some peace of mind about accountability, we still have our unanswered questions about the events following the shoot down. This GAO investigation lacks the authority and clout of Senator Roth's committee, for the GAO doesn't have the power to issue subpoenas. Without that, how can it question the unknowing colonels and the uncaring generals who orchestrated the chain of events of the investigation, military justice, and accountability after the shoot down?

The most important issue is we can now turn over all the documents we have collected, all the notes we've made, and all the questions we have to someone else who has the resources to conduct a more thorough investigation on a higher level. We know we've taken this search further than we had ever expected, and certainly further than the Pentagon would have predicted, but now we are at the end of our possibilities. We believe we now know everything we will ever be allowed to know of what happened on April 14, 1994, and we're reasonably certain even the investigators will find nothing of significance that is not already known about the events leading to the shoot down. What we don't know will never be divulged to us, and we aren't at all certain the Department of Defense will allow even this prestigious Senate investigative team, with its powerful tool of subpoena power, into its inner sanctum. The department could contend the information is too classified, too integral to the military to be made public, because we believe what we are seeking is too damaging to ever be released into the public domain. It strikes at the heart of the integrity, honesty, and honor of the entire military system.

Thus, in the middle of September Senator Roth's chief investigator, Eric Thorson, and the chief counselor of the Permanent Subcommittee on Investigations come to San Antonio. It is an ironic twist that Eric has come to do this investigation that is so important to us. Although we have just a passing acquaintance with him, he and Danny graduated in the same class at the Air Force Academy. Eric had gone on to pilot training, flown combat missions over North Vietnam, and then resigned from the Air Force to start his own executive aviation business. In the 1980s he had been appointed assistant secretary of the Air Force for Readiness Support. During this time Danny had crossed paths with him at the Pentagon. This past month we have spoken with Eric several times over the telephone. Initially he had told us, "Senator Roth is committed to finding the truth and will spare no effort to do so. Your concerns and this investigation are in the best of hands." But Danny and I already know this, and we also know it was Eric who, behind the scenes, was responsible for the Fielder friendly fire investigation. If anyone can crack the inner sanctum of the Department of Defense, it is Eric.

We learn they have already read the 110 report to familiarize themselves with the events and main characters of the shoot down. So, for what we hope will be the last time, we sit at the dining room table and share the results of this past year's journey. They peruse documents, attach yellow sticky notes, ask questions, and make copious notes. After several hours of intense conversation they pack up all the information that could possibly offer insight into their investigation. Lastly, just before they leave, Eric discusses the focus of their investigation: "We're going to look at this entire incident from the time of the shoot down until the end of all the judicial proceedings. You need to know it isn't proper for us to second-guess the findings of Captain Wang's court-martial, where a judge and jury have reviewed the evidence in a court of law and passed judgment. From the evidence we have already looked at, we don't believe there's a smoking gun, but there is a possibility the 110 investigation, the 110 report, and some important aspects of the military justice system were orchestrated and manipulated by a higher authority. The question is, if that was done, who was that higher authority? How far up in Washington did this go? We're going to take a look at everything and investigate each issue, including the Article 32 hearing for Lieutenant Colonel May."

It is early evening as they leave to catch the next flight back to Washington. Danny and I walk out to their car and watch them drive away. Hesitantly, I begin to walk inside the house, but for now, I can't face the stacks of documents on the dining room table. Opening the side gate, I walk into the backyard and sink into a comfortable chair on the deck. The sun has begun to drop down below the horizon, and the Texas blue sky is streaked with gorgeous deep colors. It has been a long time since I've noticed the beauty of the sky. This past year it has been a reminder of life's insignificance, filling me with sadness and emptiness. Now I can sense the promise of another new day and feel a spirit that compels me to go on with my life. This means much more than checking off the investigation objective. Today is a personal milestone for the official end of our efforts this past year. I believe we have honored the memory of Laura and have done the best anyone could do under these trying and unusual circumstances. Perhaps now I can move forward.

The sun has disappeared, the day is over. I enter the house, return to the dining room, and turn on the lights. Quickly and efficiently I pack the twenty-one volumes of the 110 report, bulging manila folders, correspondence, and newspaper clippings into boxes. Next, I dust and wax every surface, polishing away the dusty imprints from the past several months.

The gorilla has left the living room. I'm sure his presence will be felt for some time, and during stressful periods he will return for visits. And that's O.K., because now I will have the strength to confront him.

37 • Zakhu, Northern Iraq
August 1996

L aura's death certificate specifies the place of her death as Irbil, Iraq. Two years ago I had to pull a world atlas off the bookshelf and search the map of Iraq with my finger until I finally pinpointed its exact location. To me, this small city was the most obscure site on the face of the earth, and I was just as sure I would never hear of it again as I was that I would never again see Laura. But today Irbil is the location for the top news story of the day. It appears to be a fairly modern city, although reminders of the Gulf War can still be seen in the semidemolished buildings and in the eyes of the Kurdish children. Now, once again, Irbil has become a dangerous and deadly place.

Saddam Hussein's army has invaded the area around Irbil. Today, with American aircraft overhead, his army rolled tanks through the streets and fired artillery at the people and the buildings. A news correspondent reports Iraq has executed at least 100 Kurdish military officers and many others who have cooperated with the Americans.

Countless millions of U.S. dollars spent, countless air sorties deployed to the skies above Irbil in the past five years, fifteen American lives given, and Iraqi tanks have broken through the sacred 36th parallel into this sanctuary of protection. For obvious reasons, I am more than interested in the details of this situation.

In 1991, after the Gulf War ended, President George Bush instituted a "Presidential Finding" for the sole purpose of getting rid of Saddam Hussein. This project had been designated "lethal," giving the Central Intelligence Agency (CIA), which is forbidden by U.S. law from making efforts to assassinate a foreign leader, the authority to use force and methods that result in the death of others. After Clinton took office he became reluctant to increase the aggression against Hussein, and this angered some of the Kurdish dissidents who had been backed by the CIA. Partly because of Clinton's lack of commitment, Saddam Hussein had been able to turn the two Kurdish parties against each other. The leaders of these two opposing Kurdish groups, Jalal Talabani and Massoud Barzani, are the very same leaders the Black Hawk helicopters were ferrying the Army commanders to meet on April 14, 1994. Barzani's party had pulled out of the CIA-backed commitment and defected to Saddam Hussein's side. The American CIA had assured the Talabani party of Kurdish freedom fighters that U.S. forces would provide air cover as they tried to defend Irbil against the Iraqi assault. Although they could hear and see the allied fighter aircraft overhead, no bombs were dropped, no missiles released.

Some say this is the end of U.S. efforts to give humanitarian aid and protection to the Kurds. Some Kurds say America's humanitarian relief program was a thinly disguised mission to cover a covert CIA action program to kill Saddam Hussein. During the past five years it has been reported that American money and allied troops did provide much needed protection and relief to the Kurdish people. But it was never reported, until this week, that Zakhu was also home base to twenty-five CIA officers who were assisted by American Special Forces troops. Many Kurds were on the CIA payroll, but the two most prestigious were Massoud Barzani and Jalal Talabani.

I think back over the past two years and try to remember how often I have heard that the friendly fire downing of the Black Hawk helicopters was part of the cost of keeping peace. Why is it that this time when that precious peace was shattered, when Saddam Hussein crossed into the protected area in broad daylight, nothing was done? Once again the United States risks the lives of America's sons and daughters in a selective peace-keeping mission.

38

San Antonio, Texas
September 1996

It has been one year since the Senate Permanent Subcommittee on Investigations began its investigation and Eric Thorson sat at our dining room table, surveyed our documents, and spoke with us. These past twelve months have been a reprieve from the exhaustion and upheaval in my life since April 14, 1994. But it hasn't been the kind of year I had set out to have, perhaps because it had begun with expectations set too high.

Turning over the responsibilities of my personal quest had provided me the time and energy to properly mourn the loss of Laura. Not surprisingly, I had skipped this step when I had made the decision to focus on the events following the shoot down instead of my private life. This past year I have put aside the torment and aggravation surrounding the events that followed this tragedy and have begun to accept the profound loss that was Laura's death.

This acceptance stage is transitory; it fluctuates more than the weather. Some days are easier than others, and occasionally the gorilla does return. Acceptance has come to mean that Laura is gone forever. I will have to live out my life with that emptiness in my heart. Survival is keeping occupied, working to the point of exhaustion with the goal of achieving uninterrupted sleep. Survival, more importantly, is being able to make a difference in the short time each of us has, and I am blessed by the opportunity to teach school and raise Sean. I've taken each day as it has come, and I have made it through another year.

We received good news this week. The investigation being conducted by the Senate subcommittee is nearing completion and should be finished by the end of this year. As Eric had told us last September, "There is no smoking gun." That turned out to be true. However, there have been several interesting and revealing events for committee members over the course of their investigation, which we have learned about through the customary calls made to apprise us of the subcommittee's progress.

One set of documents that had interested Eric from the beginning were the affidavits from the two pilots who had flown the reenactment of the visual identification in Turkey as part of the 110 investigation. The results had shown Wickson and May could not have seen enough detail to determine either the nationality or the type of helicopter. Because this was such important evidence, the subcommittee had commissioned its own recreation of the visual identification with the help of the U.S. Army. The committee members were astounded to find that at the distance and angle Wickson and May had flown on April 14, the most prominent feature that could be distinguished from the cockpit of the F-15s was the faint whirling rotors of the helicopters.

When the investigators had questioned Major General Andrus about why this reenactment of the visual identification was omitted from the 110 report, he was unable to give an adequate explanation. "It was part of the evidence we submitted. I can't explain why it's not in there."

The 110 report had concluded that the F-15 pilots did not violate the rules of engagement. However, Major General Andrus's investigation did not focus on the rules of engagement. This is difficult to understand because one of the primary reasons those rules were so conscientiously constructed was to prevent a friendly fire incident. Therefore, shouldn't they be a paramount issue? Even after Captain Wickson had testified that he had not been able to determine the national origin of the helicopters, Andrus didn't pursue the issue. Why not? Not only is it standard procedure for most ROE, it is just common sense to determine what country the unidentified target belongs to before a pilot releases a missile and blows it up. When Eric had questioned the general about this serious oversight, he replied that he'd accepted Wickson's conviction that he had seen a Hind helicopter and that had been enough to conclude he had followed the rules of engagement. Obviously, Andrus is not a bumbling idiot who had become confused about the investigation's objective. He is a general who had been promoted above countless others because of his superior capabilities. It was also interesting that Major General Andrus had remarked several times during his deposition that his chief investigator, who conducted the 110 investigation, was the best F-15 pilot in the world. Yet upon being questioned by the Senate investigators, the general said, "You guys sure know how to ask the right questions."

As the Senate investigation progressed Lieutenant Colonel May had been called to give a deposition before the subcommittee. After lengthy questioning, when asked why he changed his testimony for his Article 32 hearing, he'd paused and shrugged his shoulders. When Eric continued to press him for an answer, May finally replied, "I don't know, I just don't know."

This week Eric calls again. Although these periodic telephone conversations with him have been compelling, now, at this point in time, we have become more interested in the subcommittee's conclusions. Before Eric has the opportunity to tell us the reason for his call, Danny takes this opportunity to ask him about the subcommittee's preliminary conclusions. Although I'm not sure I am prepared to hear them, I listen on the extension, feeling the nausea return to the pit of my stomach. I want to be right about my suspicions, I want them to confirm I hadn't wasted almost two years believing assumptions that are false, but at the same time I also want to be proven wrong. During this past year's intermission I had come to realize the danger of having public institutions that report to no one and have almost unlimited power to cover up mistakes and manipulate information.

These thoughts are interrupted by the serious tone of Eric's voice: "You have been more than patient, and you should be apprised of some of our initial conclusions. First, there is enough evidence to support the belief that the 110 report and some of the proceedings were manipulated for the sole purpose of never holding the pilots accountable for their actions. Both pilots were negligent in the manner in which they conducted the visual identification, and both of them violated the rules of engagement. Additionally, we ascertained Captain Wickson was prematurely given a grant of immunity that neither he nor his legal counsel had requested. We surmise this was done because the Air Force had come to believe Wickson was too straightforward in his answers and thus could blow the pilots' cover and the Air Force's legal strategy. When we called Wickson in for questioning, he admitted he did it wrong and he was, after the shoot down, prepared to take the consequences. In most legal proceedings the least culpable is given immunity. In this instance the Air Force immunized the most culpable, Captain Wickson, because it didn't want him on the witness stand, under oath, admitting he had done anything wrong, thereby assuring himself of a conviction."

Before Danny or I can interject he continues, "We believe both pilots should have been brought up on charges in a court of law. An act that involves the deaths of twenty-six people is a very grave and serious issue. The F-15 pilots' guilt or innocence should have been resolved by a court-martial, where others could see all of the evidence that existed."

At this moment I grieve for what should have been. It is too late to go back and change anything. The Air Force denied my family and the other Black Hawk families the right to see those responsible brought to trial. For almost three years this has caused us to doubt ourselves during a time when we were so emotionally vulnerable. These actions have caused us undue suffering and prevented all of us from reaching closure.

But most of all, and this makes me so angry, the Air Force has dishonored Laura and the others who were killed. In my mind, this is tantamount to hauling their burnt, broken bodies to the dump and letting vermin feed on them. What good does the full military funeral and burial achieve when almost before the grass can grow over their graves our military leaders desecrate the memories of those killed by treachery and lies?

While I have been lost in my personal thoughts, in the background I hear Eric say, "We know some of the AWACS crew were incompetent beyond belief, and there is more than adequate evidence to conclude that several crewmembers were grossly negligent."

Danny asks him about evidence left out of the 110 investigation. Eric replies, "Yes, there was critical evidence that was not included and questions that were never asked. But the other area where we found serious misactions was Lieutenant Colonel May's Article 32. The Article 32 investigating officer mischaracterized testimony and distorted his report to Major General Santarelli, who was the convening authority, when he failed to mention May's reversal of testimony. He also relied on his personal opinion when he found May to be more credible than Wickson. We believe the resulting report was inaccurate and misleading."

Eric pauses to let this information sink in, then continues with the purpose of his call. "Today I have another reason for calling you. Although the Air Force has been allowed to have an officer present in the room each time we called a witness to give a deposition and it was this officer's responsibility to report back to the Pentagon, up until now the investigation has gone well. The Air Force has been reasonably cooperative in supplying us with the witnesses we have requested and allowing us access to classified documents."

I think, "O.K., that's the good news. Now what's the bad news?"

Eric's voice drops: "Now our subcommittee has run into a very serious stumbling block. After reviewing thousands of documents and conducting dozens of interviews, last week we requested the Air Force produce the last four witnesses. These final four are senior Air Force officers who were involved in the legal proceedings that precede a court-martial. It is not proper for us to second-guess the findings of a court-martial case, but it is both proper and necessary to review the actions of these officers who participated in what the Department of Defense has come to call a 'quasi-judicial process.'"

Danny interrupts to ask, "Who were they, what were their names, what were their job titles?"

Reluctantly Eric replies: "Major General Eugene Santarelli, the convening authority for the F-15 pilots; Brigadier General John Dallager, the RCM [regimental court-martial] 303 inquiry officer for the F-15 pilots; Colonel Edward Starr, the Article 32 investigating officer for the F-15 pilots; and Colonel C. G. Mangin, the legal adviser to Major General Santarelli.

"We requested that Secretary of Defense Perry voluntarily produce these four officers for questioning. The Department of Defense refused this request because they have come to believe it might create an adverse public perception of the independence of the military judicial system. I told them, yes, that possibility does exist, but only if we find evidence of wrongdoing. If we find the legal proceedings were conducted fairly, this will only enhance the reputation of the military justice system.

"This week, on September third, Senator Roth received a letter from the deputy secretary of the Air Force, John White. He further requested these officers not be deposed. This is where we stand right now. I want to assure you Senator Roth will not hesitate to issue subpoenas if it becomes necessary."

After we hang up I discuss with Danny the possibilities this situation presents. Past experience has proven to me that no one beats the Department of Defense at this game. And I have come to believe that, to the department, it is a game. Probably as I am thinking this the Air Force legal team is gathered around a large table in a Pentagon conference room, coming up with the ultimate strategy to eventually win this round. I would like to say it doesn't matter because the important issue is Eric's confirmation of what I had come to believe previously, which I now know is the truth. While I admit there is a measure of closure that comes with this, in a larger sense this does matter to me, because it is part of the checks and balances I teach my students about in the American system of government. Maybe I've been naive, but I want to believe our government works, and most of all, I want to believe there is truth and honor with service in our military. Even now, even after what we have been through.

39. Washington, D.C.
October 30, 1996
Wednesday

Throughout October the Senate Permanent Subcommittee on Investigations has continued to dicker with the Pentagon's legal team. Now, by the end of the month, the general counselor for the Department of Defense, Judith Miller, has become the subcommittee's point of contact. Ms. Miller continues to hold firm on the Department of Defense's decision not to produce the crucial four witnesses because of the now quasi-judicial interest of the investigation and also because military officers have never before been compelled to testify about their involvement in the legal process. The Senate subcommittee has reassured her it would pose only questions of fact resulting from statements and documents relating to the shoot down, not about the officers' individual thoughts. The staff of the Subcommittee on Investigations defined the options available to the Department of Defense as follows:

1. The officers could voluntarily appear before the subcommittee.
2. Ms. Miller could accept service of the subpoenas on behalf of the officers.
3. The U.S. Marshals will serve the subpoenas to the individual officers.

Today, October 30, Air Force Deputy Secretary John White telephones Senator Roth. Senator Roth's staff informs an irate Secretary White that the senator never discusses an ongoing investigation with any of the parties involved. The staff again informs Secretary White of the available options: "Produce the witnesses, or subpoenas will be issued."

On Halloween, October 31, the Investigative Subcommittee becomes involved in an unusual version of "trick or treat." Early in the morning Senator Roth receives another letter from Secretary White, who again

253

brings up the "threaten the integrity of the military justice system" argument. With Senator Roth's approval the chief counselor for the subcommittee calls the Department of Defense at 11:40 A.M. and says, "Produce the witnesses by 2:30 this afternoon, or we will issue subpoenas!"

Everyone on the Investigative Subcommittee holds their breath. In all the investigations they have done over many years, there has never been a situation this dramatic. They certainly don't expect the four witnesses to walk through the door at 2:29, but the clock continues to tick and the minutes pass slowly. At precisely 2:30 the telephone rings. The Pentagon says that a letter from Secretary White to Senator Roth will be delivered in thirty minutes and that the Department of Defense has not yet reached a decision. Prepared for this contingency, the subcommittee's legal counsel informs the Department of Defense, "As a direct result of the department's failure to make a decision, this subcommittee is forced to issue subpoenas to produce the witnesses."

The next morning, November 1, four subpoenas are delivered to the Pentagon to be served to the Air Force. The Air Force is outraged and refuses to accept the subpoenas on behalf of the four officers. As a result, the subpoenas must be given to U.S. Marshals to effect service. Eric Thorson places a courtesy telephone call to Major General Santarelli's office in Hawaii to inform him he will be served with a subpoena today. His secretary answers the phone and tells Eric that the general is on an Air Force plane headed for Hickam AFB. Eric replies, "I'm telling you the Air Force has refused to accept General Santarelli's subpoena. Your general will be served by U.S. Marshals when he lands." The secretary exclaims, "Oh my God!"

A few hours later the associate chief of the Air Force Litigation Division finally has no choice but to accept the subpoenas on the Air Force's behalf.

For the next twelve days there is no communication with the Department of Defense. On the morning of November 13, the day the first subpoenaed witness is scheduled to testify, a letter is delivered to Senator Roth from Ms. Miller. The message infuriates Senator Roth:

> You have signed subpoenas that would require four officers to appear before your staff to justify their quasi-judicial acts. We have been advised by the Department of Justice that these subpoenas lack legal force

and effect because they were issued after the adjournment of *sine die* of the 104th Congress. Accordingly, each of the concerned officers has been directed not to appear at the times and places stated in the subpoenas.

Two days later Roth sends a letter to Secretary of Defense Perry stating, "It is my conclusion that the objection is without merit and wholly untenable. . . . I therefore overrule the objection made in Ms. Miller's letter and direct the witnesses to appear for their depositions."

Senator Roth, one of the most honorable senators in Washington, is now being deluged by calls from other senators to drop this entire issue and cooperate with the Department of Defense. Even his most loyal colleagues make this request because if the truth becomes known to the general public, it will be devastating to the Department of Defense and its system of justice. Senator John McCain of Arizona, a former naval officer and Vietnam prisoner of war, personally sends a letter to Senator Roth asking him bluntly to back off. The Senate subcommittee notices that some of the paragraphs in Senator McCain's letter are reproduced verbatim from the earlier letter sent by Deputy Secretary White. Roth has always held Senator McCain in high esteem, and this request is hurtful because Roth believes McCain's first loyalty should be to the Black Hawk families, not to the Department of Defense. He wants the truth to prevail, but in Washington telling the truth is the rarest of the virtues.

On November 20, Judith Miller sends a final letter to Senator Roth:

> . . . This responds to your letter to the Secretary of Defense dated November 15, 1996. . . . We have carefully considered your arguments that your Subcommittee's subpoenas, issued after the Senate had adjourned *sine die*, are nonetheless valid. After review with the Justice Department, we adhere to our position that the subpoenas lack legal force and effect. . . . Beyond this procedural issue, we reiterate that your attempts to depose these officers pose a grave risk to the integrity of the military justice system and to the separation of powers principle. . . . Accordingly, the officers concerned have been directed not to appear in response to the subpoenas issued by your Subcommittee on the dates specified.

The concept of "separation of powers" in the U.S. government allows only the Congress—and specifically in this case, only the Senate's legal counsel—to determine the validity of congressional subpoenas. Senator Roth thus has two choices. He can choose the constitutional approach, which means going through the appropriate legal channels and allowing the Federal District Court to rule on the subpoenas. Secondly, he can take the political approach: let the matter drop and allow the Department of Defense to have its way.

Additionally, "the clock is ticking," and the Department of Defense is more than aware that time is running out. Senator Roth is scheduled to leave the chairmanship of the Permanent Subcommittee in December. In January, when the new session of Congress begins, he will become the chairman of the Senate Finance Committee. He simply does not have enough time left in his current position to enforce the subpoenas using the constitutional approach. Also, the Justice Department has told him that if he does take the matter to court, "Attorney General Janet Reno will not prosecute."

During this time Roth's Republican colleagues continue to inundate him with letters and telephone calls telling him to back off. Senator Roth now has no political support to enforce the subpoenas. Therefore, he decides not to challenge the Department of Defense and the Department of Justice.

For the first time in the history of the United States, the Department of Defense does not comply with subpoenas issued from the U.S. Senate. It is highly debatable among legal experts that the integrity of the military justice system would have been violated. Indeed, if the Air Force's legal procedures and actions had been proper, the military justice system's actions would have been validated. But it is certain the Department of Defense's refusal to comply with Senate subpoenas violated the integrity of all the uniformed services.

Danny and I had been routinely apprised of the subpoena sequence, but we were powerless to do much except be sideline observers. Again we recalled President Clinton's words from the April 1994 memorial service: "They're all heroes and we owe it to them to honor their lives and to answer the questions of their families, to find the answers which they rightfully seek." What could be more powerful than the promise of an American president made on national television before millions of people?

But in the event President Clinton has forgotten that day and that promise, Danny sends him another personal letter requesting he intercede on behalf of the American service members who gave their lives for their country and for their families who will live with that loss forever. Danny never received any response from the White House.

40 The Pentagon
January 1, 1997
Wednesday

Today the Pentagon announced the beginning of Operation Northern Watch and the end of Operation Provide Comfort. This new mission is exclusively designed to enforce the No Fly Zone over northern Iraq. Turkey approved two six-month extensions but says this will not become a permanent mission. The operational details of this mission remain classified.

Since August the Combined Task Force of Operation Provide Comfort has assisted the U.S. Department of State in evacuating 6,493 pro-American Kurdish people. The Kurds were brought to Incirlik Air Force Base, where they boarded airliners destined for Guam. As the last Kurdish refugee boarded the plane on December 13, 1996, humanitarian aid to the Kurdish population in northern Iraq ended.

On Christmas Day the Turkish Grand National Assembly approved a new, smaller operation to replace OPC. France announced it would not participate in this new venture because it would not include humanitarian aid to the Kurds.

Operation Provide Comfort officially ended yesterday on December 31, 1996. As the last aircraft touched down on the runway at Incirlik, the United States Air Force had completed 42,000 sorties. The entire task force had flown an additional 20,000 fixed-wing and rotary-wing sorties. Six years of constant flying had included four countries, hundreds of aircraft, and over sixteen tons of supplies provided to the Kurdish people. For a complicated operation over this length of time, the safety record had been remarkable with the exception of the Black Hawk tragedy. If anyone were to access the Department of Defense's Air Force Internet link, they would learn the cause of the shoot down: "Tragedy struck the task force on 14 April 1994 when two F-15Cs confused two U.S. Army UH-60 Black Hawks flying in the No Fly Zone for Iraqi helicopters." Funk and Wagnalls *World*

258

Almanac says, "The two U.S. war planes shot down two Army helicopters because the helicopters' transponders had not been functioning. Secretary of Defense William Perry says the pilots' decision to fire without warning had been authorized by the Rules of Engagement."

There is no mention that countless other pilots were able to identify Black Hawk helicopters. There is no mention that these pilots broke the rules of engagement, did not determine the type or nation of origin of the helicopters, and were extremely negligent in conducting their mission that day.

41

San Antonio, Texas
August 23, 1998
Sunday, 9:30 A.M.

After the hottest, driest Texas summer on record, it is raining this morning. The large raindrops signify giant teardrops. Today marks the end of my personal endeavor to record this chain of events that not only changed the lives of so many families, but the United States Air Force. This journey has taken me places I never wanted to revisit, and emotionally it has been more difficult than I thought. Until nine months ago I was determined to never write this book. To prevent myself from doing so, I had consumed my life with numerous unending, sometimes meaningless, tasks. Last November Sean was researching an English paper and, as thirteen-year-old boys do, strayed from his main objective and began searching the Web. He came downstairs and showed me the information he was able to retrieve off the Internet on the Black Hawk shoot down. He'd said, "Mom, you know this isn't even close to the truth. How can you live with yourself if you don't write a book and tell how this really happened? But most of all, you owe this to Laura."

Sean was right, and I think I've known all along this was something I had to do, not for closure, but for an accurate record of the truth. Additionally, I had been unsure I was intellectually capable of accomplishing the task. But I had to try, and I told Sean I would begin after Christmas, in January. I cleared off a small desk in a guest bedroom, moved the computer upstairs, unpacked boxes of documents, and with a pounding heart I began. Initially I had set an unrealistic deadline for completion, in June, but that was not to be, and I continued writing all summer. While the temperatures climbed to over 100 degrees every day, I was sequestered in a small upstairs room, researching and writing. School had begun two weeks ago, and still I wasn't finished. A few nights ago, in a telephone conversation with my older son, Dan, he had asked, "Mom, how are you going to end the book? What is the conclusion?" That night I couldn't give him an answer because there is no tidy ending, and I've come to realize this conclusion is like most endings in real life: "If you are extremely lucky, life just continues on."

The Black Hawk families are still in touch with one another, although not quite as often as before. We were never an official, legally organized group—just parents, wives, husbands, siblings, and extended family who refused to accept the tarnished legacy imposed by the U.S. government. Together we have achieved more in accomplishing the objectives we had originally set than possibly any other group that has had a major face-off with the Department of Defense. We did get the Purple Heart and we did get a measure of accountability, although too long after the fact. By that point the Air Force had realized it had made a mistake both morally and politically.

Who orchestrated the events after the shoot down? It could have gone as high as the secretary of defense or even the White House. I've come to believe, along with other Pentagon insiders, it was General McPeak, Air Force chief of staff during the shoot down, the stern "godfather of fighter pilots," who instigated this grand scheme of not holding the F-15 pilots accountable. He was an authority figure no one dared to question, not if they wanted to hold on to their careers. A few lies seemed like such a small thing, but those lies corroded the integrity of the Air Force's top leadership.

Gen. Ronald Fogleman took over as chief of staff midway into the instigation of this grand scheme. After the final event of Captain Wang's court-martial, he enforced new Air Force standards and held eleven officers accountable. An editorial in the *Air Force Times* had said, "It was intolerable that Fogleman had to intervene in 1995 to ensure that some of the officers responsible were not promoted." And it was. McPeak left Fogleman holding the bag and ultimately responsible for his huge indiscretions in the cover-up of the shoot down. Fogleman not only held the officers accountable, he instituted new standards of accountability. He did this, I believe, because the situation forced him to preserve some measure of integrity for the Air Force. This message was grandly publicized and the words were clear: "If you make a mistake, the Air Force is going to hold you accountable." The pendulum had swung and the Air Force changed. But some said the pendulum had swung too far, and they began to call it the "One Mistake Air Force."

Also, this tangled chain of events resulted in two separate investigations. Rarely has one military incident merited this response. These investigations focused, not on the events of the shoot down, but on the improprieties that ensued. The Black Hawk shoot down was not the first time a branch of the armed services manipulated evidence and the military justice system to save careers and maintain integrity, and it won't be the last. By refusing to honor subpoenas issued by the Senate of the United States, not only did the Department of Defense make history, it technically won the last round. However, our audacity to question the Air Force's actions and our tenacity caught everyone off guard. Their decisions and actions taken after the shoot down and especially the events connected with the legal proceedings were done in secrecy, as if it were none of the public's damned business. T. R. Fehrenbach, a military historian and columnist in our San Antonio paper, wrote about the legal events of the shoot down, "The military bureaucracies have forgotten an important point: Justice must not only be done, but be seen to be done."

The General Accounting Office released its official report last November. As expected, it didn't include much that was damaging to the Air Force. The true essence of this report was in the disclaimer at the bottom of page 2:

> However, the Department of Defense prevented the GAO from interviewing key officials in the process, including the Convening Officials and the Inquiry and Investigating Officers. The Department of Defense voiced the belief that "any Congressional intrusion" into the UCMJ deliberative process would compromise the independence of the military justice system. The GAO did not evaluate the appropriateness of the disciplinary or corrective actions taken.

The last page of the fifty-four-page report contained a letter written by Judith Miller, general counsel of the Department of Defense. She wrote, "The Department appreciates the opportunity to comment on the draft report. . . . We concur with the GAO's conclusions."

The Senate Permanent Subcommittee on Investigations also finished its report, but it was incomplete due to the Justice Department's and Attorney General Janet Reno's refusal to allow the four subpoenas to be enforced. I have since learned that the Department of Defense heavily leaned on Reno to make this unusual ruling, just a further example of the Department of Defense's long arms of influence in Washington. As a result, this costly, time-consuming, and crucial Senate report on the Black Hawk shoot down was never released.

Immediately after the scandal with the subpoenas, Senator Roth moved up to become chairman of the Finance Committee and was replaced by Senator Ted Stevens, Republican, from Alaska. Stevens, who has a mean and nasty reputation, had met with Senator Roth in the early fall of 1996 to specifically review why the Black Hawk investigation was still in progress.

Stevens walked into Roth's office and first noted that Eric Thorson and the chief counselor of the Permanent Subcommittee on Investigations were in the room. Ignoring them, he seated himself in front of Roth's desk and proceeded to list the reasons why the Black Hawk investigation must be terminated. Finally Stevens said in an angry, impatient tone, "They [the F-15 pilots] were allowed to shoot those helicopters down!" Senator Roth nodded to Eric for a reply. Eric said, "Sir, the rules of engagement were broken. The pilots were not authorized to shoot down those helicopters." Stevens turned and said to Eric, "I suppose you are some kind of pilot and you know about rules of engagement!" As Senator Roth watched in amusement Eric replied, "Yes, sir, I flew over North Vietnam, Cambodia, and Laos for two years." Senator Roth quietly said, "Ted, we're going to go ahead with this." Senator Stevens has gone on to become one of the most powerful men in government. He currently serves as chairman of the Senate Committee on Appropriations.

In January 1997, Senator Fred Thompson from Tennessee took over the responsibility of the Permanent Subcommittee's investigations. He was specifically tasked to investigate the improprieties of campaign finance. This issue was given high priority and was thought to be a very high-interest item with the American public. The Black Hawk investigation was terminated, and anyone on the Permanent Subcommittee who had worked on it was either reassigned or ordered not to discuss it, ever.

I'm told by some of Senator Roth's confidants that he feels he let down the Black Hawk families because he was unable to enforce those final four subpoenas. I wrote him a letter that I hope will provide him comfort:

> In our darkest days, we were comforted by the knowledge that the best and most honorable people in Washington were conducting a

search for the truth. We know you have stood alone and swam against the tide of political persuasion. I'm sure you have even questioned yourself, "Has it been worth it?" We answer for all the families with a resounding, "Yes." We now believe there are a few honest leaders in Washington who care about the truth and, most importantly, care about the average citizens who send their children to foreign soils in the name of America and what she stands for.

As a token of our family's appreciation, I also sent him a shepherd's lamp Laura had purchased in Turkey shortly before she was killed. I'd said, "It is fitting you should receive this because you exemplify the honest man Diogenes was searching for with his lamp. Your integrity will always be remembered."

Senator Roth has framed my letter and keeps it in his office with the shepherd's lamp and Laura's picture as a reminder of all the families who have sacrificed their most precious possession. I'm grateful some in Washington make this acknowledgment, even if they are not in the Department of Defense.

This summer, as I was immersed in writing this book, Congressman Lamar Smith, from Texas, chairman of the Subcommittee on Immigration and Claims, held a hearing on the compensation issue. Several of the Black Hawk families testified, and Congressman Smith grilled the Department of Defense lawyers. He asked, "Under the provision that you made this financial humanitarian gesture to the foreigners, is there any wording that disallows paying the American families?" The lawyers couldn't give him an answer. He said, "I'll only allow you ten minutes to make one phone call to see if you can get an answer." The Department of Defense lawyers made that phone call and couldn't provide the subcommittee with any reason the American families could not be paid. Although the subcommittee has yet to make a decision, many of the Black Hawk families are encouraged.

I am not so encouraged, for Congressman Steve Buyer is vehemently opposed to paying this compensation to the American families. As mentioned previously, not only is this the same Steve Buyer who was having breakfast with General McPeak at the Pentagon when he was notified about the shoot down, but this is the same Steve Buyer who told the families during the hearing held by the House National Security Subcommittee for

Military Personnel in the summer of 1995, ". . . there is a great degree of uncomfortableness from me when there are those who seek the military court martial system for forms of accountability under Friendly Fire." Steve Buyer is the prime example of a congressman who doesn't represent the American people, but the Department of Defense.

Over the past four years I've had ample time to reflect on many of these events, and the Department of Defense's actions were not that surprising, except to us. Even though Danny was retired, we still considered ourselves part of the Air Force family and this legacy was passed on to our two oldest children. Until April 14, 1994, we were proud of and secure in this family. We are now not the only ones who feel an estrangement. In a recent editorial the *Air Force Times* said it best: "There is a sense the Air Force as a family is fraying around the edges. The bond between the leaders and the led—the very glue that holds the Air Force together—seems to have weakened. The sentiment is difficult to define and quantify, but talk to the troops and you can't help but feel it."

In 1994 the Air Force had reached a crisis in leadership. The top echelon of leadership was staffed by a brotherhood of fighter pilots who had promoted others like themselves into prominent positions. These were not bad men, just misguided men—men who went to Vietnam and wouldn't hesitate to provide air cover or take a bullet for their buddies. Compared to a bullet, fabrications and distortions become minimal distractions. Lies and cover-ups become part of the cost of doing business, as long as it is done for the good of the many. Fyodor Dostoyevsky wrote in *The Brothers Karamazov*, "Above all, don't lie to yourself. The man who lies to himself and listens to his own lie comes to such a pass that he cannot distinguish the truth within him, or around him, and so loses all respect for himself and for others." I'm sure to this very moment the Air Force brass believe they did the right thing.

Many people wonder and some have even asked me if I am angry and bitter with the military establishment. Surprisingly, I am not. After twenty-six years of military life I know firsthand it is staffed by some of the best and brightest people in America. However, I strongly believe they deserve the same honor and integrity from their leaders as their leaders require from them.

After a tragedy of this magnitude, if you're lucky, life does continue. And our family has continued on with our lives, at first under great adversity from not only Laura's death, but the subsequent events orchestrated by the Pentagon. However, we have not only persevered, we have even come to once more excel in life. Danny still works for the same insurance and banking company here in San Antonio and has accepted that there is life after the Air Force. Our son Dan, who was just graduating from the Air Force Academy when this all began, is now a captain in the Air Force. Stationed in California, in love with life and the opportunities California presents, he is at that crossroad all young captains come to. Soon he will have to decide whether to continue with an Air Force career or enter the civilian sector. He continues to be a great inspiration to me and a superb example for Sean.

Perhaps through all of this it is Sean who has had to overcome the most. Losing Laura broke his heart, and living with parents who have had to hurdle so many obstacles took precious time away from his youth. He knows there are issues that separate us from normal families, but he has come to accept those differences. Losing Laura is a part of who we are. Last spring Sean decided to leave his close circle of friends and apply to a math and science magnet school across town. He was accepted and had the courage to start this new school, with higher-than-average standards and where he knew no one. I told him how proud I was of his independence because it takes great courage to pull away from what is comfortable in life and take a risk. But that's what successful people do.

I have also continued on. Last year I helped open a new elementary school and now teach fifth grade. This year begins my sixth year of teaching, and I still look forward to each day. Teaching has been a big factor in my recovery. It is true I'm a different person now, but there is some good in that. In many ways I am stronger and my priorities are more focused. If I can survive what I've been through for the past four years, I've come to believe I can survive anything. I see the world through different eyes than many, and perhaps I've become more of a realist than a cynic. At least I hope so. Although I will always carry Laura in my heart, I have come to accept she is gone. This summer I'd said to my mother, "It is almost as if Laura has been vaporized from the planet. Even though I think about her all the time, she doesn't appear in my dreams. I've spent four years looking for a sign that signifies her spirit exists, and I've found none. Perhaps those signs are part of the fictional representation of death in movies and books."

Recently I finally found the courage to tell my friends and colleagues I was writing this book. Most thought I was doing it for closure, but I was at peace with my emotional equilibrium and had already achieved closure. At first I was writing for the higher purpose of leaving a written record of the Black Hawk shoot down with details not recorded in official reports and media accounts. But as I progressed I began to feel that perhaps I was being guided by Laura's spirit.

One night as I was sitting at the computer, the words just wouldn't come. I started twisting the heavy gold bracelet on my left wrist, the same bracelet Laura had sent for my birthday one week before she was killed. Four years ago, after opening the package, I had immediately put it on and to this day have never removed it. As I was fingering the heavy gold links, unconsciously I began to count them. Twenty-six links held together by a gold clasp. Perhaps my exhaustion and the late hour allowed me to read too much into the significance of this simple coincidence. Before, the bracelet had been just a tangible reminder of Laura; but now, after writing this book, the significance is deeper. To me, each of the links represents an individual killed on the Black Hawks. The twenty-sixth link—the link that has the clasp, the link that holds all the other links together—represents Laura. And for the rest of my life, this bracelet, so innocently purchased by Laura in Turkey, will represent the chain of events that changed my life.

EPILOGUE

U.S. Air Force Academy, Colorado
November 25, 1999
Thanksgiving Day

It has been five years since I last visited Laura's grave and the Air Force Academy. During the long journey since Laura's death, I have often questioned the decision to bury her at the Academy. It had been a decision made in emotional haste, and although it seemed right at the time, I've had some regrets. Often I've wondered if she should have been buried closer to home, where our family could have visited her grave and perhaps been comforted by her presence. Coming to terms with this decision has prevented me from returning. Avoiding the Academy, not thinking about this sadness and perhaps regret, has gotten me through this difficult period.

A few weeks ago Danny suggested it was time to return. At first I rebuffed this idea, but in my heart I knew the timing was right. I knew all of what I would ever know about the circumstances of Laura's death, and most importantly, I had accomplished what I had set out to do. I had written this book and found a publisher who would allow me to tell this story. Just last week I had finished the revised manuscript and packed my files and notebooks into boxes. For better or worse, it was time to come to terms with the past.

As my plane prepares to land, the weather is gloomy and the landscape dusted with snow. Most of all, I notice the suburban sprawl that has enveloped Colorado Springs and reaches north to the boundaries of the Air Force Academy. Danny and Sean meet me in the arrival area. They had driven in from a Kansas hunting trip yesterday afternoon in the midst of the snowstorm.

Driving north, the huge cookie-cutter subdivisions, Wal-Marts, and fast-food restaurants disguise the beautiful city we had come to love. I focus on the pristine snowcapped mountain peaks that beckon us toward the Academy high above the city. Abruptly the sprawl ends as we approach the main gate. Driving past the airfield and the stadium, the clouds dissipate and the sun comes out. Very little has changed since Danny first arrived here thirty-seven years ago. Time begins to stand still, and memories return from some of the happiest and the saddest periods of my life.

We take a left-hand turn off Academy Drive, and the cemetery comes into view on the right. Today the Academy is deserted, there is no traffic, and the silence seems appropriate for this occasion. A flock of wild turkeys crosses in front of us as we circle the drive that takes us by the flagpole and to Laura's grave. The snow has covered the grave markers, everything seems untouched. Danny and Sean had made an initial visit late yesterday. Sean, who had been only ten when he was last here, was able to plod through the snow and locate Laura's marker. Today his footprints are the only sign of a human presence.

Now, as I follow in those same footprints and stand before Laura's grave, I feel a reverence as images from the past flash through my mind. I am surprised by the peace that comes with closure and acceptance. I try not to think of what could have been, but of what was, and I feel thankful for Laura and the joy she brought to my life. Danny dusts the snow off the marker and lays red roses across the top. Sean plants an American flag in front. There is closure and acceptance because we have done all we could do to honor Laura. We, along with the other Black Hawk families, have gotten the Purple Heart, accountability, and most importantly, the truth.

This week an additional unexpected event reinforces this feeling of closure. Last Friday night we were informed that Congress had passed legislation authorizing payment of compensation to the families of the American Black Hawk victims. The families had worked for five long years writing letters, making telephone calls, sending faxes, and visiting Washington to get this compensation. Five years that could have been spent mending their families and coming to terms with losing a loved one. Again it had taken an act of Congress to rectify the Department of Defense's error of judgment. With any victory there is usually a hero. Certainly Representative Mac Collins from Georgia, who sponsored the bill, deserves recognition, but the real hero is our congressman from Texas, Lamar Smith. He had never forgotten the Black Hawk families and had worked tirelessly for this compensation. Many times the legislation had been stalled, but last Friday he had gotten it through the House of Representatives and immediately attached it to a Senate bill that was passed in the early evening. This had taken all of us by surprise, and it reminds me there are a few lawmakers who do care.

We drive to the cadet area and walk up the ramp that leads to the Graduate Memorial Wall in the Air Gardens. We've made this homage many times over the years to pay tribute to Danny's classmates who never made it home from Vietnam. Always I would say a silent prayer of thanks that Danny did return and that our family had remained unscathed during those turbulent years. Now Laura's name is inscribed on the black marble below these familiar names. I never dreamed it would end this way.

Walking past the chapel and up the far end of the ramp, we enter Arnold Hall. During Danny's cadet years we had attended movies and concerts in the auditorium and dances in the ballroom on the first level. We see the familiar Air Force memorabilia displayed in glass cases: the silver goblets representing the Doolittle Raiders, artifacts from the Hap Arnold collection, and athletic trophies. To the right is a display of Academy women who have become trailblazers in today's Air Force. Laura's picture is on the second shelf with an inscription that reads, "First female cadet to die in a combat area, first female cadet to receive the Purple Heart." I'm grateful the Academy has honored her memory.

We spend the remainder of the day sight-seeing and eating Thanksgiving dinner. In the evening at twilight I return alone to the cemetery. Off in the distance I see a small herd of elk. As I walk in Sean's footsteps to Laura's grave, their hoof marks are imprinted between the grave markers. Not only is this one of the last bastions of primordial eastern-slope Colorado, it still remains a special, a now sacred place to our family. Kneeling in the eerie silence, I see clearly that the decision made five years ago had been the right decision. Although this is where Laura's remains are interred, she is not here. Her spirit exists, but it extends beyond these grounds. I don't need to visit her grave to prove its existence, because her spirit surrounds my soul. She is with me, always.

Bibliography

Affidavit, 110 Investigation, "Reenactment of Visual Identification of F-15 Pilots," April 1994.

AFR 900-48, "Eligibility for Purple Heart," March 15, 1989, Table 3-9.

Aircraft Accident Investigation Board, "Briefing Prepared for the Family of Laura A. Piper," report, 1994.

Aircraft Accident Investigation Board, "U.S. Army UH-60 Black Hawk Helicopters 87-26000 and 99-26060," report, 21 vols., 1994.

Anderson, Jon, "Pipers Express Growing Concern About Whitewash," *Air Force Times*, October 17, 1994, 14.

Article 32 Investigation, *United States v. May, Investigating Officer's Report*, 1994.

Article 32 Investigation, *United States v. May, Summary*, 1994.

Article 32 Investigation, *United States v. Wang*, 40 vols., 1994.

Associated Press, "U.S. Backs Down After Tragedy," *San Antonio Express News*, April 15, 1994, 1.

Associated Press, "Families Get Payments in Copter Deaths," *San Antonio Express News*, August 1994, 3A.

Associated Press, "F-15 Pilot Testifies in Friendly Fire Case," *San Antonio Express News*, November 8, 1994, 3A.

Associated Press, "Turkish Soldiers Slay 82 Kurd Rebels in Raid," *San Antonio Express News*, April 13, 1995, 10A.

Associated Press, "GIs Whose Unit's Fire Killed Americans Were Honored," *San Antonio Express News*, April 16, 1995, 13A.

Auster, Bruce, "The Perils of Peacekeeping," *U.S. News & World Report*, April 25, 1994, 28–30.

Auster, Bruce, "Strange Justice, Air Force Style," *U.S. News & World Report*, May 15, 1995, 42.

Auster, Bruce, and Edward Pound, "A GI's Death in the Fog of War," *U.S. News & World Report*, April 24, 1995, 40–41.

AWACS RCM 303 Inquiry Officer Report, *Rules for Courts-Martial 303 Inquiry into the Shoot-down of Two US Army UH-60 Black Hawk Helicopters in Northern Iraq on 14 April 1994*, 3 vols., 1994.

Barry, John, and Russell Watson, "Raising the Stakes," *Newsweek*, September 23, 1996, 32–34.

Bird, Julie, "Friendly Fire," *Air Force Times*, May 2, 1994, 1.

Bird, Julie, "A Question of Leadership," *Air Force Times*, November 7, 1994, 14–15.

Bird, Julie, and Bryant Jordan, "Fine Tuning Accountability," *Air Force Times*, May 18, 1998, 3.

Borowiec, Andrew, "U.S. Continues Backing Turkey as Strategic Ally," *Washington Times*, July 20, 1994, 15.

Breslau, Karen, Melinda Liu, and Evan Thomas, "Saddam's Dark Threat," *Newsweek*, November 24, 1997, 25–33.

Captain Wang, Jim, 963 Airborne Air Control Squadron, Tinker Air Force Base, Oklahoma, record of trial, 40 vols., 1995.

"The Challenge Ahead," *Air Force Times* editorial, August 1, 1994, 35.

Compart, Andrew, "The Air Force Way of Life Kept Me," *Air Force Times*, November 7, 1994, 4.

"Copter Tragedy Taped," *Atlanta Constitution*, April 21, 1994, 8.

Cox, Jerry, "A Pilot's View of What Went Wrong," *Air Force Times*, May 16, 1994, 33.

Cox, Jerry, "Good Leaders Should Accept Blame," *Air Force Times*, February 6, 1995, 33.

Crawley, Vince, "Mystery Hovers Around Disaster," *Stars and Stripes*, European ed., December 22, 1994, 1.

Crawley, Vince, and Kevin Dougherty, "The Day Triumph Turned to Tragedy," *Stars and Stripes*, European ed., December 21, 1994.

Dacey, Alan, "Bundled out of Baghdad," *Newsweek*, November 24, 1997, 29.

Department of Army, Armed Forces Institute of Pathology, "Autopsy Report," Washington, DC, April 16, 1994.

Department of Defense, Public Affairs, "Memorial Service Remarks by President William J. Clinton, Secretary of Defense William J. Perry, and Chairman of the Joint Chiefs of Staff General John M. Shalikashvili, USA, on April 25, 1995, at Ft. Myer, Virginia," News Release No. 222-94, April 25, 1994.

Department of Defense, Public Affairs, "Operation Provide Comfort Accident Investigation: News Release," July 13, 1994.

Department of Defense, Public Affairs, "Air Force Chief to Review Black Hawk Actions," News Release No. 414-95, August 1, 1995.

Department of Law, U.S. Air Force Academy, *Law for Commanders* (Washington, DC: Government Printing Office, 773-001/10032, 1990).

Dickey, Christopher, and Gregory Vistica, "Mission Impossible," *Newsweek*, September 23, 1996, 38–39.

Diehl, Alan, "Complaint to Chairman and Ranking Minority Members of Armed Services Committees," cover letter, October 22, 1994.

Diehl, Alan, telephone conversation, May 12, 1995.

Diehl, Alan, "Safety Problems Lead to More Losses," *Air Force Times*, June 12, 1995, 38.

Diehl, Alan, *Silent Knight*, forthcoming.

Dougherty, Kevin, "Agony of Iraq Downing Also Felt by Fellow Fliers," *Stars and Stripes*, European ed., October 2, 1994, 1.

Dougherty, Kevin, "Assessing the Threat," *Stars and Stripes*, European ed., December 22, 1994, 4.

Driver, Don, "Air Force Captain Acquitted in Deaths," *San Antonio Express News*, June 21, 1995, 1.

Elliott, Michael, "The Sick Man Coughs Again," *Newsweek*, April 17, 1995, 55.

Fehrenbach, T. R., "We've Forgotten Responsibility Can't Be Delegated," *San Antonio Express News*, July 16, 1995.

Fogleman, General Ronald, "A Message from the New Chief," *Air Force Times*, November 14, 1994, 33.

Fogleman, General Ronald, "Air Force Standards and Accountability," speech transcript and videotape, August 10, 1995.

Fulghum, David, and Jeffrey Lenorovitz, "Iraq Shootdown May Trigger Legal Action," *Aviation Week & Space Technology*, May 2, 1994, 18–19.

Gillis, John, "Will the Real Air Force Please Stand Up," *Air Force Times*, July 11, 1994, 31.

Gun Camera Tape: Wing Pilot Randy May, April 14, 1994, videotape.

Hackworth, David, "Don't Blame the Fighter Jocks," *Newsweek*, April 25, 1994, 27.

"A Hard and Risky Course," *Air Force Times* editorial, 1998.

Harris, John F., "U.S. General for Iraq Mission Removed After Probe into Downing of Copters," *Washington Post*, July 15, 1994, 7.

Hastings, Robert, "The Station and Other Gems of Joy," Springfield, Illinois: self-published, 1993.

Hedges, Chris, "Kurds Flee Turkey and Unrest," *New York Times*, July 10, 1994, 10.

Hedges, Chris, "Turkish Forces Report Surrounding Rebel Kurds in Iraq," *New York Times*, March 25, 1995, 3Y.

Hitchens, Christopher, "Struggle of the Kurds," *National Geographic*, vol. 182 (August 1992), 33–60.

"Into Uncharted Skies," *Air Force Times* editorial, January 5, 1998, 32.

Jones, Tamara, and Michael Shear, "Young Officer Killed in Iraqi Skies Was on Path to Realizing a Dream," *Washington Post*, April 19, 1994, 1B.

Kang, Stephanie, "She Understood the Consequences," *Air Force Times*, May 2, 1994, 16.

Kern, Tony, *Darker Shades of Blue: The Rogue Pilot* (New York: McGraw-Hill, 1999).

Komarow, Steve, " 'Screwups' Kill 26," *USA Today*, April 14, 1994, 1.

Komarow, Steve, "Purple Hearts but Few Answers for Officers' Kin," *USA Today*, April 15, 1995.

"The Kurdish Killing Fields," *New York Times*, July 4, 1994, 18.

Kurdish Tape, Part I: Shoot Down of Trail Black Hawk, April 14, 1994, videotape.

Kurdish Tape, Part II: Black Hawk Crash Site, After Shoot Down, April 14, 1994, videotape.

"Letters to the Editor," *Air Force Times*, June 13, 1994, 35.

Liu, Melinda, and Weston Kosova, "Reading Saddam's Mind," *Newsweek*, September 23, 1996, 34.

Loh, John Michael, "What It Takes to Be a Commander," *Air Force Times*, October 17, 1994, 41.

Markstein, cartoon, *Newsweek*, April 25, 1994, 19.

Martin, Gary, "Navy Boss Denies Cuts to Blame," *San Antonio Express News*, April 16, 1994, 7A.

May, Randy, "I Accept Responsibility," *Stars and Stripes*, European ed., October 2, 1994, 1.

McPeak, Merrill, "General McPeak Offers Condolences," *Goodfellow Monitor* (Goodfellow AFB), April 29, 1994, 3.

McPeak, Merrill, and Sheila Widnall, "Tragedies Won't Defeat Air Force," *Air Force Times*, August 1, 1994, 37.

Melengoglou, Constantine, "Focus on the Kurds," *Time*, April 17, 1995, 8.

"The Month That Was," *Air Force Times* editorial, May 2, 1994, 33.

Muradian, Vago, "The Unspeakable Happens Again," *Air Force Times*, April 25, 1994, 3.

Muradian, Vago, "Report Blames Pilots, Controllers in Iraq Shoot Down," *Air Force Times*, July 11, 1994, 3.

Muradian, Vago, "Five Face a Range of Options as Case Proceeds," *Air Force Times*, October 24, 1994, 9.

Muradian, Vago, "They Are Good Officers and Good Crewmen," *Air Force Times*, October 24, 1994, 8.

Muradian, Vago, "Evidence Illustrates Leadership Problems in Black Hawk Deaths," *Air Force Times*, November 7, 1994, 16.

Muradian, Vago, "F-15C Pilot in Shoot Down Faces Hearing," *Air Force Times*, November 14, 1994, 6.

Muradian, Vago, "Is U.S. Intelligence Being Misused?" *Air Force Times*, December 12, 1994, 20.

Muradian, Vago, "Why Incirlik Is Crucial," *Air Force Times*, December 12, 1994, 22.

Muradian, Vago, and Julie Bird, "Shootdown Challenges Rise," *Air Force Times*, August 14, 1995, 15.

Muradian, Vago, and Steven Watkins, "When Is a Mistake a Crime?" *Air Force Times*, October 17, 1994, 14.

Myers, Gene, "The Day the Black Hawks Went Down," *Air Force Times*, May 2, 1994, 35.

Mylroie, Laurie, "Unfinished Business in Iraq," *Wall Street Journal*, April 20, 1994, 1.

"News of Black Hawk Tragedy Ripples Through Community," *Stars and Stripes*, European ed., April 16, 1994, 1.

Pine, Art, "U.S. in Dilemma over Pilots Who Downed Copters," *Stars and Stripes*, European ed., June 18, 1994, 5.

Piper, Danny, "Victims of Iraq Shoot Down Now Victims of Semantics," *Air Force Times*, January 30, 1995, 28.

Poindexter, G. W., "Profound Thanks from a Nation," *Air Force Times*, May 2, 1994, 16.

Reuters News Service, "British Gulf War Commander Calls for Compensation," *Los Angeles Times*, September 12, 1994, 9A.

Risen, James, "FBI Reportedly Suspected CIA Scheme to Kill Iraqi," *San Antonio Express News*, February 15, 1998, 20A.

Risen, James, "U.S. Undertakes New Strategy to Unite Foes Against Saddam," *San Antonio Express News*, July 25, 1998, 8B.

Ruane, Michael, "Friendly Fire Death Torments Military Family," *San Jose Mercury News*, November 26, 1994, 27A.

Schmitt, Eric, "Copter Deaths: Pentagon Finds Failure," *New York Times*, July 1, 1994, 1.

Schmitt, Eric, "Pentagon Acts to Bar Repeat of Copter Loss," *New York Times*, July 14, 1994, 1.

Scowcroft, Brent, "Why We Stopped the Gulf War," *Newsweek*, September 23, 1996, 37.

Thompson, Mark, "Way, Way Off in the Wild Blue Yonder," *Time*, May 29, 1995, 32–33.

Thompson, Mark, "So, Who's to Blame?" *Time*, July 3, 1995, 27.

U.S. General Accounting Office, *Operation Provide Comfort Review of U.S. Air Force Investigation of Black Hawk Fratricide Incident* (Washington, DC: Government Printing Office, 1997).

U.S. House Committee on National Security, Subcommittee on Military Personnel, *Friendly Fire Shootdown of Army Helicopters over Northern Iraq*, 104th Congress (Washington, DC: Government Printing Office, 1995).

Wacker, Bob, " 'Friendly Fire' Whose Fault?" *The Retired Officer Magazine*, December 1994, 27–31.

Watkins, Steve, "AWACS Crew Unlikely to Face Harsh Discipline," *Air Force Times*, August 29, 1994.

Watkins, Steve, "Crew Member in Shoot Down Makes Statement," *Air Force Times*, October 10, 1994, 6.

Watkins, Steve, "What the New Chief Is Planning," *Air Force Times*, November 7, 1994, 3.

Watkins, Steve, "Perry Refuses to Intervene in Trial," *Air Force Times*, January 9, 1995, 3.

Watkins, Steve, "Scapegoat," *Air Force Times*, March 6, 1995, 14.

Watkins, Steve, "Are Investigations Mishandled?" *Air Force Times*, May 29, 1995, 3.

Watkins, Steve, "Beyond the Verdict," *Air Force Times*, July 3, 1995, 12–15.

Watkins, Steve, "Getting Tough," *Air Force Times*, August 28, 1995, 12.

Watkins, Steve, "Panel Orders Testimony in Shootdown," *Air Force Times*, March 18, 1996, 3.

Weiner, Tim, "Court-Martial Nears in Case of 2 Helicopters Shot Down," *New York Times*, April 15, 1995, 10Y.

Widnall, Sheila, "Poised to Meet New Challenges," *Air Force Times*, January 9, 1995, 43.

Widnall, Sheila, "Review of Actions Taken Following the Aircraft Accident of April 14, 1994," memorandum for the Deputy Secretary of Defense, August 11, 1995.

Wilson, George, "Military Leaves Justice Undone," *Air Force Times*, July 10, 1995, 54.

Wolf, Jill, *Helicopters* (Yellow Springs, OH: Antioch Publishing, 1991).

Zarembo, Alan, "Tale of an Iraqi Turncoat," *Newsweek*, March 23, 1998, 43.

Index

Accident Investigation Board, 67–68
accountability, 185, 217, 220, 222–23,
    226; Air Force and, 232, 239–40,
    261; media and, 221–22; Perry on,
    100–101, 107, 189, 221
admonishment, letter of, 222
AIM-9 heat-seeker missile, 33, 76
Air Force: accidents in, 108, 136–37;
    and accountability, 232, 239–40,
    261; charges brought in shoot
    down, 153–54, 180; handling of
    families, 63–65, 81, 87, 127–28, 155,
    197; handling of investigation, 101,
    134, 221, 249–51; memorial service
    for shoot down victims, 97–98,
    100–101; Piper family and, 1–2,
    131–32, 154–55, 159–64, 265;
    protection of pilots, 188–89, 223,
    228, 244, 249–50, 261; and Senate
    investigation, 251, 254; Special
    Operation Forces, 74–79
Air Force Academy, 94–95, 111–15,
    268–70; Wall of Honor, 113, 134
Air Force Regulation 110-14
    investigation, 67, 83–84, 108, 117;
    irregularities in, 72, 77–78, 227–28,
    249–50; report on, 123, 126–32,
    192–93, 248
Air Force Times, 107–9, 125–26, 161,
    265
Air Tasking Order (ATO), 17
Alfred P. Murrah Federal Building,
    205
Amnesty International, 143
AMRAAM, 33, 76
Andrus, James, 227–28, 235–36, 248
area of responsibility (AOR)
    frequency, 23
Article 32 hearings: on AWACS crew,

160–61, 165–72, 250; irregularities
    in, 184; on May, 177–85, 187, 250
AWACS (airborne warning and
    control system) crew, 6, 10–11, 22,
    28, 132, 209, 211, 216, 250; Article
    32 hearing on, 160–61, 165–72, 250;
    blind zones of, 17–18; charges
    against, 153–54; discipline of, 186,
    222; and media, 193–94; normal
    procedures for, 72–73; reactions to
    shoot down, 35–39, 68–70;
    testimony of, 130–31

Barzani, Massoud, 20, 246
Bass, Cleon, 91, 164, 186, 193, 196–97,
    234
Bass, Connie, 91, 164, 167–68, 186,
    193, 234
Bass, Cornelius Anthony, 21, 91
Bass family, 126–28, 201, 205–6, 208
Bell, Dierdre "Dee," 23–24, 29, 38, 52,
    208–9
Bergmann, Georgia, 174–75, 193, 234
Black Hawk families, 132, 140, 163,
    175, 231, 261; activism by, 164, 190,
    196, 226; and anniversary of shoot
    down, 196–99; and AWACS hearing,
    165–72; and charges, 154; and Con-
    gressional investigations, 234; and
    Department of Defense, 189; goals of,
    241; and media, 159–60, 192–94; pos-
    sibility of lawsuit by, 132–33, 226;
    and Purple Heart, 157–58, 174, 190–
    91, 197; and Roth, 263–64. *See also*
    compensation of families
Black Hawk helicopters, 6, 11–12, 21;
    crew and passenger list for, 50;
    misidentification of, 30–31, 170,
    228–29

Black Hawk pilots, testimony of, 210
Black Hawk shoot down, 22–34; Air
    Force memorial service for, 97–98,
    100–101; anniversary of, 196–99;
    cover-up of, 7–78, 184, 188–89, 223,
    227–28, 244, 249–50, 261; early reac-
    tions to, 35–50; events leading up
    to, 10–24; Kern on, 230; Kurdish
    video of, 77, 107, 176–77; reenact-
    ment of, 227–29, 248; reprimands
    handed down in, 222–23; site of,
    74–79; time line for, 51–53
blood chit, 19
briefing guide, 17–18
British families, compensation of, 145–
    46, 148–49
Bush, George, 5, 245
Buyer, Steve, 54, 235, 264–65

Caldwell, Bryan M., 166–68, 171
Casualty Affairs, 81, 87
Cathy, Mark, 23–24, 35–36, 209, 211
Central Intelligence Agency (CIA),
    245–46
Ciller, Tansu, 56
cleared to shoot, 18
Clinton, Bill, 54–55, 62, 101, 225, 245,
    256–57
CNN, 48, 59, 62, 129
Colbert family, 237
Cole, Richard, 36, 40–42, 47, 69–70
Collins, Mac, 269
compensation of families, 87, 145–46,
    148–49, 236–37, 264–65, 269
Congress: approach of, 235; and com-
    pensation of families, 269; early re-
    action to shoot down, 54–57; investi-
    gation by, 223–26, 231–37, 243–44,
    247–57, 263; and Purple Heart, 197
court-martial, of Wang, 186, 188,
    191–92, 203–20
Cox, Jerry, 109–10
Croker, Stephen, 186

Dallager, John, 251
Delta Point system, 37, 43, 213
Department of Defense: and
    compensation of families, 264;
    handling of families, 189; leak on
    charges, 151; and Senate
    investigation, 251, 253–57, 262–63.
    See also Perry, William
Department of Justice, 254–56
Diehl, Alan, 200–204
Donaldson, Sam, 192–94
Dornan, Bob, 232–36, 242
Dostoyevsky, Fyodor, 265
Dougherty, Mark, 42–43
"Duke" role, 13, 41

Ellner, Mark Anthony, 174–75
Emery, Curtis, 162, 222
enroute frequency, 23, 210, 213
European Union, 144
Exon, James, 57

Fairchild Air Force Base crash, 136
Fehrenbach, T. R., 262
F-15s, mission of, 213–15
Fielder friendly fire investigation,
    223–24, 243
fighter pilots: Danny and, 131–32;
    expectations of procedure, 69–70,
    109–10, 212; and reenactment of
    shoot down, 227–29; reputation of,
    83, 214; rogue, 230; support for
    Wickson and May, 155–57
flight procedure review, 56
Fogleman, Ronald R., 232, 239–40, 261
French families, compensation of,
    145–46, 148–49
friendly fire, 49, 64; precautions
    against, 70; trial for, 177–78
Fuller, Chris, 35–36, 211

General Accounting Office, 224, 242,
    262

Gingrich, Newt, 56
"The Girl on the Tarmac" (Piper), 104–6
grief, 112, 123, 138, 219, 247
Guard frequency, 25

Hackworth, David, 103
Halcli, Joseph M., 14, 36–37, 209; and Article 32 hearing, 161; and Black Hawk shoot down, 22–24, 36–37, 51, 53; charges against, 154; discipline of, 186, 222; testimony of, 211
Hall, Michael, 21
Harris, Deborah Shelton, 224
Hastings, Robert, "The Station," 94
Have Quick frequency, 25
Herbin, Gregory, 35
Hind helicopters, 30–32, 41, 47–48, 103, 213
Holland, Bud, 136
House of Representatives, hearing by, 231–37, 242
HUD (heads-up display) tape, 19, 32, 34, 46, 48
Hussein, Saddam, 5, 22, 245–46

IFF (identification friend or foe), 71
immunity: for Tracy, 216; for Wickson, 163, 169–70, 181, 249
Incirlik Air Force Base, 3, 5–6, 15; early reactions to shoot down, 67–73; Search and Rescue Squadron, 49
Integrated Countermeasures Suite (ICS), 26
Interim Safety Board, 49
Iraq, 56, 245–46
Irbil, 245–46

Johnson, Sam, 54
Joint Tactical Information Data System (JTIDS), 12
Joulwan, George, 119

Kenya crash, 108
Kern, Tony, 230
Kurdish No Fly Zone, 5
Kurds, 102, 245–46, 258; Democratic Party, 56; early reaction to shoot down, 75–77; families of victims, compensation of, 145–46, 148–49; lawsuit by, 132–33; Turkey and, 143–45; video of shoot down, 77, 107, 176–77

Lippmann, Walter, 93
Loh, John, 163–64

Major, John, 55
Mangin, C. G., 251
Martin, Douglas, 13–14, 22, 25, 29, 36–37, 52, 222; and Article 32 hearing, 161–62; charges against, 154; early reaction to shoot down, 41, 69–70
Mass Casualty Response Team, 74–79
May, Randy, 15–19, 22, 43; Article 32 hearing on, 177–85, 187, 250; and Black Hawk shoot down, 25–28, 31–34, 38, 53; charges against, 153, 180, 188; comment by, 34, 156; early reaction to shoot down, 45–47; further career of, 196, 223; mistakes made by, 215; Piper's investigation of, 124–26; protection of, 188–89, 223, 228, 244, 249–50, 261; reprimand of, 222; and Senate investigation, 248–49; statement by, 156–57; testimony of, 130, 140–41, 182–83, 228–29, 231; treatment of, 119–20; witnesses on, 168
McCain, John, 255
McGeehan, Mark, 136
McKenna, Patrick, 11–12, 33
McPeak, Merrill, 101–2; and fighter pilots, 83, 119–20, 163, 261; "A Message to the Troops," 136–37; receipt of news, 54

media, 54–55; and accountability, 221–22; Black Hawk families and, 159–60, 192–94; and charges, 155; and compensation of families, 149–50; Pipers and, 82–83, 85, 90–91, 103–4, 161, 174; on shoot down, 48–49, 102–3, 129; and Simpson-Goldman murders, 118, 146; and Tracy, 216; and Wang, 192

merge, definition of, 18

"A Message to the Troops" (McPeak and Widnall), 136–37

Miller, Judith, 253–54, 262

Mission Command Forward, Zakhu, Iraq, 8, 11, 20

Mitterand, François, 55

Mortuary Affairs Team, 78

Mounsey, Erik, 21–22

Mounsey, Kate, 164–65, 193

Mounsey, Sarah and Ray, 165

Mulhern, Richard, 20

Murray, Dan (fiancè), 1–2, 7–9, 88–90, 113; early reactions to shoot-down, 44–47; eulogy for Laura, 92, 94; and investigation, 84–85, 90, 142; and Laura's apartment, 115–16; and pilots, 16–17, 166

Murray family, 88

Murray, Sherry, 66

negligence, 184–85, 230–31

Neuser, Steven, 43–47

North Atlantic Treaty Organization, 144

nullification, 220

Nunn, Sam, 57

Oaks, Robert, 67–68, 71–72, 117, 126

O'Brien, James, 42–43, 222

O'Brien, Rusty, 162

Office for General Counsel, 146

Ojeda family, 64, 93, 98–99, 123

Ojeda, Renee, 63, 85–86, 89

Oklahoma City, 205

Operation Northern Watch, 258

Operation Provide Comfort, 3, 6, 143, 145; end of, 258–59

Pentagon, and Senate investigation, 232, 239–40

Perry, William, 54–56, 67, 191, 206; on accountability, 221; and compensation, 145–46, 148–49, 237; and investigation, 124–25, 129–30, 251, 255; promise of accountability, 100–101, 107, 189; and Purple Heart, 133–34

Pilkington, Jeffrey Scott, 13, 101, 131, 184; admonishment of, 222; and Article 32 hearing, 162; early reaction to shoot down, 42, 48–50, 67, 70–73; further career of, 202–3; relieved of command, 132; testimony of, 211–14, 229, 235–36

Piper, Dan (brother), 2, 260, 266; graduation of, 113; receipt of news, 60, 84; at Wang court-martial, 205–18, 220

Piper, Danny (father), 1, 266; and Air Force, 131–32, 155, 159; and compensation, 149, 237; and Congressional investigations, 231–34, 251; and Diehl, 200; and media, 104; and Purple Heart, 133–34, 157, 173–74, 190, 197–99; reactions to news, 81, 83; receipt of news, 58–66; on vacation, 234–38, 241, 268; and Wang verdict, 219–20

Piper, Ed, 92

Piper family: adjustment to Laura's death, 97–110; and Air Force, 1–2, 154–55, 159–64, 265; and Air Force report, 122–35; and anniversary of shoot down, 196–99; and Clinton, 225, 256–57; and media, 82–83, 85, 90–91, 103–4, 161, 174; and memorial service and funeral, 92–96; and return of Laura's body, 87–90; trip to Europe, 81, 111–21

Piper, Hal (reporter), 104–6

Piper, Joan L.: and book, 260–61, 266–68; bracelet from Laura, 1, 3, 267; commitment to investigation, 90, 103; eulogy for Laura, 82, 89, 92–94; investigation of Black Hawk shoot down, 124–26, 137–38, 141–42, 175–76, 200–204, 243–44; reactions to news, 80–86; receipt of news, 58–66; relationship with Laura, 4; as teacher, 58, 60–61, 80, 98–99, 137, 147–50, 194–95, 202, 234, 252, 266; thoughts of vengeance, 202; at Wang court-martial, 204–18

Piper, Laura A.: autopsy report on, 138–41; career of, 1–2, 7–8; in days before shoot down, 1, 3–4, 7–9, 20–22; Defense Meritorious Service Medal, 87–88, 93; funeral of, 86, 94–95; German apartment and household goods of, 81, 87, 111, 115–16, 120–21, 152–53, 230; grave of, 113–14, 122, 268–70; Hal Piper on, 104–6; Memorial Fund, 113; memorial service for, 86, 92–94; orders for mission, 134–35; postcards from, 99–100; relationship with Sean, 61–62, 199; return of body of, 84–96

Piper, Sean, 2–3, 123; and Air Force report, 127; and book, 260; and media, 103–4; reaction to news, 84; receipt of news, 60–64; relationship with Laura, 61–62, 199; at school, 98, 147–50, 198–99, 241–42, 266; on vacation, 129, 204, 219, 234–38, 241, 268

Piper, Vernitia, 89, 91–92, 187–88

Pope Air Force Base collision, 108

Purple Heart, 87, 157, 173–74, 190–91, 197–99; criteria for, 133–34

Randolph Air Force Base, 58–59, 197–99, 201; Legal Office, 132–33

Reno, Janet, 262

reprimand, letter of, 222

Request SIF, 38

Richardson, Douglas, 162, 222

Robinson, Ricky, 21

Roth, William, 224–25, 232, 235, 251, 253–56, 263–64

rules of engagement (ROE), 13, 29, 32, 41, 56; investigation on, 69–70, 212–13, 215, 248

Sanders, Donald, 20–21

sanitization, 18–19

Santarelli, Eugene, 163, 179, 184–85, 188, 223, 250–51, 254

Saylor, James, 12, 23–24, 69

Schell, Barbara, 20, 104

Senate investigation, 224–25, 232, 235, 243–44, 247–57, 263

Shalikashvili, John, 54–56, 67, 100, 130, 189

Simpson-Goldman murders, 117–18, 146

Sklute, Nolan, 221–22

Smith, Lamar, 264, 269

Special Missions, 143–44

special packages, 22

sponsors, 11, 170

Starr, Edward M., 179–80, 183–85, 251

"The Station" (Hastings), 94

Stevens, Ted, 263

subpoenas, 232, 251, 253–56

Talabani, Jalal, 20, 246

target designator (TD) box, 28

Thompson, Eileen, 157–58, 160, 193, 234

Thompson, Fred, 263

Thompson, Jerry, 11, 20, 42–43, 78, 157

Thorson, Eric, 243–44, 248–51, 254, 263

threat-of-the-day brief, 17

Tinker Air Force Base, 204–18

Tourette's syndrome, 168–69, 193

Tracy, Lawrence, 10, 12–14, 130, 207–9; and Black Hawk shoot down, 22, 24, 29, 35, 38; charges against, 154; reprimand of, 222; testimony of, 171, 216–17

Turkey, 56, 143–46, 258

Turkish families, compensation of, 145–46, 148–49

Uniform Code of Military Justice, 130, 185

U.S. government: early reaction to shoot down, 54–57; handling of investigation, 119–20

U.S. Marshals, 254

Voltaire, 198

Wang, Jim, 12–14; and Black Hawk shoot down, 22–24, 28–29, 31, 38, 51–52; charges against, 154; court-martial of, 186, 188, 191–92, 203–20, 222; and media, 192; testimony of, 171, 216–17; on verdict, 220–21

Washington, George, 198

White, John, 251, 253–54

Wickson, Eric, 15–19, 22; absence of charges against, 154, 188, 231; and Black Hawk shoot down, 25–34, 38–39, 52–53; early reaction to shoot down, 45–48; further career of, 196, 201–2; immunity for, 163, 169–70, 181, 249; mindset of, 214–15; mistakes made by, 215; Piper's investigation of, 124–25, 141–42; possible nervous condition of, 168–69, 172, 193, 203, 215; protection of, 188–89, 223, 228, 244, 261; reprimand of, 222; testimony of, 130, 141, 164, 166–68, 181–82, 206–8, 228–29; treatment of, 119–20

Widnall, Sheila, 54, 114, 131, 232; and May's court-martial, 191; at memorial service, 88, 92–93; "A Message to the Troops," 136–37

Wilson, Ricky L., 52, 69, 130, 216; and Black Hawk shoot down, 23–24, 26–28, 31, 38; charges against, 154; further career of, 223; reprimand of, 222; testimony of, 210–11

Zahrt, John Wagner, 74